D0842811

DATE DUE

Published by John Wiley & Sons, Inc., Hoboken, New Jersey.

Published simultaneously in Canada.

For general information on our other products and services or for technical support, please contact our Customer Care Department within the United States at (800) 762-2974, outside the United States at (317) 572-3993 or fax (317) 572-4002.

Wiley also publishes its books in a variety of electronic formats. Some content that appears in print may not be available in electronic books. For more information about Wiley products, visit our web site at www.wiley.com.

Library of Congress Cataloging-in-Publication Data:
Cortese, Amy, 1961-
    Locavesting : the revolution in local investing and how to profit from it / Amy Cortese.
        p. cm.
    Includes index.
    ISBN 978-0-470-91138-9 (cloth); ISBN 978-1-118-08580-6 (ebk);
    ISBN 978-1-118-08579-0 (ebk); ISBN 978-1-118-08578-3 (ebk)
    1. Small business–Finance. 2. Investments. 3. Community development. I. Title.
    HD2341.C67 2011
    332.6—dc22

                                                          2011005647

Printed in the United States of America
10 9 8 7 6 5 4 3 2 1

Contents

Preface

Starting Anew

I t was early September 2009, the first anniversary of the collapse of Lehman Brothers, which precipitated the worst economic downturn since the Great Depression. Fifteen million Americans were out of work and the economy was still shedding massive numbers of jobs each month. Millions of people owed more on their homes than they were worth and faced foreclosure. All over the country, small businesses—the engines of job creation and innovation—were starved for credit and growth capital.

Yet on Wall Street things were looking up. The S&P 500 was rebounding. After a $700 billion taxpayer-funded infusion and trillions more in emergency lending and guarantee programs, the nation's biggest banks were doing swimmingly. The top four banks emerged with an even greater share of the pie, counting 60 percent of all bank deposits between them. Goldman Sachs had recently posted the largest quarterly profit in its 140-year history, largely fueled by proprietary trading gains in a volatile market. Bonuses were back to boom levels. Morgan Stanley set aside a whopping 62 percent of its revenue to lavish on employees.

That massive disconnect between Main Street and Wall Street was starkly clear as I flew to Santa Fe to attend the inaugural national gathering of Slow Money, a Slow Food–meets-finance organization whose goal is to "bring money back down to earth." Hundreds of social investors, entrepreneurs, farmers, and citizens had assembled to see if we couldn't somehow begin to create new models for investing in local, small-scale food and agriculture enterprises—the kinds of enterprises that create things of value and help build healthy communities.

The moment was ripe with possibility. People everywhere were hungering for solutions. Although I didn't find any in Santa Fe, at least not fully formed and ready to go, the air was electric with ideas and energy. Local stock exchanges, new community-based funds, municipal bonds that would finance local food and agriculture—these were just some of the proposals being dreamed up to begin rebuilding our local economies and foodsheds. Slow Money chapters were springing up across the country, from Boston to Boulder.

As a journalist, I had covered many emerging trends that would go on to fundamentally reshape business and society: the rise of the Web, the green business and cleantech pioneers, and the growing shift toward a socially responsible way of doing business. There was something similarly significant afoot. As the country was casting about for solutions to pull us out of our economic morass, maybe the answer was right in our own backyards, in the small businesses that anchor our communities and economy.

What would the world be like if we invested 50 percent of our assets within 50 miles of where we live? Woody Tasch, the founder of Slow Money asked.

It was the most interesting question I'd heard in a while.

■ ■ ■

This book is about alternatives.

Long before the global financial crisis exposed the flaws of our complex, intertwined, profit-at-any-cost system, a profound movement had been building that is centered on building resilient, sustainable, and healthy communities. It can be seen in the surge of "buy local" sentiment, farmers markets, and "locavore" diets.

Today, we are buying local and eating local, but we still aren't investing local. There just hasn't been an easy way for individuals to put money into worthy small businesses in need of capital.

The truth is, our financial markets have evolved to serve big business—when they serve business at all, that is. Of all the trillions of dollars madly flying through the financial markets, less than 1 percent goes to productive use, in other words, to providing capital to companies that will use it to hire, expand, or develop new products. The rest is sucked into the voracious maw of trading and speculation. And that tiny fraction of productive investment goes mainly to companies big enough to issue shares in initial or secondary public stock offerings—an increasingly exclusive club. When small enterprises create three out of every four jobs and generate half of GDP, that is not an efficient allocation of capital.

At the same time, the traditional funding sources for small businesses—savings, friends and family, venture capital, and bank credit and loans—have become mighty scarce since the financial crisis. It's more than a temporary freeze. Long-term trends—such as accelerating consolidation in the banking industry and less risk taking among venture capitalists (VCs)—do not bode well for the nation's small businesses. And decades-old securities regulations make it difficult for average investors to put money into private firms. Indeed, it's easier for most folks to invest in a corporation halfway around the world than in a small business in their own neighborhoods.

But that, I saw, was about to change. Just as "locavores" eat mostly foods that have been raised or grown in a radius of 100 miles or so, some people are now investing the same way. I call them locavestors. The idea is that, by investing in local businesses, rather than faceless conglomerates thousands of miles away, investors can earn profits while supporting their communities.

The more I looked, the more I saw the signs of a grassroots stirring. In Brooklyn, New York, where I live, residents had rallied to support two local bookstores, becoming part owners in the ventures in addition to being regular customers.

In Clare, Michigan, nine burly cops—the town's entire police force, actually—banded together to buy a 111-year-old bakery that was on the verge of closing. The renamed Cops & Doughnuts now employs 19 people and has helped revitalize downtown Clare.

In northwest Washington, the Local Investment Opportunity Network, a loose-knit group of residents, has been investing in local enterprises from bike shops to creameries. And in little Hardwick, Vermont, community financing has helped create a vibrant local food scene—and 100 jobs.

Cooperatives—businesses based on a model of democratic ownership that arose out of the dislocations of the Industrial Age—are enjoying a revival in everything from energy to food. In Wisconsin, as an epic clash between unions and a budget-slashing governor played out in the state capital, the state's rural cooperatives were demonstrating that more harmonious and productive models are possible.

As with everything, the Internet is bringing new power and reach to the idea of local investing, and social networking is broadening the concept of community. Kiva (www.kiva.org) and Kickstarter (www.kickstarter.com) have showed how the small donations of many people can have a big impact on the lives of others. Now this peer-to-peer crowdfunding model of aggregating many small sums promises to unlock new opportunities for investing in businesses whose needs are not being met by conventional sources.

Social media is also reviving the direct public offering, or DPO, a little-known method of selling shares directly to the public, without Wall Street underwriters. By cutting out expensive middlemen and lowering costs, these do-it-yourself IPOs put public offerings within reach of smaller companies and allow individual investors to get in on early stage investment opportunities typically reserved for angel investors and VCs. Ben & Jerry's raised early capital through a DPO.

Meanwhile, communities from Lancaster, Pennsylvania, to the Hawaiian islands are attempting to bring back local stock exchanges, like the ones that thrived in the United States from the 1830s until the mid-20th century, to provide liquidity and spur investment in their regional economies. Compare that to today's public markets, which facilitate speculation over investment and have all but abandoned smaller firms, and this seems like an idea whose time has come again.

■ ■ ■

Local investing is not a panacea. Small business can be risky, and no one is suggesting that investors sink all of their money into the local farm or flower shop. Nor will local investing ever replace our global financial system. It should be viewed as a complement—and a necessary one. Without strong local economies we cannot have a healthy national economy.

But there is a very compelling case to be made for local investments as an asset class in a diversified portfolio. In a world of sprawling multinational conglomerates and complex securities disconnected from place and reality, there is something very simple and transparent about investing in a local company that you can see and touch and understand. As investing guru Peter Lynch has counseled, it makes sense to invest in what you know.

In addition to financial rewards, local investing can bring a much richer set of returns. In an age of global volatility and peak oil, a strong and varied local business base reduces vulnerability and helps make communities more self-reliant. The spending and profits generated by a locally owned company tend to stay in the area, recirculating in ways that benefit the local economy, rather than being sucked out to a distant headquarters. "Buy local" campaigns have found that a simple 10 percent shift in purchasing from chains to locally owned merchants can generate many times the amount in economic benefits. What would a similar 10 percent shift in investments yield? Or even 5 percent?

Part One of this book sets the stage for the local investing revolution. Chapter 1 details how, as a society, we are failing our small businesses, through everything from government policies that favor big business to a gross misallocation of capital. Chapter 2 explores how securities regulations have evolved to hamper local investment and how the financial industry has come to dominate our economy to a dangerous degree. Chapter 3 lays out the case for locavesting, and Chapter 4 takes a closer look at the types of companies we are talking about and why they are so vitally important to restoring balance to the economy and society.

The rest of the book is devoted to exploring various models that are emerging to reconnect local investors with local businesses. The first two chapters in Part Two deal with the traditional and most established options for investing for local impact—community banks and community development loan funds. But as you'll see, even these mainstays of small business funding face uncertain futures.

Chapters 7 through 13 explore a progressively more comprehensive range of solutions, from ad-hoc community-supported and -financed enterprises to crowdfunding to cooperatives to direct public offerings and local stock exchanges. At the end of each chapter, I've included information that will help investors who wish to more actively pursue these ideas.

■ ■ ■

It is still early days for local investing, and if you are looking for get-rich-quick schemes this book is probably not for you. Most of these investment models have kinks that need to be worked out. Some, such as crowdfunding and local exchanges, must navigate the complex and confusing thicket of federal and state securities regulations. In all cases, a balance must be struck between facilitating the flow of capital to small, community-rooted companies and safeguarding investors from scams and unreasonable risk.

The challenges are truly daunting. But they are challenges that we, as citizens, must rise to if we want to support job growth, broadly shared prosperity, and economic independence. Isn't this the sort of financial innovation we should be encouraging? Rather than synthetic collateralized debt obligations (CDOs) and computerized robo-trading, which serve no social purpose, why not put our brainpower to work creating vehicles that allow people to invest in real companies producing real things that create real jobs?

While we will talk about investing, this book is fundamentally about fixing our broken economic system and restoring a more just and participatory form of capitalism, one that allocates capital to productive, socially beneficial use. It's about creating an alternative to the zero-sum, winner-take-all economy and the race to the bottom it engenders. It's about rebuilding our nest eggs, our communities, and, just perhaps, our country.

Indeed, there was something auspicious about the beginnings of this movement amid the financial turmoil of the last few years. As the plotters of the Slow Money insurrection gathered in Santa Fe, the city was preparing for its annual fiesta, which kicks off with a decades-old tradition known as the burning of Zozobra, or Old Man Gloom, a spectral 50-foot muslin-and-paper puppet that flails and groans. The quirky ritual was started in the 1920s by Santa Fe artist Will Schuster as a way to banish the negative memories of the past year. It attracts thousands of revelers, many of whom bring personal gloomy reminders they would like to see go up in flames. As Zozobra's roars and moans floated across the clear desert air that September evening, it was as if we were piling the CDOs, credit default swaps, and ill-gotten gains of the subprime debacle onto the pyre. It was time to start anew.

Introduction

Cereal Milk for the Gods

Walk by Momofuku Milk Bar in New York's East Village any day or evening, and you're likely to find a small horde. Foodies, hipsters, and students come for a fix of chef David Chang's addictive pork buns and the whimsical confections of his protégé, Christina Tosi, like the crack pie (described simply as "toasted oat crust, gooey butter filling") and the compost cookie (pretzels, potato chips, coffee, oats, and butterscotch and chocolate chips), which manages to satisfy all of your snack food cravings in one chewy, crunchy, salty bite. But the real draw is the soft-serve ice cream, piled in generous, creamy spirals that threaten to topple their little paper cups. Tosi dreams up a constantly changing lineup of out-there flavors, from old-fashioned doughnut to the signature cereal milk, which, as advertised, tastes like a luscious version of the milk left in the bowl after you've finished your cornflakes.

But then, that's exactly the sort of thing helped establish Chang's reputation as the irreverent maestro of the budding Momofuku empire, which has grown from a single noodle bar in 2004 to five unique but equally worshiped temples of dining. Their casual atmosphere belies the meticulous detail that goes into Chang's food and the insistence on the best, locally sourced ingredients. So who do Chang and Tosi entrust for their soft serve? The answer is proudly scrawled on the chalkboard menu: *All dairy is organic and comes from Milk Thistle Farm, Ghent, NY.*

Not bad for a small, upstart dairy run by a farmer who is not yet 30. In fact, providing the house milk at the Milk Bar is hardly the only honor bestowed upon Milk Thistle Farm by this food-obsessed city. *New York* restaurant critic Adam Platt declared Milk Thistle's whole milk "cereal milk for the Gods," while the magazine's "Best of New York" issue in 2010 gave its yogurt top honors in that category. It's the milk of choice for the Tom & Jerry eggnog-like cocktail at the trendy Pegu Club lounge. One blogger described Milk Thistle as "a milk with decided substance; *philosophy*, even."

What *is* it about this milk that inspires grown people to gush breathlessly and line up at farmers markets to pay $7 for a half-gallon? The first thing you notice is the old-fashioned returnable glass bottle, printed with a quotation from biodynamic farming guru Rudolph Steiner ("In its essential nature, a farm is a self-contained individuality"). The milk inside is not merely organic; it comes from grass-fed cows. Happy cows. Milk Thistle's herd of 50 mostly Jersey cows graze on pesticide-free pastures year round and come and go into the barn as they please. Their diet, supplemented with hay in the winter months, is free of antibiotics and synthetic hormones. Dante Hesse, Milk Thistle's slight, soul-patched young proprietor, prides himself on knowing each of his "girls" by name. A brown Swiss cow with a bossy streak is named Bronx.

The milk has a high cream content and is gently processed and pasteurized to retain the flavor and nutrients. Momofuku's Tosi says the flavor varies subtly from week to week and season to season, reflecting what the cows have been eating and inspiring her soft-serve creations.[1]

Hesse has successfully navigated the notoriously difficult economics of the dairy business. When he started out five years ago, he sold his organic milk in bulk to a bigger dairy operation. But after a couple of years of red ink, he realized he was on the fast track to ruin. That's when he stumbled across a postcard-perfect, 80-acre farm in bucolic Ghent, two hours north of New York City in the Hudson Valley. Hesse and his wife, Kristen, rented the farm, renovated old barns and repaired fences, and moved into a little house on the property with their three young kids. By 2008, Hesse was selling his milk directly to the public at New York City farmers markets, to immediate acclaim.

Milk Thistle is sold at an expanding number of farmers markets—Hesse can net $3,000 a day, cash, at the bigger ones. The iconic glass bottles are also sold at Whole Foods stores throughout New York, and retailers in neighboring states are clamoring for them as well. The strong demand has helped propel Milk Thistle to around $750,000 in annual sales in just a few short years.

Hesse knew he wanted to farm since he was a young boy, but he still seems a bit awed by his success. "When we started this farm almost five years ago, never did I imagine that we would end up running as big a business as we are running," he says.

■ ■ ■

Milk Thistle soon hit a wall. The farm was operating more or less at capacity. Hesse was selling all of the product he could make, and was already supplementing his herd's output with milk from other local farmers to meet demand. Because his cows are free ranging, he requires about an acre per cow for grazing.

Hesse doesn't own the land he farms on—the Hudson Valley's proximity to New York City has priced it out of his reach. Nor does he own a processing facility. Instead, he trucks his milk 15 miles to a small, aging plant, where it is processed and bottled.

With more land and his own processing facility, Hesse figures he could expand into new product areas like ice cream, butter, cheese, and additional varieties of yogurt. That would allow him to sell more products into each Whole Foods store and farmers market, maximizing profits and even perhaps lowering his lofty prices. He hopes to soon become licensed to sell in additional states, including New Jersey and Massachusetts, where Whole Foods has indicated it will carry his products. "If we had the production to fill all that demand, it would reduce our unit costs by 80 percent," he says, sounding more businessman than farmer.

But expanding production costs money—at least $700,000, by Hesse's estimates. He made the rounds to banks, which turned out to be an exercise in futility. "Banks won't touch us," he explains. "No collateral." Besides, he's got deeper reservations about bank loans, as many small farmers struggle under heavy debt loads. "This thing about farmers borrowing and borrowing and borrowing," he sighs. "It only works if the farm has been in the family for generations." The banks, he says, "will put a blanket lien on all of your equipment, land, etc. It's immoral."

So Hesse did what seemed to him the natural thing to do. He turned to those who appreciated him most: his customers. One autumn day in 2008, as the financial markets were tumbling around him, he stuck a small sign on his stand at the farmers market:

> Dear customers,
>
> It has become necessary for us to pursue purchasing or building our own bottling facility in the very near future. We are actively seeking investors for our new venture. Please let us know if you would like to see our business plan or if you know of funding sources we should look into.
>
> Thank you,
> Dante and Kristen Hesse

A reporter who frequented one of the farmers markets noticed the sign, and Milk Thistle Farm was featured on National Public Radio. Speaking from a market in Brooklyn's Carroll Gardens, where Hesse was setting up one chilly March dawn, the reporter explained Hesse's plight in grave tones. "He's offering 6 percent interest for an investment of a thousand dollars. Now, there's not much to back up that investment. He's still got no collateral, he's got no cosigners. The only thing he owns is a herd of cows. Anyone who invests in his farm has to take it on faith."[2]

Even with that caveat, the story of the struggling farmer-entrepreneur resonated with listeners, and hundreds of e-mails offering support—and often money—poured in from across the country.

Little did Hesse know he was on his way to becoming a white-collar—or make that overalls-clad—criminal. By putting up his sign, Hesse had unwittingly violated a major tenet of securities law. The Securities and Exchange Commission, the financial market watchdog, prohibits private businesses like Hesse's from soliciting funds from the public unless they go through a costly registration process. The natural impulse of a farmer to turn to customers who value organic farming, and of those individuals to want to support something they believe in that provides a financial return, does not fit easily into that legal view. Hesse escaped trouble, thanks to the intervention of a Hudson Valley lawyer who took him under his wing, and was ultimately successful in raising money from a customer-led group of investors. But his story illustrates a larger truth.

Hesse has succeeded, in large part, by tapping into a powerful movement that is centered on promoting locally produced food and supporting healthy, sustainable communities. It can be seen in the surge of "buy local" sentiment, farmers markets and "loca-vore" diets sourced close to home. But he has also bumped up against its limits. Today we are buying local and eating local, but we still aren't investing local. It is easier for an individual to invest in a company halfway around the world than in a small enterprise down the street—or up the Hudson River. In the meantime, millions of businesses like Milk Thistle Farm are going begging for capital, unable to expand and hire, and holding back an important pillar of a full throttled economic recovery.

The good news is, there *are* ways to invest in local companies. But relatively few investors, entrepreneurs, or even lawyers are familiar with them. By exploring local investment success stories and strategies, this book hopes to point the way forward to a more inclusive and prosperous form of capitalism.

PART

I

The Economics
of Local

Motherhood, Apple Pie, and Political Theatre

How We Are Failing Our Small Businesses

If we've learned anything from our near economic collapse and its aftermath, it's that small business is right up there with motherhood and apple pie in the pantheon of American ideals. Just ask any politician, from either side of the divide.

President Obama preached the gospel of small business as he crisscrossed the country in 2010 pushing his $30 billion small business stimulus package. A typical venue was the Tastee Sub Shop in Edison, New Jersey—a town, the president noted, that was "named after somebody who was not only one of history's greatest inventors but also a pretty savvy small business owner." Addressing a crowd that included local business owners, he intoned: "Helping small businesses, cutting taxes, making credit available. This is as American as apple pie. Small businesses are the backbone of our economy. They are central to our identity as a nation. They are going to lead this recovery."[1]

Just two months later, ahead of the midterm elections, a dozen House Republicans took to Tart Hardware ("Everything to Build Anything") in a suburban Virginia industrial park to unveil their "Pledge to America," a 45-page glossy pamphlet brimming with lofty promises to cut taxes and regulation that read like a Big Business wish list. "We are here to listen to the small-business people who are facing the same kind of uncertainty that small-business people all over the country are dealing with," declared then-minority leader John Boehner, who likes to remind folks that he is just a small business guy himself who "stumbled into politics."[2]

The rush to the nearest mom-and-pop store, camera crews in tow, in times of economic adversity is a political tradition. If we had a dollar for every time a politician delivered small-business bromides against the backdrop of a patriotic banner, we could retire the national debt. No doubt some genuinely hold this view, but politicians are nothing if not savvy. They are playing to the deeply held belief in small business that is central to how we view ourselves as a nation—less a melting pot than an audacious mashup of immigrants, commerce, and ambition.

From its earliest days, the country relied on and admired its independent business people—the merchants, farmers, and artisans that plied their trades in the colonies. Benjamin Franklin, the son of a soap maker turned eclectic entrepreneur and patriot, so valued independence and self-reliance that he bequeathed 2,000 pounds sterling (a small fortune in those days) to the cities of Boston and Philadelphia to establish loan funds that would help young artisans and apprentices start their own businesses. He specified a fixed interest rate of 5 percent to deter excessive profit making from the loans. In his will, Franklin explained his motive, noting that he had been trained as a printer in Philadelphia and that "kind loans of money from two friends" served as "the foundation of my fortune, and all the utility in life that may be ascribed to me."[3] (This generous act led one observer to dub Franklin "the inventor of microfinance."[4])

Many of us are descended from self-made businesspeople and entrepreneurs. My grandfather Ralph arrived at Ellis Island as a young boy in 1906, just one family among a wave from southern

Italy looking for better economic opportunity. He never went to college, but like many of his generation, he was a tinkerer, experimenting with new electrode technology in his basement. After working at Westinghouse, in 1930 he founded his own company, Engineering Glass Laboratories. EGL built a thriving business producing electrodes, tubing, and other components for neon signs—a French innovation introduced to the United States in 1923. The company became the market leader, with a significant export business, and continues today.

My maternal great-great-grandmother, Mary Moore, serves as a reminder that American entrepreneurship is open to all. She ran a boarding house in rough-and-tumble New York for the scores of young men arriving from Ireland in the late 1800s through the turn of the century, becoming something of a local powerhouse with her ability to deliver the vote among that fast-growing population.

We all have stories like this to tell. And many of us aspire to someday, perhaps, unchain ourselves from our corporate overlords and go into business for ourselves. That impulse is what led Sagar Sheth and Kory Weiber, two young engineers with promising careers at General Motors, to strike out on their own. Their company, Moebius Technologies, manufactures high-tech medical equipment in a plant in Lansing, Michigan. "It's one of these things where you realize you have to try, or you'll always wonder what could have been," Sheth, whose parents were born in India, told me. "To a large extent the American Dream is about entrepreneurs. What's beautiful about this country is that anyone can be an entrepreneur—that's very different from most places in the world." Indeed, business ownership has been the escalator to the middle class for generations of ambitious immigrants.

If we've canonized small business entrepreneurs, it's for good reason: They provide real economic benefits. What Franklin and his Revolutionary peers no doubt understood, and what our contemporary leaders intimate, is the value that local businesses bring to a community. They are engaged in the community's civic life and add to its diversity, identity, and independence. They contribute to the community's prosperity by employing local workers and spending profits locally, allowing that money to recirculate in the community—what is known by economists as the multiplier effect. Studies have shown that a dollar spent at a locally owned enterprise generates three times more direct, local economic activity than the same dollar spent at a corporate-owned peer.[5] And their tax contributions help pay for local services. (It's a pretty good bet that the owner of your local hardware store isn't stashing his profits in a tax shelter in the Cayman Islands.)

While Wall Street has increasingly chosen fast, speculative profits over productive investment, small businesses are the engine of the *real* economy, the firmly on-the-ground Main Street. Broadly defined by the Small Business Administration as firms with 500 or fewer employees, small businesses make up 99 percent of all U.S. companies. They range from sole proprietors and mom-and-pop shops to established, locally owned companies that employ hundreds of workers. Also among their ranks are high-growth startups that have the potential to become corporate powerhouses themselves someday. Collectively, these 27.5 million companies employ half of all private sector employees and contribute half of private GDP—about $5.5 trillion annually. That's more than the entire economic output of Germany and the United Kingdom combined. They're innovative, producing 16 times more patents than their larger counterparts. And, most significantly in these days of high unemployment, they are responsible for more than two out of every three jobs created.[6] From 1990 to 2003, small firms with fewer than 20 employees generated 80 percent of net new jobs.[7]

A study by Harvard professor Edward L. Glaeser highlights the link between firm size and employment growth. Analyzing census data from 1977 to 2007, Glaeser found that the U.S. counties with the smallest firms experienced job growth of 150 percent. As average firm size increased, job growth decreased almost in lockstep. Counties in the middle quintile had 90 percent employment growth, while those with the largest companies added just 50 percent more jobs.[8]

Large corporations create a lot of jobs, to be sure, but they eliminate more—at least domestically—making them net job destroyers.[9] Indeed, in their drive to cut costs and boost margins, some of our biggest and most iconic corporations seem locked in a cycle of job destruction. In June 2010, Hershey Foods shuttered its historic chocolate plant in the Pennsylvania town that bears its name and moved production to Mexico. IBM abandoned its birthplace of Endicott, New York, earlier in the decade. And, like many Silicon Valley firms, Apple employs 10 times more workers in China than it employs at home. Big corporations moved quickly to cut jobs during the recession. Citigroup shed nearly 60,000 workers. In January 2009 alone, America's largest public companies, including Caterpillar, Pfizer, Home Depot, and Sprint Nextel, sent pink slips to more than 160,000 employees. Even before then, the trend was clear. Collectively, U.S. multinational corporations shed 2 million domestic jobs from 1999 to 2008, an 8 percent decrease. Over the same period, their overseas hiring swelled by 30 percent, aided in part by tax breaks that encourage them to keep profits and investment overseas. The 1.4 million jobs that domestic corporations added overseas in 2010 would have lowered the U.S. unemployment rate to 8.9 percent, according to the Economic Policy Institute.[10]

Benjamin Franklin, or my grandfather for that matter, could hardly have imagined the vast scale of the multinationals that rule global commerce today. But small enterprises are still the underpinning of our towns, communities, and nation, enriching us culturally and economically. So it's no wonder politicians and special-interest peddlers want to wrap themselves in small business' warm glow.

Sticking Up for the Local Butcher

The problem is that for all of the flag-waving rhetoric, we have treated our small businesses dismally. Everything from federal tax policy to investment allocation to local development initiatives has favored the largest, most powerful enterprises—at the expense of the small entrepreneur. The photo op at the mom-and-pop has become a hollow ritual.

For a vivid illustration of where our national priorities lie, look no further than the bailout of Too Big to Fail financial institutions engineered in late 2008 by then-Treasury secretary Henry Paulson. As we know, hundreds of billions of taxpayer dollars went to prop up megabanks and those that enabled them, such as insurance giant AIG. All told, with federal lending programs, debt purchases, and guarantees factored in, the total assistance reached $3 trillion by July 2009, according to Neil Barofsky, inspector general for the Troubled Asset Relief Program (TARP).[11]

That bailout likely averted disaster. But rather than stimulate lending and economic activity, as hoped, it seems to have served mainly to fuel the record trading profits of its recipients and leave them larger and more systemically important than ever. Prominent critics, such as Nobel Prize–winning economist Joseph Stiglitz, have argued that TARP money would have been better spent supporting smaller financial institutions that did not engage in the reckless behavior that precipitated the crisis and might have actually used the money to make loans. It wasn't until September 2010—after a protracted battle with some of Congress' self-professed champions of small business—that President Obama signed the Small Business Jobs Act, establishing a $30 billion fund to spur local bank lending to small business as well as a smattering of tax breaks to aid struggling entrepreneurs. It was a welcome boost. But that's tens of billions for small business, trillions for Too Big to Fail business.

As outrageous as the bailout was for many Americans, it's just the tip of the iceberg. Each year, a staggering amount of subsidies, grants, and tax breaks go to our most profitable and politically connected corporations—an estimated $125 billion—with little economic or social payoff. There are farm subsidies to Big Agriculture ($10 billion to $30 billion a year, paid mostly to industrial-scale and absentee farmers); tax breaks for oil and gas companies (more than $17 billion a year); and tens of billions more proffered by state and local officials to woo large corporations to set up plants, offices, and stores within their borders.

Policy debates (or what passes for them these days) concerning everything from health care to financial reform to tax cuts, have been framed in terms of what is good or bad for small business owners. All too often, though, Joe the Small Business Owner is simply a prop, providing cover for an entirely different agenda driven by big business interests. The Chamber of Commerce, for example, actually claimed in a $2 million ad campaign that the creation of a Consumer Financial Protection Bureau intended to protect the public from abusive credit card and loan products would have a chilling effect on the local butcher.[12] And the few programs aimed at giving smaller firms a fair shake often end up being perversely exploited by big corporations.

It hardly matches the rhetoric.

Sadly, this is not a new phenomenon. As a delegate to a 1980 White House Small Business summit told the *New York Times:* "Our problem is small business has always been a 'motherhood' issue—everybody is for it, but everybody ignores it."[13] And Republicans since Ronald Reagan have been trying to kill the Small Business Administration, the one government agency dedicated to helping the nation's entrepreneurs.

Indeed, the crisis has simply illuminated what has been going on quietly for 30 years: federal economic, tax, and fiscal policy is crafted by and for the largest corporations, which are increasingly disconnected from any U.S. locale. This unholy alliance is bound by campaign contributions, lobbying muscle, and a revolving door among powerful corporations and the government agencies that oversee them. (Consider that the cost of winning a House seat has risen more than threefold since 1986, to $1.3 million in 2008, while senators in 2008 spent an average of $7.5 million.)[14] In this cozy pay-for-play system, the little guy doesn't stand a chance.

A Growing Capital Gap

It's more than politics working against small business. As investors, we have let them down as well. The link between investors and businesses has largely been severed, with Wall Street acting as the intermediating force, extracting fees—or rent, in economic jargon—every step of the way. More and more small business owners are falling through the widening cracks of our financial system. Without access to capital, products go undeveloped, expansion is put on hold, hiring is snuffed out, and innovation suffers. A lack of capital is a key reason why half of new businesses don't last more than five years.

Entrepreneurs have always scrambled to raise funds, bootstrapping their ventures by tapping credit cards, personal savings, and home mortgages, hitting up rich relatives, and eventually securing bank loans and lines of credit. High-growth ventures batting for the fences have been able to seek equity infusions from angel or venture capital investors. But those customary sources of early funding, never ideal, have all but dried up since the financial crisis. And the long-term trends are not promising.

Venture capital, for example, has always been reserved for a rarified category of companies—tech-savvy startups with game-changing potential. Think Google, Apple, and Facebook. Fewer than 2 percent of all entrepreneurs seeking funding from VCs or angel investors get it.[15]

But even for high-growth startups, venture capital has become scarce. VC firms from Silicon Valley to Boston retreated during the recession. Venture investments plunged 37 percent in 2009, to $17.7 billion, the lowest level in a dozen years. And despite a brief spike, investment fell again in 2010.[16] When they did invest, VCs preferred less risky, later-stage companies with proven potential, continuing a pattern started well before the crisis. The move upstream is, in part, a reflection of the ballooning size of venture funds. As $1 billion funds have become common, venture capitalists need to do larger deals, often investing tens of millions of dollars at a time. (In January 2011, the two-year-old online coupon site Groupon raised $950 million from about 10 venture firms).

The situation is similar with angel investors—wealthy private investors who typically invest smaller sums in early stage companies ahead of VCs. In the first half of 2010, total angel investment was $8.5 billion, a 6.5 percent decline from the previous year, according to the Center for Venture Research at the University of New Hampshire. Seed- and startup-stage investing declined the most, hitting its lowest level in several years as angels followed VCs up the food chain. "Without a reversal of this trend in the near future, the dearth of seed and start-up capital may approach a critical stage, deepening the capital gap and impeding both new venture formation and job creation," warned Jeffrey Sohl, director of the Center.[17]

Venture investors may have lowered their ambitions, but not their profit targets. A 2010 study by Pepperdine University's Graziado School of Business Management found that venture capitalists expected a whopping 42 percent return on their money, while private equity groups planned on a 25 percent profit.[18] A bigger obstacle for many entrepreneurs is the level of ownership and control that venture capitalists typically demand. It is said that one out of two founders of early stage venture-backed companies are fired within the first 12 months.[19]

And friends and family? Unless you've got relatives at Goldman Sachs, who's got any with tens of thousands of dollars to spare these days?

Left Behind

That leaves banks, the mainstay of small business funding, whose loans and lines of credit provide a crucial lifeline for growing firms. Yet here again, the story is grim. Stung by losses and scurrying to build up reserves, banks of all sizes cut back on lending after the subprime mortgage meltdown in 2008. Some $40 billion worth of small business loans evaporated from mid-2008 to mid-2010.[20]

Just 40 percent of small businesses that tried to borrow in 2009 had all of their needs satisfied, according to Federal Reserve Chairman Ben Bernanke.[21] The situation hadn't improved terribly in 2010: More than 75 percent of small businesses that applied for a loan during the first half of the year did not receive the credit they needed. After years of loose credit, financial institutions swung to the other extreme, tightening credit standards for small businesses every quarter from the start of 2007 through the first quarter of 2010. Standards began to ease a bit in mid-2010, but they are expected to remain tight compared to historical norms for some time.[22]

The biggest cutbacks came at the largest banks—the very ones that were bailed out by taxpayers and still benefit mightily from their ability to borrow virtually free money from the Fed. The 22 largest recipients of TARP funds collectively trimmed their small business lending by almost $2 billion each month from April 2009, when the government began requiring them to file monthly reports on their lending, to the end of the year. JPMorgan Chase, for example, reduced small business loans over the seven-month period by 3.7 percent, to $962 million. At the same time, it set aside nearly $30 billion for employee bonuses, an 18 percent increase.[23]

It calls to mind Robert Frost's observation that a bank is a place where they lend you an umbrella in fair weather—and ask for it back when it begins to rain.

Fully four out of five small business owners were hurt by the credit crunch, according to a 2010 midyear survey by the National Small Business Association (NSBA).[24] Economic uncertainty was by far their biggest challenge, but 29 percent of surveyed business owners cited a lack of available capital as their biggest worry. Nearly 60 percent were unable to obtain adequate financing to meet their needs. When we're expecting the nation's small businesses to pull the economy out of its slump, as they have in previous downturns, that is a problem. Among small business owners for whom capital availability has been a problem, 40 percent said they had been unable to expand their business, while 20 percent were forced to reduce staff.

"Since 1993, when we began asking these questions, there has been a direct correlation between access to capital and job growth—when capital flows more freely, small businesses add new jobs," the NSBA wrote.

For their part, banks counter that loan applications have dropped off and there is a dearth of creditworthy small business borrowers to lend to. They have a point. Small business owners have seen their credit standing hammered by the recession. Many use their homes or other property as collateral for loans, so plummeting real estate values hit them hard. And when banks decreased credit lines, as they did throughout the crisis, in a stroke, they inflated companies' debt ratios, further impairing their credit scores. Unlike their bigger brethren, small enterprises don't have the cash reserves, foreign divisions, or ready borrowing facilities to tide them over in hard times.

Banks are flush again, but economic growth is still restrained by a lack of credit, especially for the smallest firms. Private companies surveyed by Pepperdine University in early January 2011 identified increased access to capital as the policy most likely to spur both job creation and GDP growth, far ahead of tax incentives and regulatory reform. That was true across all size groups except for the largest: Private companies in excess of $1 billion favored tax incentives and regulatory reform over increased capital access.[25]

Beyond the crisis-induced credit freeze, a deeper and more worrisome trend threatens the long-term health of small business. A decades-long wave of bank consolidation, spurred by deregulation and accelerated in the recent financial crisis, is choking off community banks—the small, locally owned institutions that have traditionally served families and businesses in their regions.

Small banks with less than $1 billion in assets hold just 15 percent of national deposits, down from 28 percent in 1995. The top four banks—each with greater than $100 billion in assets—have grown in the same timeframe from 7 percent of all deposits to 44 percent today.[26] Despite the painful lessons about what happens when the economy depends upon a few, systemically important institutions, the biggest banks emerged from the financial crisis even bigger and more powerful. These megabanks, with their computerized lending models and management from afar, aren't well suited for local lending and have all but abandoned it. Despite their smaller market share, small banks represent 34 percent of small business lending, compared to 28 percent for the 20 largest banks.[27] As a 2007 study concluded, "Credit access in markets dominated by big banks tends to be lower for small businesses than in markets with a relatively larger share of small banks."[28]

The net of all these trends is that more companies are falling into the capital gap—the no-man's-land between bootstrap funding (like credit cards) and higher-ticket investments (like venture capital)—just when they most need capital to grow. "The small business owner, and our innovation economy, are being left behind," says John Paglia, associate finance professor at Pepperdine University. "That doesn't bode well for our economic future."

A Massive Market Failure

Those lucky entrepreneurs who do make it through the early company-building years have typically looked forward to the ultimate prize: an initial public offering, or IPO. By selling shares to the public, companies are able to raise long-term equity capital to sustain their growth and reach new scale, while allowing early investors to cash out. But the IPO is no longer the rite of passage it once was for generations of entrepreneurial firms.

Like other avenues of funding, the IPO window narrowed to a slit after the financial crisis. Just 61 companies went public in 2009, one of the lowest turnouts in four decades.[29] The number nearly doubled in 2010, but it was still less than half the typical volume and down from a peak of 756 IPOs in 1996. And the market debutantes in recent years tended toward mature companies like VISA, "re-IPOs" like General Motors, or foreign-based firms such as Spain's Banco Santander or Ming Yang Wind Power Group, one of dozens of Chinese startups to debut on U.S. exchanges. Young, high-growth domestic companies—the quintessential IPO candidates—were mostly missing in action. The lack of an important "exit" strategy is one reason that VC funding has suffered. Venture capitalists were forced to funnel more resources to existing portfolio companies, leaving them less for new investments.

IPO markets are cyclical, of course. And the pipeline was building for 2011, including the widely anticipated debuts of tech stars such as Groupon and Facebook. But there are longer-term forces at work leading to a decline in the total number of companies listed on U.S. public markets, especially among smaller firms, and a general decrease in the deployment of productive capital.

More private companies are eschewing the IPO route because of the public scrutiny, loss of control, and focus on short-term results that comes with it, as well as the increasing volatility of the markets. (Facebook, for example, has been reluctant to go public, but it may be forced into an IPO by its swelling ranks of private shareholders.)

At the same time, the hurdles to going public have risen. For many small businesses, the requirements and costs associated with listing on the New York Stock Exchange or NASDAQ are prohibitive.[30] The median IPO size 20 years ago was $10 million; in 2009, it was $140 million.[31] In recent years, the underwriting of IPOs has taken a back seat to more profitable activities such as high frequency trading and creating and selling derivatives at Wall Street investment banks, which now take on only the most lucrative IPOs. The IPO market is effectively closed to 80 percent of companies that need it, according to an alarming report by David Weild and

Edward Kim, capital markets advisors with Grant Thornton LLC. (Weild is a former vice chairman and executive vice president at NASDAQ.) "Capital formation in the U.S. is on life support," the authors write. The lack of new listings "is a severe dysfunction that affects the macro economy of the U.S.—with grave consequences for current and future generations."[32]

The dire assessment underscores a fundamental failing of our 21st-century financial system: the massive misallocation of capital away from its most productive uses and toward unproductive, even harmful, ones, such as speculative trading, subprime mortgages, and the latest bubble *du jour*.

By one gross measure, of the trillions of dollars that flow through our stock markets, just 1 percent goes to industrious use—that is, to funding companies through initial and secondary offerings so they can innovate and expand. The other 99 percent is trading and speculation. For example, companies raised $8.8 billion in IPOs and $6 billion in secondary offerings on NASDAQ in 2010—a total of $14.8 billion. That represents just 1 percent of the $2.9 trillion in shares that traded on the exchange that year.[33] The situation is similar on the Big Board. The imbalance has worsened since 1996, when an SEC advisory committee warned that capital raising amounted to just 2 percent of total market activity.[34]

Not all trading is speculative. But the staggering rise in volume—to more than 6 billion shares traded per average day from a billion or so in 1997—has little to do with long-term investing (and a lot to do with high-frequency trading, in which sophisticated computer algorithms fire off thousands of trades per second to exploit fleeting price imbalances). Meanwhile, most of that 1 percent of productive capital flows to relatively large companies: Small and medium-sized enterprises with under $500 million in sales generate roughly 45 percent of the country's business revenues, but they account for less than 5 percent of total capital markets activity, according to Morgan Stanley. The percentage drops off to less than 1 percent of capital markets activity for companies under $25 million in sales.[35]

Just think about where your 401(k) or retirement account is invested. It's most likely in the stocks and bonds of big corporations, with maybe some U.S. Treasuries or emerging market plays. Michael Shuman, an economist, author, and leading agitator in the local movement, notes that Americans collectively hold $26 trillion in stocks, bonds, mutual funds, pension funds, and life insurance. Yet, he says, "not a penny of that goes into local business."[36]

We've all been taught the efficient market theory—that markets allocate capital to its most productive use. But if that's the case, shouldn't we be allocating at least half of our investment dollars to the small companies that make up half of GDP and more than two-thirds of job creation? As Shuman puts it: "It amounts to a massive market failure."

Postcards from the Edge

Like Dante Hesse of Milk Thistle farms, entrepreneurs across the country are being held back by a lack of funding.

In Fort Meyers, Florida, locally owned Storm Industries has been a bright spot in a foreclosure-ravaged economy. Demand for the company's innovative weatherization and hurricane protection products for homes, such as its clear storm panels and cooling sun screens, has been strong. It employs more than 100 workers and does all of its manufacturing locally using domestically sourced materials. Storm Smart president Brian Rist wants to expand into energy-efficient products, such as thin solar film shades that collect energy while keeping homes cool. But despite his company's 16-year track record and healthy growth, local and national banks are reluctant or unable to lend, at least on reasonable terms, he says. "We have plans to hire people at good-paying jobs and develop new products, but it all takes capital—and that's where I'm up against a wall," says Rist. He doesn't want to dilute his family ownership with private equity investment, so he will probably plow his own savings into the company.

In Lancaster, Pennsylvania, Wolfgang Chocolates has been serving sweet tooths in the region for four generations. The company, which once peddled its chocolates strictly through fundraisers, operates a thriving retail and private label business that employs 150 people. Sales have grown by 30 percent a year, and Wolfgang is developing seven new private label products for a major drugstore chain. But that requires an investment in new manufacturing lines, molds, and packaging, says Michael Schmid, Wolfgang's managing partner. While the company is in expansion and reinvestment mode, cash flow is tight. And credit is hard to come by. "Banks are not investors. They want to give you money based on assets and they want to know when they can get it back," says Schmid. "They don't care what you're going to do in the future." On the other hand, his company is too small for typical VCs and is not plugged into angel networks. Still, Schmid is determined to find a way. "This is what I know to be true: I don't believe the solution is to stop the growth or slow down the business," he says.

And then there's Sagar Sheth, the cofounder and president of Moebius Technologies in Lansing, Michigan. Sheth and his partner, Kory Weiber, bought an ailing auto racing supplier in 2007 and retooled it for the fast-growing medical device market, a welcome development in an area where two manufacturing plants had recently closed. Moebius' contract manufacturing business was growing and orders were flowing in, but Sheth and Weiber ran into a brick wall trying to obtain a loan for new equipment to fill the orders. The company's bank pulled its credit line, and more than a dozen other banks turned them down. They finally obtained a $237,000 loan from the Lansing Economic Development Corp., a local government-backed agency. "When we took this venture on, we knew it was going to be hard to get financing," says Sheth. But the pair figured they could use the collateral of the business they were buying to back a loan while they grew the business. "We were pretty well aware of the traditional methods of going after funding. What we weren't aware of was what was about to come, which is this whole industry and way of doing a startup falling apart. The financial environment has been changing almost constantly since we started."

It all seems so shortsighted. Some of our biggest and most successful corporations were established in difficult, recessionary environments, including companies as varied as Burger King, Hyatt Corp., CNN, MTV, FedEx, and General Electric. But things were different then. One can only wonder what great companies never got a chance to fulfill their potential for lack of funds in the Great Recession.

2

Blue Skies, Pipe Dreams, and the Lure of Easy Money

Our Financial Legacy and Its Unintended Consequences

It wasn't always this way. From the country's earliest days, businesses were built by marshalling a region's surplus savings into local ventures run by people known to the community. Often the funds came from wealthy merchants and wholesalers, as well as farmers, mechanics (the geniuses of the Industrial Age), and ordinary citizens. Together, they helped create entire new industries, whether mechanical clocks in Connecticut or machined-powered textiles in Massachusetts, that built on the region's strengths, expertise, and social connections, much like Silicon Valley today.[1] Cities established regional stock exchanges to facilitate the flow of capital to area businesses. The problems, for the most part, came when people began investing in more speculative ventures farther afield.

To explore the roots of our modern financial failures, we must travel back to the early 1900s, when my grandfather Ralph was just making his way to America and our modern system of financial regulations was about to be created. In those days, the country's freewheeling markets were the financial equivalent of the Wild West, with snake oil swindlers roaming the land peddling all manner of speculative investments and get-rich schemes, from exotic oil fields and silver mines to lucrative land development. These can't-miss investments were typically in distant locales, making them conveniently impossible to vet. The smooth-talking hucksters especially liked to target farmers, widows, and other residents of western states, who were persuaded to invest their savings in these dubious or fraudulent schemes. Many were wiped out.

In Kansas, J. N. Dolley, the state's larger-than-life bank commissioner, had had enough. By Dolley's reckoning, hundreds of hucksters operated in Kansas, bilking residents out of $3 million to $5 million a year. Newly wealthy Kansas, he said, made for "fat picking." In a *Saturday Evening Post* article from 1911, he told of just one example:

> An old farmer I used to know came up to Topeka to see me. He'd sold his Kansas farm and had the money in the bank. A couple of smooth gentlemen came along and persuaded him to invest the money in developing a magnificent tract in New Mexico that was just about to be irrigated. He invested; and, after waiting patiently a good many months for the promised returns, he came up to see me. I advised him to invest some more money in a railroad ticket and go down and look at his land personally. He did go down there. He got off at the railroad station that was to be their shipping point and walked half a day through the sagebrush, and then climbed some bare, mountainous hills until his wind gave out. The land he'd invested in was still higher up. The only way to irrigate it would be from the moon. That was only one instance out of a good many.[2]

Dolley led the charge for legislation that would curb these abuses. In 1911, at his urging, Kansas passed pioneering legislation aimed at protecting investors from what he called "fakers and blue sky merchants" pushing investments backed by "nothing but the blue skies of Kansas."

The law required any company selling stock, bonds, or securities of any kind in Kansas to file a detailed application with the bank commissioner, who had broad discretion to approve or reject the application. Dolley is said to have approved just 7 percent of the applications filed the first year.[3] Those who got the green light had to file twice-yearly financial updates with the commissioner's office.

The common-sense law was controversial at the time, with opponents arguing that it was paternalistic and would create "a nation of fools and weaklings," according to one account. But Dolley's argument, that the law would keep "Kansas money in Kansas" and help local farmers and small businesses rather than enriching "New York Stock Exchange speculators and gamblers," prevailed.[4]

Other states followed suit. By the early 1930s, every state save for Nevada had its own "Blue Sky" laws. The laws varied, but the intent was the same: preventing unscrupulous salesmen from promising unrealistic returns and misleading investors about risk. The Blue Sky laws were the bane of the fast-money men, but speculation didn't dry up. It simply moved to more legitimate theatres. During the latter half of the Roaring '20s, the action was on the stock market. Installment loans had recently been introduced, giving people a chance to buy, for the first time, big-ticket items like appliances and cars on credit. The newfound taste for credit carried over to the stock market, where investors leveraged themselves to the hilt, buying stocks on margin. Why not? Stock prices were rising and, like all leadups to massive speculative crashes, a collective delusion had taken hold that risk no longer existed and markets would rise inexorably. (Sound familiar?)

Two Tiers of Investors

The stock market crash of October 29, 1929, began America's rapid descent into the Great Depression. The Hoover administration's ineffective response to this national tragedy led to the election of Franklin Delano Roosevelt. Within days of assuming office in March 1933, Congress passed his administration's Emergency Banking Act of 1933, which took immediate measures to restore calm to a nation gripped by a bank panic.

A flurry of legislation followed that would lay the groundwork for our modern financial system. The Banking Act of 1933, more commonly known as the Glass-Steagall Act, insured commercial bank deposits, but in return prohibited commercial banks from speculating in securities—a prudent separation that was repealed in 1999 under the Clinton administration. That was followed by the Securities Act of 1933, the nation's first comprehensive legislation regulating the offer and sale of securities. The law required full disclosure of material facts so that investors could make informed decisions. Next came the Securities Exchange Act of 1934, which regulated secondary trading and established the Securities and Exchange Commission (SEC) to oversee the securities industry.

Since then, disclosure has been at the heart of our regulatory system. Any securities sold to the public——whether debt or equity—must be registered with the SEC and a detailed prospectus made available to investors. Once public, the issuer is subject to regular filing of audited financial statements, in the form of 10Qs and the like (and more recently, internal audits required by the Sarbanes-Oxley Act). It was a logical system, but one that has had unintended consequences for small businesses seeking to raise capital.

When Congress passed the '33 and '34 Acts, it acknowledged the state Blue Sky laws and let them stand, creating an even more complex regulatory thicket. There have been efforts to make the laws more uniform over the years, and the SEC has deemed certain offerings exempt from state regulations. But for the most part, companies that want to offer shares to the public must comply with SEC regulations as well as the unique regulations of each and every state they want to offer securities in.

The Securities Act of 1933 created another lasting legacy: the creation of a financial elite. The '33 Act distinguished between sophisticated investors, such as company insiders and institutions who could "fend for themselves" (as a later legal case put it), and ordinary individual investors. That concept was further expanded and codified in 1982 in the form of Regulation D. Reg D was intended to ease the regulatory burden on private placements and certain smaller, more limited public offerings by exempting them from federal regulations. It also created an "accredited investor" category. In addition to insiders and institutional investors, the definition encompassed affluent individuals who, by dint of their wealth and the financial sophistication that implied, did not require the protective coddling of the SEC. Private companies were now free to raise money from these well-heeled investors without going through a costly registration process.[5]

Just like that, the universe of investors was cleaved in two. If you had a net worth of $1 million or more, or annual income of at least $200,000 (later amended to $300,000 for couples), you were among the top 2 percent of Americans and could invest in pretty much anything you like.[6] The rest—the vast majority of Americans who failed to meet that standard—were free to buy publicly traded stocks, bonds, and mutual funds but were effectively barred from a wide range of investment opportunities in small, private ventures deemed too risky. Hereon, there would be two sets of rules for investing.[7]

To use Michael Shuman's colorful analogy, it was the same philosophy that led to Prohibition: If you cannot be trusted to drink responsibly, we will ban drinking. If investors could not be trusted to invest their money wisely, the SEC would ban them from risky investments. Happily, reasonable minds prevailed and Prohibition was repealed in 1933. But we are still left with our dual-class investor system.

To be fair, it is not an outright ban. The SEC over the years has carved out exemptions that make it easier for small companies to raise money from the public without the burdens of registration and ongoing reporting requirements. But there is an Alice in Wonderland-like madness to the rules, which inspire as many interpretations as there are legal experts. Reg D contains three different exemptions for small offerings of under $1 million or $5 million. But two of them (Rules 505 and 506) limit the number of nonaccredited investors to 35, and those folks must be supplied with similar documentation and disclosure as would be required in a registered offering, so many companies stick to accredited investors to simplify matters. There are also prohibitions on soliciting the general public (as Dante Hesse did when he put up a sign at a farmers market). And those are the simplest exemptions. Regulation A exempts public offerings of less than $5 million from registration, but it is so little understood that it is hardly ever used. There have been a grand total of 36 Reg A offerings since 2005, according to the SEC.[7] The commission has also given a pass to offerings that are contained to one state—like Ben & Jerry's first stock offering in the mid-1980s in Vermont—leaving them to state regulators.[9] But they are equally rare.

Finally, the people closest to an entrepreneur—the proverbial friends and family—are free to invest in his or her venture, due to their preexisting relationships. But this, too, easily spills into a gray area—especially in the Facebook age, when people have hundreds of "friends."

To revisit Shuman's Prohibition analogy, it's more like regulating the saloon so that it can serve ordinary customers only after it obtains an expensive license and provides detailed audited reports on the dangers of each libation. Meanwhile, the martinis flow freely in the VIP room.

The practical effect has been to shut small investors out of a large part of the market where their money could be put to productive and profitable use.[10] Rather than keeping money local—or "Kansas money in Kansas," as the original Blue Sky law proposed—some of these well-intentioned rules have hampered local investment. Thus, when he needed capital, Dante Hesse could not simply turn to his customers for help, and they in turn were unable to invest even a small sum to ensure a continued supply of his Cereal Milk for the Gods.

Modern-Day Blue Sky Merchants

For most of the postwar era, that arrangement has worked out just fine for investors. As America became a global economic powerhouse, the stock markets both fueled that growth and were themselves propelled by it. The Dow Jones Industrial Average rose steadily from around 200 in 1950 to 1,000 in the mid-1980s, before spiking to nearly 11,000 by the turn of the century. And investors big and small came along for the ride. There were downturns, but overall, individual investors shared broadly in the prosperity and stability.

That's not to say that the Blue Sky merchants that Dolley railed against had been entirely vanquished. There will always be scam artists, whether shady boiler-room operators or Ponzi-scheme artists masquerading as financial magicians, trying to make a buck off of some rube. Greed may be an enduring aspect of human nature and financial markets—bankers have gotten a bad rap since at least Biblical times, and the Rothschild bank was called "a vast, black octopus stretching its tentacles around the world"[11] more than a century before Matt Taibbi famously labeled Goldman Sachs a "vampire squid wrapped around the face of humanity" in the pages of *Rolling Stone*. But for the most part, the securities and banking regulations put in place starting in 1933 kept the abuses in check, facilitating the flow of growth capital to businesses and fostering widespread confidence in the financial system.

But as many investors sense, something fundamental has changed. In little more than a decade, investors have been buffeted by a string of scandals. There was the dot-com frenzy of the late 1990s, when investment banking analysts hyped companies their employers were taking public despite the fact that they had little revenue, much less profits, and were privately characterized as "dogs." In 2001 and 2002, a wave of accounting scandals exposed the cooked books of prominent companies like Enron, WorldCom, and Tyco. Shares of Enron, the energy trading giant, went from $90 in mid-2000 to $1 just five months later, wiping out $11 billion in shareholder value. Those blips, of course, are overshadowed by the derivatives-fueled subprime mortgage meltdown that nearly took down the entire global economy six years later, on the 75th anniversary of the Securities and Banking Acts of 1933. Trillions of dollars' worth of wealth evaporated almost overnight. For the first decade of the 21st century, the markets delivered negative returns. The Dow was down 9.3 percent, the S&P lost 24 percent, and the NASDAQ ended the decade a whopping 44 percent below where it started. And that includes dividend income.[12]

Indeed, the most breathtakingly reckless and deceitful practices over the past decade or two (let's not forget the savings & loan crisis of the late 1980s) have taken place not deep in some boiler room, but right under our noses at the nation's top financial institutions. As we know all too well by now, mortgage brokers pushing "no-doc" loans on unqualified home buyers, investment bankers peddling highly leveraged inscrutable securities packed with toxic garbage, and rating agencies that stamped it all Triple-A, collaborated to pull off perhaps the biggest Blue Sky scam ever perpetrated.

The fact is, Wall Street today is a very different place than the one contemplated by the crafters of the 1930s regulations. Indeed, it's hardly a place at all. It's more a swirling vortex of profit-seeking electrons. With the dismantling of key regulations starting in the 1970s, the shifting of risk from investment firms to shareholders, and an explosion of financial engineering and risk taking, the financial sector morphed from a productive industry that enabled the growth of business and promoted an inclusive prosperity to one that puts its own profit above all else, including clients, business, and society at large. As Philipp Meyer, a former Wall Street trader turned writer, told *Time* magazine: "With a trader, the goal of every minute of every day is to make money. So if running the economy off the cliff makes you money, you will do it, and you will do it every day of every week."[13]

Today, individual investors are playing in a market that, despite SEC oversight, is increasingly rigged against them. (As Bernie Madoff told *New York* magazine from his jail cell: "I realized from a very early stage that the market is a whole rigged job. There's no chance that investors have in this market.")[14] The Dodd-Frank Wall Street Reform and Consumer Protection Act attempts to reign in some of the riskier practices. Banks will have to divest much of their proprietary trading and maintain higher capital cushions, for example. And a good portion of the $600 trillion worth of derivatives will be forced to trade on regulated exchanges. But having succeeded in watering down the final bill with a blizzard of lobbying dollars, entrenched Wall Street interests are now working to make sure that the final rules maintain their profits and market dominance. In a case of the fox guarding the henhouse, the biggest banks are poised to control the new derivatives exchanges, keeping them opaque and preserving their fat margins.[15] The risk is still with investors and taxpayers.

Meanwhile, sophisticated investors have been piling back into risky investments in search of higher return. Junk bonds, hedge funds, and emerging markets have seen huge inflows of capital. Some sophisticated investors are even investing in lawsuits for a piece of the potential winnings.[16] Helped along by the ability to borrow money on the cheap, the "smart" money is once again taking on dangerous levels of debt. Leveraged buyouts—where private equity investors borrow massive amounts of money to take over an undervalued company, squeeze costs out of it, saddle it with debt, and pay themselves enormous fees for the favor—are staging a comeback. And the potentially destabilizing high-frequency trades fired off by computer algorithms now make up almost three quarters of trading volume.

Is it any wonder that prominent economists from Joseph Sitglitz to Nouriel Roubini have warned that another financial meltdown is likely in the coming years?

How Wall Street Ate the Economy

Ordinary investors had little hand in creating the crisis, aside from those who took out mortgages they didn't understand or couldn't afford. Rather, the crisis was the product of the so-called sophisticated investors and the anything-goes universe they operate within, where synthetic securities ginned up by financial engineers allowed them to pile up speculative bets and risk and feed the Wall Street profit machine.

The rationale for exempting sophisticated investors from regulation is that, being wealthy and financially savvy, they can fend for themselves. Further, since they are trading among themselves, it is argued, their actions do not affect ordinary investors. Their risk taking was even helped along by Congress and the SEC. In 2004, for example, at the request of the biggest investment banks, the SEC lowered the net capital requirement, or cash cushion, for Bear Stearns, Lehman Brothers, Goldman Sachs, Merrill Lynch, and Morgan Stanley, allowing them to leverage themselves to the hilt. For every dollar invested, the banks borrowed about $30. It was Happy Hour in the VIP room, the equivalent of 30-for-1 drink special. (It is little coincidence that three of those banks did not survive the subprime crisis, while the remaining two were propped up with taxpayer money.)

It is painfully clear that the actions of sophisticated investors trading among themselves with little oversight can have disastrous results for the entire global economy. It is also clear that many so-called sophisticated investors—managers of pension funds, state and city treasuries, and sovereign funds—in fact did not understand the risks embedded in the opaque securities Wall Street was pushing. Even the chiefs of some of the biggest banks claimed they did not grasp the implications of the financial wizardry taking place within their organizations.

For the most part, though, the financial chiefs and their traders walked away unscathed, with bonuses intact. Wall Street is back to record-level profits and pay, while Main Street is still suffering. Unemployment is stuck in the high single digits, and the ranks of the long-term unemployed continue to grow. Some 2.5 million more Americans were expected to lose their homes in 2010 and 2011. Between November 2008 and April 2010, about 39 percent of households had either been unemployed, had negative equity in their house, or had fallen behind on house payments.[17] Many consumers have seen their credit card interest rates hiked even as their savings accounts earn less than the cost of inflation. Companies won't hire until they see signs of a pickup in the economy, but without jobs, consumers, who make up the biggest piece of GDP, are reluctant to spend. American innovation and entrepreneurship is in peril.

We did not get into this situation overnight. In many ways, the prosperity of the last decade or so was an illusion. The housing bubble inflated home prices, which in turn drove consumer spending, as homeowners used their houses as ATMs by borrowing against their value. Real wages were down, and job growth, from a historical standpoint, was atrocious. Between May 1999 and May 2009, private sector employment rose by 1.1 percent, the lowest 10-year increase since the Depression.[18] But consumer spending was on a tear.

While we were on our collective debt-fueled bender, the manufacturing sector—long a pillar of the economy and middle class—continued its long decline as jobs and skills were shipped overseas.

In its place has arisen an industry that creates little of real value and contributes only to the prosperity of a few. Manufacturing accounted for just about 30 percent of GDP in 1950. By 2003, it had shrunk to less than 13 percent, and by 2009, 11 percent. Over the same time frame, the financial services sector has doubled, from 10 percent of GDP in 1950 to around 20 percent today. Its profits have grown even faster; financial services generated a whopping 40-plus percent of U.S. corporate profits in recent years.[19] As Arianna Huffington writes in *Third World America*, the financial sector is "supposed to serve our economy, not *become* it."[20] At the same time, power in the financial sector has concentrated to a degree not seen since the days of the robber barons—a fact the financial reform bill has done nothing to address. Bank of America's assets are equal to 16 percent of GDP, and JPMorgan Chase's, 14 percent.[21]

Economists have a term for this: financialization. The word refers to the reduction of nearly anything of value—from home mortgages to life insurance—to a tradable commodity. But it also describes the dangerous degree to which the financial sector has come to dominate our economy. The broader economy is now subservient to finance. Public companies march to the tune of maximizing shareholder profits and short-term results, prompting them to seek the lowest cost labor, even if it means slashing benefits and shipping American jobs and expertise overseas. Over the past decade, we have imported $4.3 trillion more manufactured goods than we have exported, and 5.6 million manufacturing jobs have vanished.[22] The ballooning trade deficit (excluding oil imports) has caused the displacement of 5.6 million jobs in 2007 alone, according to one study.[23] Meanwhile, American wages have actually declined even as productivity has soared—defying a historic relationship under which the two measures have moved in more or less lockstep. Real average hourly earnings (not including benefits) are at roughly 1974 levels.[24]

This is not a path to prosperity. We are destroying the middle class and outsourcing our future. The credit has stopped and there is no economic engine to pull us out of our malaise. Without a more diversified, productive economy, we will not be able to grow ourselves out of our economic rut.

A Return to Value

As the fast-money mores of Wall Street have pervaded our culture, manufacturing has lost its appeal among young entrepreneurs. Sagar Sheth, the young cofounder of Moebius Technologies, has spent a lot of time thinking about this. "Manufacturing requires a lot of work, a lot of up-front investment, a lot of the things that younger people don't care about anymore. And I think that's the scariest thing about where the U.S. is right now. There's very little value placed on making things," says Sheth, whose company employs eight full-time employees in a hard-hit neighborhood in Lansing, Michigan. While Moebius hasn't yet turned a profit, orders have been flowing in.

Sheth, a thoughtful 33-year-old, has bigger concerns. "Culturally, we have lost a sense of respect for what brought us here, what got us to this place as a country—building things that the world can use," he continues. "We've created this image that there are ways to make easy money—you know, where you can sit in a college dorm room and write a social networking site and become a billionaire. Or you have these smart kids coming out of school and going to Wall Street and making a lot of money playing around with numbers. These are the pipe dreams that so many young people are aiming towards. They're no longer going out and trying to start companies that can make hundreds of thousands of dollars a year. They're now looking for ventures that can make millions upon billions of dollars a year, and that require very little upfront cost. We could buy stuff from China—we know that. We could sell it back in the U.S., make our 30 percent margins and build a big company around it. The reality is, it's not what we believe in."

Globalization is here to stay. But isn't it time for a backup plan? We've seen what unfettered free markets and financialization have wrought. The question now is, how do we begin to create a more diversified and resilient economy that supports the betterment of society? How do we once again channel capital to the innovative entrepreneurs that make things of value and create jobs? How do we keep at least some Kansas money in Kansas? In this, we all have a role to play.

CHAPTER

3

Buy Local, Eat Local . . . Invest Local

Reconnecting Investors and Businesses

or many Americans, the lesson of the financial crisis is that neither Wall Street nor the government can be trusted to look out for the interests of Main Street. The system is just too entrenched and self-reinforcing. If we are concerned about the direction of the economy and our country, it is up to each and every one of us to be part of the solution, even if on a small scale.

This book is about alternatives. Alternatives to the Wall Street casino. Alternatives where investors can put their money to productive, profitable use. Alternatives for small business owners who are begging for capital so they can expand and hire. And alternatives for a country desperate for solutions that will create jobs and help us regain our economic prosperity.

Across the country, people are figuring out ways to invest in their local businesses and communities. In the process, they are rebuilding economies, revitalizing downtowns and rural Main Streets, and establishing a sense of shared purpose and wealth. It's capitalism writ small. Or as I call it, locavesting. Just as locavores eat food grown or produced in their region, locavestors invest in enterprises that are rooted in their areas. In doing so, they earn profits while supporting their communities.

The locavore metaphor is an apt one. As consumers and eaters, we have become disconnected from our food sources, to the point where some children grow up believing that food actually springs from the supermarket in its shiny shrink-wrapped form. The local food movement and organizations like Slow Food have begun to reestablish the links between farm and table and rebuild local food systems. When we buy locally produced food—whether from a farmers markets or community-supported agriculture (CSA) or grocery store—our dollars directly support those producers. Local investing takes that one important step further. Like any small business, local farmers and food producers need capital if they are to grow and compete with the mass-market muscle of industrial-scale farms. A lack of capital is the main drawback for new farmers and small scale food producers.

Locavesting goes beyond food, however. It is a recognition of the vital role that community-rooted businesses of all kinds, from mom-and-pop merchants to high tech firms to hometown manufacturers, play in our local economies. As we'll see, these companies create enormous economic and social value for their communities—measured in jobs, a healthy tax base, charitable giving, civic engagement, quality of life, and the distinct sense of place and identity they foster. But they are exactly the types of companies that fall through the cracks of our bigger-is-better financial system. As with the industrial food complex, our global, disembodied financial system has severed the links between investors and companies, borrowers and lenders—links that fostered trust and accountability. The consequences have often been disastrous. When our most sophisticated financial institutions cannot even figure out who owns the mortgages they originated, you know things have gotten too complex.

Locavesting attempts to restore a sense of connection, intimacy even, to financial transactions, and to broaden the concept of "return." Rather than zero-sum finance, where my win requires your loss, local investing aims for mutual benefit. Instead of supporting monocrops, monocultures, and monopolies, locavesting helps build robust local economies, competitive markets, and lively, self-sufficient neighborhoods. We're not talking about an idealistic look backward, but a pragmatic look into the future and what it will take to recreate the regional diversity and prosperity we've lost. The adage that what's good for General Motors (or GE or IBM) is good for the country may not hold true in these days of outsourcing, downsizing, and wage stagnation. But what's good for the local family farm, merchant, or startup truly is good for the community.

The Case for Locavesting

Let's be clear: No one is suggesting that people rush out and sink all of their money into the local dry cleaner (and they're already very well financed, in my neighborhood at least, thanks to the Korean *kye* system, in which groups of Korean-Americans lend money to one another). Small businesses are risky, to be sure. Due diligence is definitely required, and not all ideas or entrepreneurs deserve to be funded.

Nor will local investing ever replace our current global financial system. It should be viewed as a complement—and a necessary one. As Leslie Christian, a Wall Street veteran and social-impact investment fund manager, puts it: "Ultimately, unless we have really strong local economies, we're not going to have a functioning global economy."

There is a compelling investment case to be made for small, private, community-rooted companies as a worthy and prudent asset class.

Local Is a Growth Business

The Buy Local movement has now reached mainstream proportions. Local, you could say, is the new organic—often commanding the same premium prices that organic products enjoy. The number of farmers markets have tripled in the past decade, and community-supported agriculture—where customers prepay a farm for a share of its harvest—has seen a 33-fold rise since 1990. Microbrewers are hopping. People are drawn to the authentic, unique, and artisanal. In Brooklyn, indie entrepreneurs are handcrafting everything from chocolate and

pickles to gin and kombucha. The idea has even taken hold on the
mass market Internet. Online bazaars such as Etsy, Daily Grommet,
and Abe's Market are thriving by emphasizing the stories of the entrepreneurs behind the unique products they offer, putting a face and
a set of values on what is typically an impersonal electronic purchase.

In a survey of 4,000 U.S. consumers conducted by the Natural
Marketing Institute in 2010, 41 percent of respondents said they
cared about products made locally. That number has been growing by 7 percent a year since 2006, said Gwynne Rogers, the institute's LOHAS business director (LOHAS stands for Lifestyles of
Health and Sustainability—a consumer demographic composed
of 40 percent of Americans, according to NMI). While the environment and health were factors (55 percent and 50 percent,
respectively), the biggest motivation was economic: 93 percent of
respondents believe local products are better for their community.

The branding firm BBMG, meanwhile, reported that 32 percent
of respondents in a recent study said it was "very important" to
them whether a product was grown or produced locally. And of
1,000 Americans surveyed by WebVisible in 2010, four out of five
said they choose to shop at a local, independent business over
a larger chain. Their reasons: supporting their community, conve-
nience, and service.

"Consumer interest in local has absolutely grown," says Peter
Rose, a senior vice president at The Futures Company, which
researches global trends. The factors driving the local movement
are diverse, he says, from a desire for transparency, quality, and
storytelling to environmental and social concerns. "All of these
things suggest that local has some real endurance."

Perhaps the clearest sign that the local movement has arrived
is the fact that giant corporations are now trying to muscle in on
the trend (as they have already done with organic).

HSBC, a global bank with assets of $2.4 trillion, dubs itself
"The World's Local Bank," while Frito-Lay TV ads feature family
farmers that grow its potatoes. A major ad campaign by Chevron
trumpets its support of small businesses and communities in the
areas around the world where it operates. These efforts, however, often add up to little more than "local washing." (Chevron,

for example, is currently fighting a suit brought by indigenous inhabitants of the Oriente, a patch of pristine Ecuadorian rain forest that Texaco, now owned by Chevron, systematically polluted over decades of oil exploration. How's that for a good neighbor?)

Other companies are taking more concrete steps. Some of the biggest Internet names are making local plays. Local content is a major pillar of AOL's growth strategy, building on its acquisition of local content sites Patch and Going. And mighty Google sent shock-waves through the online world with its $6 billion bid for Groupon, a two-year-old startup that offers targeted coupons and aims, in the words of its founder, to "transform the way local business is done."[1]

Retailers have gotten the local religion, too. After gobbling up and homogenizing many of the country's once-proud regional department stores, Macy's has decided to inject some local flavor into its stores with indigenous brands and products tailored to local tastes. That might mean Frango chocolates in Chicago or white church outfits in Atlanta. Macy's believes "going local" is the key to its future growth.[2] And Overstock.com last year introduced a new online Main Street Store that will carry products from small businesses.

Even the biggest retailer of them all, Walmart, has jumped on the bandwagon. In late 2010, Walmart, the world's largest grocer, announced it would stock its shelves with more locally grown products from small and midsized farmers. The company plans to double sales of locally sourced produce in the United States to 9 percent by 2015. (Walmart defines "local" as products produced in the state where the store is located.) Even a small increase could have a big impact, considering that food sales make up more than half of Walmart's $405 billion in annual revenue. The goals are higher in other countries, such as Canada, where Walmart's grocery business is brand new. Overall, the retailer hopes to sell $1 billion worth of locally produced food by 2015.

In announcing the program, Walmart portrayed it as a way to help struggling small-scale farmers, build stronger local economies, reduce the company's food miles, and provide customers with fresher food. That may be so. But there's also a clear-eyed economic rationale. Sourcing closer to stores saves Walmart money. And, as the company's web site says: "Buying locally grown produce is a hot marketplace trend, with customers increasingly reaching for staples such as tomatoes and corn that grew in local soil."

Familiarity

Investment guru Peter Lynch has long advised "Invest in what you know." Berkshire Hathaway's Warren Buffett adheres to a similar principle of sticking to his "circle of competence." That might mean investing in the company that makes your favorite minivan (in Lynch's case) or cherry soda (in Buffett's). Each investor's area of expertise will differ. But there is one thing we are all familiar with: our own backyards. By that I don't mean the tomatoes growing in the garden, but the local and regional companies we walk or drive by every day, read about in the news on a regular basis, and that are a familiar part of our environment. The flow of information about local establishments, both in the local news media and on an informal basis, tends to be much greater for a nearby company than for a distantly based one. And that, as any financial expert will tell you, is a big plus.

"Knowledge is currency," says Ben Marks, president and chief investment advisor at Marks Wealth Management in Minnetonka, Minnesota, which runs a fund that is heavily weighted in Midwestern companies, such as Minneapolis-based General Mills and Medtronic. "If you can know more about what you're investing in, it increases the probability of success." That's especially true for smaller companies, which can often offer the greatest returns but for whom information is generally less available than large companies. "Local investors have an advantage," says Josh Silverman, a wealth management advisor with Northwestern Mutual Financial Network in Charleston, South Carolina, who advocates a 100-mile investing strategy. "You can find out a lot of timely information."

In his book *Enough* (John Wiley & Sons, 2009), John Bogle, the legendary Vanguard founder, tells of a community banker who, every Sunday after church, likes to drive past a local company he's lent to, just because he *can*. That's something that J. N. Dolley's unfortunate Kansan could not easily do when he invested in a speculative New Mexico land deal. But even with modern communication and transportation systems, investors today are often similarly in the dark. Who among us can truly comprehend the Byzantine structures and operations of the typical Fortune 500 corporation?

"There's something about investing in local businesses that you can read a 15-page business plan and understand, as opposed to putting money into a company like General Electric, where you could have every degree under the sun and spend two years reviewing their books and records and still not really understand what they're doing," says Eli Moulton, a lawyer based in Vermont who has helped many small companies in the area raise money from customers and local residents. "And yet, as a society, whether it's driven by special interests or not, the focus in this country is to push money into the public markets. I think in many respects it is to support this huge financial industry we have."

Local Companies Are Profitable

Small and midsized companies do not share the economies of scale of their larger counterparts, but neither do they have the bloated overhead and bureaucracy of big corporations. That shaves a layer of cost and allows them to be more nimble and responsive to their markets. Many locally owned companies are firmly established in their regions and enjoy strong brand recognition and loyalty—lessening or eliminating the need for costly advertising campaigns. They also represent much greater growth potential than supersized corporations that have already saturated their markets. According to the federal government's Statistical Abstract, sole proprietorships—the business structure favored by many small businesses—are nearly three times more profitable than corporations.

Companies that operate in a smaller geographic area and use local suppliers have lower shipping and logistical costs, and are buffered from rising oil prices. In an age of peak oil, climate change, and rapidly growing global demand, that is a significant advantage that will only grow in importance. The Middle East is once again in turmoil, and oil prices were beginning a roller coaster rise in early 2011, driving down shares of many oil-dependent companies. Someday in the not too distant future, we could be looking at $200-a-barrel oil and $6-a-gallon gas, in which case the local model will be looking pretty smart. Prices at the gas pump aside, there is a growing recognition that there is a steep cost to carbon-based fossil fuels, and that cost will increasingly be imposed on its biggest users.

At the same time, thanks to the Internet, it is easier and cheaper than ever for small businesses to broaden their customer base.

And what about returns? Many investors assume double-digit stock market gains over time, but the reality may be quite different. Volatility has skyrocketed and, in a bubble-fueled environment, big run-ups are likely to be followed big sell-offs. Many experts say that mid-single digit returns are a more realistic expectation for the years ahead—making the modest returns offered by some smaller companies more competitive.

Here's one more data point: While large-cap stocks turned in a negative performance for the decade ended in 2010, the S&P 600, a small-cap index, actually gained an average 7.1 percent per year.[3]

Local Companies Are Less Risky Than You Might Think

There is a strong perception that small companies and startups are extremely risky—that's the reason, after all, the SEC created such high hurdles for these companies to raise money from ordinary investors. But do they really pose such hazards? Sure, there is no guarantee they will survive or thrive. As noted, only half of new businesses last longer than five years (although not always because they failed—the statistics reflect the natural flux of self-employed people moving back into the job market). But every behemoth, from Apple to Procter & Gamble, was once an ambitious startup. And there are also plenty of established businesses with strong track records—companies like Wolfgang Chocolates in York, Pennsylvania, and Storm Smart in Fort Myers, Florida—that are poised for growth.

Larger companies may have the resources to better weather a downturn, but size no longer guarantees safety, if it ever did. Who would have thought that Lehman Brothers, a 158-year-old investment firm that had just had logged its most profitable years, would vanish virtually overnight? Or that Arthur Andersen, a global consulting company founded in 1913, would be dissolved in disgrace after the envy-inducing profits of one of its clients, Wall Street darling Enron, were revealed to be phony? At least you can rest easier knowing that a local business probably isn't dabbling in highly leveraged derivative trades or special-purpose investment vehicles or engaging in risky, complex activities that could blow up—quite literally, as BP shareholders discovered after the Deepwater Horizon oil rig exploded in April 2010, killing 11 workers, unleashing millions of gallons of oil into the Gulf of Mexico, and evaporating $88 billion of shareholder wealth in a matter of weeks.[4]

Diversification

As an asset class, local companies can help diversify a portfolio. Locally rooted companies are less likely to be buffeted by the global disruptions and Wall Street mischief that rock the markets with increasing frequency. The flip side, of course, is the concentrated geographic risk: If an area is hit by a natural disaster or a localized economic setback, investments in that area would be impacted. That's why most locavestors invest just a portion—anywhere from 5 percent to 20 percent, although some have gone much higher—of their investment dollars in local and regional enterprises.

Diversification is an accepted strategy to minimize risk in an investment portfolio. But what about an economy? Local investing can help us move away from the systemic risks embedded in our Too Big to Fail system. For the nation as a whole, a more diversified, distributed economy—just like a smart, distributed electric grid or computer network—makes for a more resilient system, less vulnerable to a shock to any one part, whether the failure of a major bank, sovereign country, or political regime. And that benefits all investors.

Indeed, sophisticated investors have been casting about for alternative investments that can earn a decent return and, more importantly, diversify their holdings so they are not so tied to the increasingly volatile stock market. In their quest, investors have poured millions of dollars into ever-more speculative and questionable investments—from catastrophe bonds that essentially bet on a gentle Mother Nature, to loans to young Dominican athletes in return for a cut of their future signing bonuses, to bets on the premature death of life insurance policy holders.[5]

Local companies, I submit, are an alternative investment class you can feel good about.

A Grassroots Movement

Don't expect to hear any of that from your mainstream broker. Local investing, for now, is a purely grassroots movement, flourishing in the cracks of the financial system. When I inquired with Charles Schwab, where I have a retirement account, about investing some of my savings locally, the pleasant advisor handling my call was stumped. Domestic or international funds she could do. But Brooklyn? She suggested that perhaps I could invest in a New York state municipal bond. (Self-directed IRAs, which are available from many banks and brokerages, offer investors a greater degree of flexibility. While conventional IRAs stick to mainly stocks, bonds, and CDs, a self-directed IRA may be invested in alternative assets such as real estate and private equity—including many of the types of investments we will discuss in coming chapters).

Nor will your broker point out the broader benefits of investing locally. As vital links in a local web, these enterprises benefit their communities in myriad ways. So when you invest in a local or regional company, the "returns" are much more than monetary.

For one, local business owners are more than business managers; they are residents and neighbors who have a reputation and stake in the community. Their kids go to the same schools as the children of their customers and employees, and they rely on the same municipal and state services. With that connection comes an implicit responsibility and accountability. While a national or multinational corporation owned by absentee shareholders is driven solely by a mandate to maximize profits, a local business owner is likely to take a broader range of factors into consideration when, say, closing a plant, voting on tax issues that might affect local services or schools, or taking action that could potentially damage the environment. In a study funded by the Environmental Protection Agency of more than 2,000 chemical plants, absentee-owned plants released three times more toxins than those based in the area.[6]

Independent, local companies are also good for local business. They patronize neighboring establishments and carry each other's goods. When they need supplies or services—whether construction, web design, accounting and legal services, cleaning, or catering— they typically use local providers, thereby creating or supporting more jobs in the area. I see this sort of cross pollination all the time in my neighborhood, where local businesses take pride in offering Brooklyn-made wares in their shops and restaurants, and you'll encounter many examples across the country in the pages to come. Independent businesses are also the mainstay of local advertising, helping to keep alive a vibrant local media that covers issues and politics of interest to the community. In an age of corporate media consolidation, that can mean the difference between cookie-cutter content and programming, and useful, on-the-ground news.

Contrast that to typical corporations and chain stores, where purchasing, advertising, and charitable giving are highly centralized operations dictated by headquarters. Their models rely on economies of scale, so they procure from large suppliers who are tuned to the same model. Their vast supply chains stretch to China but bypass local vendors. Big corporations also tend to advertise in national venues and give to national charitable organizations.

Terry Lutes, chief operating officer of the Illinois Department of Commerce and Economic Opportunity, refers to these intangible qualities as social capital. "If you go to a local Little League ballpark, you'd see all the kids out there playing," says Lutes, "and you would notice that it's a local establishment sponsoring them." (Hmm. Anyone ever seen Team Target?) "We've also noticed that it's usually the local business people making good on giving to local charities and supporting local causes," he adds. Indeed, local businesses give 2.5 times more to local charities per employees than nonlocal firms, according to one tally.[7]

In addition, as members of the community, local business owners are more likely to contribute in a time of need. A study of assistance in the wake of Hurricane Floyd in Pitt County, North Carolina, found that local branches of national chains were less likely than locally owned franchises to provide assistance to employees adversely affected by the storm. The national chains were also less likely than local businesses to contribute to relief and recovery efforts.[8] In Bay St. Louis, Mississippi, the lone locally owned radio station, WQRZ-LP, was the only broadcaster operating after Hurricane Katrina, providing a critical source of news when commercial stations went silent.

A healthy independent business base is also critical to a region's tax base. Many large corporations employ sophisticated tax strategies to dodge their fair share of taxes, taking advantage of corporate tax loopholes large enough to drive a Brinks truck through and off-shore tax havens that are little more than a post office box. And the taxes they do pay often abruptly vanish when the company decides to close a plant or store or move to greener (cheaper) pastures.

The Local Multiplier

It makes intuitive sense that a robust independent business presence benefits communities. And research backs that up. A strong body of research dating back to the 1940s makes a persuasive case that communities with a diversified economy comprised of many locally owned businesses have a higher quality of life, civic engagement, and income equality than similar communities that are reliant upon on a few large employers.[9]

More recent studies have shown that money spent at a local retailer, as opposed to a national chain, circulates locally rather than being "leaked" out of the community to the coffers of a distant headquarters. This economic boost is known as the local multiplier effect.

Civic Economics, an economic development consultancy, has been at the forefront of measuring the direct and indirect benefits of independent businesses on their locales. "Usually it's an emotional argument," explains Matt Cunningham, a principal at Civic Economics. "We thought there was an economic argument, too." The firm has conducted several studies since 2004 comparing locally owned, independent merchants and service providers with their national chain peers. In each case, the independents generated more local economic activity—measured in wages, jobs, local spending, taxes, and charitable giving—for each dollar of revenue, up to three times more activity than the same dollar spent at a neighboring chain. This is because a greater portion of their hiring, purchasing, spending of profits, and charitable giving takes place in the local area. The results are specific to each locale and the types of businesses studied, says Cunningham, but "it's definitive that a locally owned business will keep more money local than a chain."

The firm's 2004 study of Andersonville, Illinois, a Chicago neighborhood with a strong independent retailer presence, is often cited. It found that for every $100 spent at a local store, a full $68 remains in Chicago. The same amount spent at a chain would net only $43. In San Francisco, a city that has preserved its retail independence, a 2007 analysis concluded that a 10 percent market share increase by local merchants could create $200 million in additional economic activity and create more than 1,300 jobs. The findings of a 2008 study of Grand Rapids, Michigan, were similarly stunning: A 10 percent shift of sales from chains to locals would result in a $137 million jolt to the local economy and 1,600 new jobs.

Now there's a stimulus package that won't cost taxpayers a dime.

A more recent study by Civic Economics, completed in September 2009, was commissioned to help guide post-Katrina development and renewal in New Orleans. The study focused on a four-block stretch of retail-heavy Magazine Street that is home to 100 independent businesses that collectively occupy 179,000 square feet of retail space. Of the $105 million in sales generated by the businesses, about a third, or $34 million, stays local. In contrast, a SuperTarget store composed of the same amount of retail square footage (not including parking) would generate $50 million in annual sales, the study estimated, of which just $8 million, or 16 percent, would remain local. Extrapolating the results out to the broader New Orleans economy, the report concluded that an all-local retail economy would generate $2.35 billion more a year in local economic activity than an all-chain economy. Neither extreme is realistic, of course, but the message is clear: Local enterprises provide more bang for the buck to their communities.

What those studies don't capture is the extent to which locally owned businesses add to the diversity, character, and appeal of our neighborhoods and downtowns. By promoting human scale commerce, local merchants facilitate chance encounters and chats with neighbors. These casual interactions are more than friendly diversions. They are essential for building the relationships and civic bonds that make for a healthy, well-functioning society and democratic process. Even as our Facebook connections have multiplied into the hundreds, studies have shown that most Americans' core networks— the people they can discuss important matters with—have shrunk and become less diverse in the past two decades. Just 43 percent of

Americans know most of their neighbors by name, and 28 percent know none, according to a Pew Research poll. Vibrant neighborhoods are key to shaking us out of our increasingly atomized existences.

They also provide relief from a soul-crushing monoculture of strip malls and highways. A study by CEOs for Cities found that, even in the midst of a housing slump, houses in areas with greater levels of walkability—measured by their proximity to stores, restaurants, and other amenities—had higher values, commanding premiums of $4,000 to $34,000.[10]

The John S. and James L. Knight Foundation's Soul of the Community project interviewed 43,000 people in 26 communities over three years to determine what makes a community a desirable place to live. The answers are important, the foundation notes, because communities that inspire a strong sense of attachment among their residents have higher local GDP. What did they find? The most desirable qualities are the presence of social gathering spots, openness and a welcoming spirit, and an area's physical beauty and green spaces.[11] It seems we are nostalgic for the idyllic small town. There is a deep sense that we have lost something vital, that the forces of corporate-led globalization have eroded the character, independence, and cultural diversity of our towns and communities. That is true in the world's most remote villages as well as its biggest metropolises. In response, grassroots organizations around the world are forming to counter that trend with "economic localization."

The signs are everywhere. Cooperatives, community gardens, and community-supported agriculture are flourishing. Slow Money, a national network modeled on the Slow Food movement, is attempting to finance the rebuilding of local food systems. The Business Alliance for Local Living Economies (BALLE), a coalition of citizens and entrepreneurs passionate about building strong local communities, is making an impact in every corner of the country. Meanwhile, hundreds of "transition towns" across the United States and other countries are marshaling grassroots resources to build resilient communities that can withstand severe ecologic or economic shocks and offer a higher quality of life.

Communities are taking control of their economic destiny. Many have created local currencies, such as Detroit Cheers or

Ithaca HOURs in upstate New York, to keep money circulating locally. The largest such system, BerkShares, serving the Berkshires region of northwestern Massachusetts, is accepted at more than 400 businesses and several banks, and 2.5 million of the notes have circulated since the scrip was introduced in 2006. The Brooklyn Torch will soon debut in North Brooklyn.

Meanwhile, local businesses are banding together to raise awareness among customers of the importance of shopping at local, independently owned enterprises. Inspired by Civic Economics' local impact studies, the 10% Shift, a campaign that encourages people to redirect a portion of their spending to independent businesses, has spread from New England across the country. Local business alliances, such as the Austin Independent Business Alliance in Texas and Local First Lexington in Kentucky, have sprung up in more than 130 cities. And they've had astounding success.

Over the 2008 holiday season, when retail sales everywhere slumped, the big chains reported punishing declines over the prior year. Sales at Borders and The Gap slid 14 percent, while Williams-Sonoma took a 24 percent hit. Independent retailers fared better. Their sales were down 5 percent overall, but just 3.2 percent in cities with active "buy local" programs, according to a survey conducted by the Institute for Local Self-Reliance. The trend continued over the 2009 holidays, with indie sales up 2.2 percent overall and 3 percent in areas with campaigns, compared with Commerce Department–reported sales growth of 1.8 percent in November and negative 0.3 percent in December for all retail sales.[12]

Shifting Fortunes

We've seen that a shift of just 10 percent of spending from corporate-owned chains to locally owned merchants can have an outsized impact on the local economy. What would a similar 10 percent shift in investment dollars from Fortune 500 to locally owned businesses yield? Or even a 5 percent shift?

Or, as Slow Money founder Woody Tasch asks, in typically ambitious fashion: *What would the world be like if we invested 50 percent of our assets within 50 miles of where we live?*

It's a powerful question, but one that begs many more. What would these micro-investing models look like? How can we ensure investors are protected? And what is a fair return? If the answers are not yet clear, the promise is. "There is the potential for an unexpected, rapid shift in investment," says Michael Shuman, that could pull a trillion dollars out of "business as usual."

Politicians will continue to battle for bragging rights as BFF (best friend forever) of the entrepreneur, and the Chamber of Commerce will push its Big Business agenda on their behalf. But the real solutions are taking shape far from corporate boardrooms and the power corridors of Washington, D.C., as entrepreneurs, investors, and citizens experiment with alternative ways of raising capital for small scale, community-centered businesses. Rather than sit back and wait for the government or some benevolent corporation to ride in to their rescue, communities across the country are taking matters into their own hands, devising innovative ways to nurture their local entrepreneurs and established businesses. They are exploring new models of ownership that align the goals of investor and business, and even blur the line between customer and owner.

Some of these ideas are simple, harkening back to the way business used to be done, such as the informal group of residents of Port Townsend, Washington, that invest in local businesses, or the democratically run cooperatives that are undergoing a resurgence. Others ideas, such as crowdfunding—where many small investments are aggregated from many people over the Internet—are more complicated and must carefully navigate the regulatory thicket to succeed. Similarly, an effort to bring back local stock exchanges—the kind that served regional communities for much of our history—faces significant legal and behavioral challenges, but offers exciting potential to reconnect local investors and businesses.

All of the efforts you will read about, however, seek to create an alternative space where citizens, investors, and entrepreneurs can come together to build healthy, resilient companies and communities less vulnerable to the machinations of global conglomerates and speculators. In doing so, they just may restore our faith in capitalism.

The Local Imperative

Leveling the Playing Field

Before we meet the innovators (and a couple of old standbys) who are creating new models for local investing, it is useful to take a closer look at what types of small businesses we are talking about and why supporting them is so important to our prosperity and well-being. Defining what exactly constitutes a small business can be tricky—and ripe for manipulation.

The Small Business Administration (SBA) defines a small business as a concern that is "organized for profit; has a place of business in the United States; makes a significant contribution to the U.S. economy through payment of taxes or use of American products, materials or labor; is independently owned and operated; is not dominant in its field, on a national basis; and is no larger than SBA's small business size standard for its industry."[1]

A definition that only a bureaucrat could love.

Generally, the size cutoff is 500 employees. But employee headcount can be misleading. A hedge fund, for example, may have three employees but rake in a half a billion dollars. So, in addition to employee headcount, the SBA also sets revenue thresholds by industry—less than $750,000 for agriculture, for example, and less than $33.5 million for building and construction—but a general rule of thumb is $7 million or less in average annual receipts for nonmanufacturing industries. These parameters are used to determine eligibility for small business loans and government procurement programs. A small business may be a sole proprietorship, partnership, corporation, or other legal form.

But the definition is malleable, and small business owners end up a convenient pawn in policy debates. Take the controversy over the expiration of the Bush tax cuts in 2010, which, if allowed to expire for top earners as proposed by President Obama, would have reinstated a higher tax rate on individual incomes greater than $250,000 a year. (In a compromise bill, the cuts were extended for another two years.) Critics of the proposal, including the Chamber of Commerce and most Republicans, argued that allowing the top tax cuts to expire would hurt the nation's hardworking small business owners. In fact, as the SBA Office of Advocacy noted, only 4 percent of the self-employed would be affected. The real issue, it seems, was the 3 percent of "small businesses" that generate half of all small business net income. Among the "family businesses" that benefit from the Bush tax cuts are oil and mining giant Koch Industries (2009 revenues: $100 billion), global consulting giant PricewaterhouseCoopers (2009 revenues: $26 billion), and private equity firm KKR (assets under management: $55 billion), not to mention many lobbyists, lawyers, celebrities, and politicians.[2] Not exactly the mental image conjured up by "small business."

How do these behemoths pass themselves off as small fry? By adopting typical small business structures—such as sole proprietorships, partnerships, and S-Corps. Businesses structured in these ways don't pay corporate taxes; instead, the profit or loss from the business is "passed through" to the owners, who are taxed as individuals. When a giant company is controlled by a small number of shareholders, this can translate into big savings.[3] The Tribune Company saved $1.9 billion by converting to S-Corp status in 2008, by the company's own account.[4] When billionaire Sam Zell bought the media company, which publishes the *Chicago Tribune* and *Los Angeles Times* among many other newspapers, in a leveraged buyout in 2007, he engineered an elaborate structure that allowed him to take advantage of a 1996 provision intended to spur employee ownership of small business.[5] (The tax holiday still didn't save the company from collapsing under the weight of its debt and mismanagement: Tribune filed for Chapter 11 bankruptcy protection in December 2008.) In 1980, before the rules for pass-through entities were loosened, the share of net business income earned by traditional corporations was 80 percent. By 2007, it had shrunk to 53 percent.[6]

Small business parameters are similarly skewed when it comes to procurement. By law, the federal government must spend 23 percent of its prime contracts with small business. Yet various loopholes have allowed some of the largest companies in the United States, Europe, and Asia, including Boeing, Northrop Grumman, Bechtel, and British Aerospace, to qualify for small business contracts—diverting $100 billion a year from small business, according to the American Small Business League. The group estimates that less than 5 percent of federal contracts are actually awarded to small business. That's a loss for us all. A Senate study suggests that every 1 percent increase in federal contracts to small businesses would create more than 100,000 jobs.[7]

For the purposes of this book, however, we are concerned with *real* small businesses making real things or providing true services. That may include sole proprietorships, mom-and-pops, high-growth startups, and established companies with a couple of hundred employees. The companies may be involved in food and agriculture, like Milk Thistle Farm, or high-tech manufacturing, like Moebius Technologies. The defining characteristic of a locavestor business is that it is locally owned and rooted in a community. It is not run by absentee owners who dictate decisions affecting a community from a far-off headquarters with the sole intent of maximizing profit. A locavestor business pays local taxes and is a stakeholder in its region. These are the small businesses that make up the fabric of our communities, adding to their diversity, character, and wealth, the businesses that we want to keep in our lives. For me, it's my favorite local wine shop, where a visit invariably involves a lively discussion of Italian food with Mathew, the owner, and the swapping of recipes before he points us to his latest finds. It's a very different experience than, say, a trip to Trader Joe's. As with Supreme Court Justice Potter Stewart's famous definition of pornography, you know a locavestor business when you see it.

It is a diverse group. According to the SBA, 29 percent of non-farm small businesses are owned by women, and 21 percent are owned by minorities (there may be overlap in the groups). But what binds them is their independence, passion, and ambition. For some, that means rapid growth and perhaps someday joining the ranks of America's top companies. Others have more measured growth goals and little interest in the "get big fast" track. In fact, only one out of five entrepreneurs seeks "maximum growth," according to an SBA study. The majority simply want to manage an enterprise that is a comfortable size and scale.[8] In an age of corporate gigantism and profit primacy, that is refreshing.

"I think business school culture, and more recently Silicon Valley culture, places way too much value on the high growth potential venture," says David Fisher, a small business consultant and former economic development official in Hawaii. "It's like saying, don't bother to take a walk in the park if you are not planning to go to the Olympics. I have helped a lot of people develop businesses that do under a half a million a year in revenue, yet have happy owners and workers and a happy community."

Locavestor entrepreneurs are often motivated by broader goals than simply extracting the most possible profit. As Sagar Sheth explains, "When an entrepreneur says 'my goal in life is to see one hundred people employed,' that's so much more valuable than a goal of seeing a million dollars in your pocket. There's something to be very proud of in that." In the three years since he and his partner started Moebius Technologies, they have not paid themselves a salary. "That's what it takes, and we understand that," says Sheth. "We know that if you're going to build a beautiful business, a sustainable company that hires people and grows, you have to make sacrifices."

And local? That, too, can be in the eye of the beholder. Local is a loose term that can be applied to a tight knit neighborhood, or the boundaries of a state. It can also extend to a geographic region with a shared identity, such as New England. The companies in your immediate community—the mom-and-pops, the farmers, the homegrown startup—are certainly at the core of what we think of when we say local. But there are also publicly traded companies in most regions that benefit the local economy.

That's the philosophy at Marks Wealth Management of Minnetonka, Minnesota, just outside of Minneapolis—a region rich with local companies that made good. The firm's core equity portfolio, composed of about 35 stocks, has a strong Midwestern flavor. Ben Marks, president and chief investment officer, says that appeals to his clients. "Midwesterners think we're a little hardier and a little more conservative, a little more honest, more hard-working," he says. "It may not be true, but we like to think it's true. But I do think the message really resonates with our clients."

In addition to pride of place, there's also a sense of comfort with the familiar. "Our clients would much prefer to own Med-tronic than some company in Japan or China that might make a similar product," says Marks. "You're not going to know the man-agement, you're just not going to know the corporate culture."

Give Darwin a Chance

Some people will argue that small businesses for generations have gotten by just fine on funding culled from savings, friends and family, credit cards, and bank loans. And that, while these sources of funding may be harder to come by today, it is just a temporary condition. But that would overlook some fundamental changes over the past few decades that have put small businesses at a distinct dis-advantage. We are dealing with structural issues and entrenched bias, not a cyclical blip that will disappear with a rise in the Dow. In fact, the Dow Jones Industrial Average was up 11 percent for 2010, thanks to record corporate profits, but small firms were still strug-gling to raise funds and unemployment barely budged.

The competitive playing field, long tilted in favor of big busi-ness, has grown even more lopsided. Large corporations and national chains enjoy a huge competitive advantage over their smaller rivals. They can raise capital more easily and cheaply, and they can draw on deeper reserves to weather a downturn. They can also promote "loss leaders" to gain a competitive edge. Due to their size, they are better able to absorb increasing regulatory costs, which cost small firms much more on a per-employee basis. And, although they need it least, our biggest corporations are the beneficiaries of generous public largesse.

This is not good old Darwinian survival of the fittest. This is the powerful and well-connected getting a generous helping hand from the government.

U.S. taxpayers fork over almost $125 billion each year in subsidies to U.S. businesses—the equivalent of all the income tax paid by 60 million individuals and families, according to Public Citizen, a nonprofit, nonpartisan group based in Washington. The subsidies come in different forms, including tax breaks, incentives, and direct government payments to offset research and other activities. And they go to some of the richest corporations on the planet. Oil companies including BP, ExxonMobil, and Chevron benefit from billions of dollars' worth of subsidies a year. Cutting just nine of their tax subsidies, as proposed by the Obama administration, would save $45 billion over 10 years.[9] The oil giants, for example, get paid to blend ethanol into the gasoline, something they are already required to do by law. The five-year cost: $31 billion.[10] And that doesn't begin to account for the external costs of pollution, environmental degradation, and a national defense policy centered on protecting oil interests abroad that is borne by taxpayers.

Agri-giant Archer Daniel Midlands also benefits mightily from ethanol subsidies. According to one calculation, every dollar in ethanol profits for ADM costs the public $2.85.[11] Forty percent of ADM's profits come from heavily subsidized crops, according to a Cato Institute study.[12] Again, the Big Ag subsidies pose external costs to society, in the form of cheap corn-based sweeteners that have infiltrated our food products and contributed to climbing obesity rates, a loss of biodiversity in favor of mono-crops, agricultural run-off, and so on.

A more insidious form of corporate welfare is the discretionary subsidies negotiated in secret by state and local officials to attract big plants, company headquarters, sports stadiums, and other developments to their areas—to the tune of an estimated $50 billion a year. The situation is especially distressing—and visible—in retail, as chain stores continue to displace the independent merchants that have long served their communities. The big boxes are viewed as lucrative prizes to many city and town officials, who offer major tax concessions, real estate deals, and taxpayer-funded infrastructure improvements to lure them.

Good Jobs First, a policy research center, has tallied more than $1 billion in development subsidies granted to Walmart stores and distribution centers alone since the early 1990s, including tax breaks, free or bargain land, and infrastructure assistance. The group says the figure is likely conservative, since there are no disclosure requirements and their research relied on published reports.[13]

The reward for all this lucre? Local jobs and tax revenues. But the reality is often starkly different, as benefits fall far short of promises.

The Big-Box Squeeze

Stacy Mitchell, a senior researcher at the New Rules Project, a program of the Institute for Local Self-Reliance, has written extensively about the corrosive effects of big box stores. In her 2006 book *Big Box Swindle,* she details the hidden costs of these one-stop-shopping meccas and supersized chains, from Home Depot to Target to Walmart. Instead of adding jobs to a region, over the long term, net new jobs may be negative as local merchants across a wide swath of specialties go out of business. Often, that means replacing good-paying jobs and benefits with lower wage, part-time work. (One study concluded that the opening of a Walmart store can drive down wages in the entire county.[14])

Given the low pay and part-time hours—a typical 34-hour a week worker at Wal-Mart will make an estimated $19,200 a year—many big-box employees often cannot afford the health-care plans they are offered.[15] These workers are often among the biggest users of taxpayer-funded health care. Massachusetts is one of the few states that tracks public health-care usage by employer.

Since 2006, Walmart has topped its list of companies with workers dependent upon health-care programs run by the state. In 2008, 5,021 Walmart workers were enrolled in such programs in Massachusetts alone. The situation is much the same in states across the country.[16]

Researchers at Loyola University tracked 306 retail businesses within a four-mile radius of a Walmart that opened on the west side of Chicago in 2006. By 2008, 82 had gone out of business, with the hardest-hit retailers being the closest to Walmart. The equivalent of 300 full-time jobs were lost. What's more, after analyzing taxable sales for nine months before and nine months after Walmart opened, the researchers found that sales receipts in the surrounding area had declined.[17]

Meanwhile, those empty downtown storefronts can lead to the decline of a once-bustling commercial district, lowering a town's property taxes and diminishing what was once its most valuable real estate. And because chains have tax strategies available to them that the independents do not (like combined reporting, which allows them report a loss even if the store is profitable in that particular state), the overall effect can be a lowering of a region's tax collections. Add to that the considerable costs of maintaining infrastructure such as roads, lights, and security that come with a big-box presence, and the expected windfall quickly disappears.

But by now, the town is totally dependent on the big-box as a revenue source, which can be a problem when, invariably, the shiny supercenter starts feeling a little old and outdated. The retailer starts looking around for greener pastures, sparking another round of frantic concessions by town officials to keep the store, and pitting one locality against another.

That's the local damage. But what about the impact on the overall economy?

As the big-boxes have grown, so has their clout, to the point where they are reorganizing large swaths of the economy around themselves. Suppliers must play by their rules—or be shut out. Costs are increasingly pushed onto suppliers, who may even be assessed a fee if their products fail to generate sufficient profits.[18]

In their relentless quest for ever-lower prices, the mega-retailers squeeze the margins of their suppliers, prompting virtually all to seek the lowest cost manufacturing overseas. Suppliers often look to make up some of the lost margin with less powerful retailers—the independents. In recent years, the mega-retailers have expanded into private label, launching their own brands, which compete with the products of their longtime suppliers. That's driven many consumer-products makers to merge with competitors or worse, into bankruptcy. Four of Walmart's top 10 suppliers in 2004 filed for bankruptcy protection by 2006.[19] In this way, the big-box squeeze has contributed to the consolidation of corporate power and the bleeding of jobs overseas.

And we haven't even touched on environmental issues such as massive runoff from the acres of parking lots that pollutes our waterways, the abandoned big-box shells that litter the landscape, and the increased car travel involved in going to the store. As Mitchell has noted, in the late 1970s, the average household drove 1,200 miles a year for shopping. That figure has tripled, to about 3,600 miles. After the 1970s, she writes, "stores got a lot bigger. Between 1982 and 2002, more than 100,000 small retailers disappeared. The big-box stores that replaced them were many times larger, far fewer in number, and thus served larger geographic areas."[20]

The Price of Power

As corporate power has consolidated in every field, from healthcare to agriculture to finance, Big Business has furthered its stranglehold on government and society. Corporations spend hundreds of millions of dollars every year on lobbying and political campaigns. Many of these corporations' executives and lobbyists end up running government agencies that oversee their former industries. Corporations not only influence legislation, they also write it.

In 2009, as important legislation from health care to financial reform was being considered by Congress, big business mobilized. Less than a year after their near-death experience, financial firms poured a record $78 million into the coffers of federal candidates and political organizations. Commercial banks alone spent more than $50 million in lobbying that year, and interested parties such as Goldman Sachs, Visa, and the Private Equity Council fielded lobbying teams stuffed with ex-government officials.[21] And even as they publicly made nice, the largest health-care organizations spent more than a half-billion dollars to influence landmark health-care legislation. The Chamber of Commerce, backed by some of the biggest corporations in the world, spent almost $80 million in just three months in the fall of 2009.

Thanks to the controversial *Citizens United* Supreme Court decision in July 2010, corporations and special interest groups can now spend unlimited sums on political advertisements without ever having to reveal their role. In the 2010 midterm elections, more than $455 million flooded into ads aimed at defeating or promoting candidates, much of it from opaque "grassroots" groups created after the ruling.

The fix is in. And what do we get in return? Outsourced jobs and offshore tax shelters that rob the country of revenue.

U.S. corporations raked in record profits in 2010—$1.6 trillion in the third quarter alone, fueled by massive cost-cutting and lay-offs and the ability to borrow on the cheap.[22] They were also sitting atop a mountain of cash totaling nearly $2 trillion. But that did not translate into jobs. Recent economic downturns, unlike those of the past, are increasingly followed by jobless recoveries. What's changed? The balance of power between corporations and their employees, according to a growing chorus of economic observers. Unions have withered, courts have become friendlier to big business, and "companies now come closer to setting the terms of their relationship with employees, letting them go when they become a drag on profits and relying on remaining workers or temporary ones when business picks up," writes David Leonhardt in the *New York Times*.

Desmond Lachman, a scholar at the American Enterprise Institute, notes, "Corporations are taking advantage of slack in the labor market. They are using that bargaining power to cut benefits and wages, and to shorten hours."[23] The diminished work conditions of the private sector are now the standard to which public sector employees—such as teachers and firefighters—are being compared.

In the meantime, millions of American jobs have been shipped overseas. The foreign subsidiaries and affiliates of U.S. multinational firms added 729,000 employees between 2006 and 2008, for a total of 11.9 million, according to Commerce Department data. Over the same two-year period, they cut 500,000 jobs at home, reducing their domestic workforce to 21.1 million.[24] (That's one reason why U.S. manufacturing employment can decrease even as exports rise.)

In addition to lost jobs, we get lost revenue. The official U.S. corporate tax rate is 35 percent, but few big companies actually pay that. According to a 2008 report by the Government Accountability Office (GAO), a quarter of the country's largest companies paid no federal income taxes in 2005 on their $1.1 trillion in gross sales that year.[25] None. General Electric raked in more than $14 billion in worldwide profits in 2010. Not only did it not pay any U.S. taxes—it claimed a tax benefit of $3.2 billion. All told, corporations accounted for just 6 percent of U.S. tax receipts in 2009, down from 30 percent in the mid-1950s.[26] With the United States facing a projected $1.4 trillion budget gap, the tax burden falls on smaller companies and ordinary citizens.

Domestic companies with global subsidiaries cost U.S. taxpayers an estimated $37 billion a year in lost tax revenue, according to Business and Investors Against Tax Haven Abuse, a coalition of small business and investor groups. Add in wealthy individuals, and the loss from overseas tax havens could be as much as $123 billion, according to the Treasury Department. At the higher range, the group points out, those funds could pay for a 12 percent tax cut for every individual.

In 2007, Citigroup had 427 tax haven subsidiaries, Morgan Stanley had 273, Bank of America had 115, Lehman Brothers had 57, JP Morgan Chase had 50, Goldman Sachs had 29, and AIG had 18, according to the GAO. In 2008, Goldman Sachs paid just $14 million in federal taxes on profits of more than $2 billion— an effective tax rate of less than 1 percent. That's less than a third of Goldman CEO Lloyd Blankfein's annual pay, Business and Investors Against Tax Havens points out.

It's not just financial companies. Eighty-three of the top 100 largest publicly traded companies park money in offshore tax havens. Google, the search giant whose motto is Do No Evil, has saved more than a billion dollars a year in taxes for the past three years by shifting income to tax havens and expenses to countries with higher corporate tax rates.[27]

Even some corporate champions are disturbed. Michael Porter, the noted Harvard business professor and corporate strategist, for one, is urging change. "Corporations are widely perceived to be prospering at the expense of the broader community," he wrote in a January 2011 article urging a more inclusive approach to creating value.[28] A recent Pew poll found that two-thirds of Americans say they have "a great deal" or "quite a lot" of confidence in small business, compared to just 19 percent who are confident about big business. (The only group to rate lower in the poll was Congress.[29])

Sitting atop their growing fiefdoms, the nation's CEOs have enjoyed staggering pay increases. Walmart's CEO makes more in an hour than some of his employees will earn in a year, according to one calculation.[30] CEO pay is emblematic of a troubling rise in income inequality. The past decade has been very good to the super rich. The top 1 percent of the country's population grabbed 23.5 percent of all pretax income in 2007, up from less than 9 percent in 1976.[31] Indeed, the top 1 percent of Americans owns more than a third of the country's private wealth—more than the entire wealth owned by the bottom 90 percent. No wonder pundits are likening the United States to a banana republic.[32]

Rethinking Old Habits

Is this the kind of world we want? Just as every purchase is a vote, every investment dollar carries a deeper message. If we care about our communities, our middle class, and the future prosperity of our country, we must rethink our behavior.

That's starting to happen in some interesting quarters. With cities, counties, and states saddled with crippling budget gaps, the economics of local is gaining adherents among economic planners and others.

This new view of economic development is sometimes referred to as economic gardening, because it emphasizes nurturing a region's existing businesses, rather than hunting for "big game." Studies have found that the cost of creating a job is dramatically lower when states focus their efforts on local companies.

In Illinois, which faces a $13 billion deficit and a woefully under-financed pension system, Terry Lutes, chief operating officer of the Illinois Department of Commerce and Economic Opportunity, and his team are trying a new approach. "For a long time everybody bought into the notion that it was all the big bang . . . bring in the big plant or a company with 200 or 1,000 jobs," he explains. "In the process, we all started to realize that we are bidding against each other and the companies are all using us. Every state has this. We've become a little more cognizant of the fact that they're playing us off against each other."

In late 2004, for example, Maytag Corp. closed a refrigerator factory in Galesburg in western Illinois to take advantage of cheaper labor in Mexico. The move eliminated 1,600 factory jobs—5 percent of the local workforce—and sent a ripple effect through the local economy, jeopardizing as many as 2,000 additional jobs.[33] The move came despite $12 million in subsidies showered on the company just a few years before by state and local governments. After Whirlpool acquired Maytag in 2005, things went from bad to worse. The company announced it would close another Maytag plant in Herrin, Illinois, eliminating 1,000 jobs—prompting the state to try to recoup almost $200,000 recently forked over by the state for improvements in the factory (a down-payment on a total $385,000 promised). And despite promises of tens of millions of dollars for a new plant and job training offered by then-governor Tom Vilsack, Whirlpool went on to close several more plants.[34]

Lutes, a former technology entrepreneur, figures that it may be more cost effective to generate small business jobs. The new math goes something like this: Illinois has 500,000 small businesses. If the state could help each one of them hire just one employee, it could reduce the unemployment rate by 5 percentage points.

Lutes says he is not completely abandoning the big companies, just taking a more "diversified" approach. But he is clearly excited by the prospects.

Some of the measures his department is considering are taxing Internet sales, which could snare $70 million (Illinois is one of many states that don't collect tax on online sales, which hurts local retailers), creating a microloan program for entrepreneurs, and helping local independent businesses create Buy Local programs and strong local branding to boost sales.

Other states, such as Vermont and Arizona, have been successful in promoting local business as a way to create jobs. "We're a follower," concedes Lutes, "but we're kind of a big follower. Larger states are still in the thrall of trying to get the big score."

An independent look at the numbers backs up Lutes' logic. From 2006 to 2008, Illinois resident companies (independents and firms headquartered in the state) added a modest 35,000 jobs. Nonresident companies, on the other hand, shed 151,000 Illinois jobs, or 10.8 percent of their state workforce, according to YourEconomy. org, a brilliant interactive database developed by the Edward Lowe Foundation. Try it and see who is creating jobs in your own state.

Now it is our turn, as investors. A *Los Angeles Time* article about the Bill and Melinda Gates Foundation called attention to the contradictions that investing often entails.[35] The foundation spends hundreds of millions of dollars on programs aimed at improving health and eradicating deadly diseases in Africa. Yet its assets were invested in oil companies whose African plants spew toxic fumes that have contributed to widespread health problems in the region. Similarly, many citizens are frustrated with the high rate of unemployment and other economic ills, but have all of their savings invested in some of the companies most responsible for sending jobs overseas and reducing worker standards.

Socially responsible investing (SRI) is a good start. But the SRI model—of screening out companies whose business involves weapons, tobacco, or troubled regions of the world, rather than proactively seeking out the kinds of companies we want to encourage— has its limits. Local investing is proactive impact investing. Think of it as a grassroots stimulus.

Locavesting is not a panacea. Many of the investment models you are about to read about are little more than grand ideas, with the hard work of hammering out the details still ahead. Some will never gain widespread acceptance or viability without changes to our securities laws. Others may work well for one community or sector but not another. Yet, they are all worth pursuing, and we ignore them at our peril. After all, what is our choice? We can continue subsidizing corporate dominance, the Wall Street casino, and foreign jobs, or we can begin to build a different world, dollar by dollar.

The local investing movement is not anti–big business. It just asks that we consider the implications of our policies and actions, and that we give local enterprises a fair shake. As Michelle Long of the Business Alliance for Local Living Economies put it: "We're not against scale. But we question it when it means violence, or outwitting your stupid customers, or squeezing your competitors." Rather, the movement celebrates the native genius of America, the resourcefulness of communities, and the inherent desire in all humans to be part of something bigger than ourselves.

PART

II

Experiments in Citizen Finance

5

The Last Real Banker?

Relationship Banking Is Not Dead—Yet

In southern Vermont, people talk of a legendary banker named Dudley H. Davis. After serving in the Navy in World War II, Davis in 1946 became a teller at the Merchants Bank in Burlington, rising through the ranks to become its president, a position he held for 36 years. Under Davis, the bank grew from a single branch with $1 million in assets to more than 30 branches across the state with over $800 million in assets. More importantly, it was instrumental in providing startup funding for many of Vermont's most successful businesses and helped many residents buy their first homes.

For a bank CEO, Davis took a personal interest in his borrowers. "All the old-time entrepreneurs talk about how, when you needed money, you'd go in, meet with Dudley Davis," says Eli Moulton, an attorney based in Burlington who helps small businesses raise capital. "He'd grill you on your business plan, and if he liked you, you got a loan. That world doesn't exist anymore."

As an editorial in *Vermont Business* noted after Davis passed away in late 2004: "He was famous for scheduling weekly board meetings and making his directors work. He was famous for knowing off the top of his head the condition of every commercial account at the bank. And he was famous for helping out a couple of guys named Ben and Jerry make it through the day with a creditor nipping at their heels." Maybe, the piece concluded, "Dudley Davis was the last real banker in America."[1]

Old-fashioned community banking, the kind based on personal relationships, is not entirely dead. There are still banks, like the family-owned Sunrise Banks in Minneapolis–St. Paul, or Broadway Federal in Los Angeles, which has been serving the area's middle-class black neighborhoods since 1946, that pride themselves on knowing their customers. Community banks are typically defined as banks with less than $1 billion in assets, although many have less than $250 million in assets, and focused on a particular geographic region. These institutions have traditionally been pillars of their communities, often for generations. Their owners and decision makers tend to be locally based, with all of the familiarity and accountability that comes with those roots.

"These are the businesses and people that go to school together and churches and synagogues together and live and work in the same community, so it's kind of a little ecosystem," says Paul Merski, chief economist for the Independent Community Bankers of America. "If the small businesses in the community are doing well, then the community bank is doing well. They're dependent on each other." For those reasons, a community bank is not going to put someone in a loan that they know they can't pay back, says Merski. (In contrast, putting people in mortgages that would later balloon in cost was precisely the business model of subprime lenders such as Countrywide Financial, now owned by Bank of America, and Long Beach Mortgage, a unit of Washington Mutual, now part of JPMorgan Chase.)

Similarly, a small business owner has a better chance with a community banker who will take qualitative factors into consideration— reputation in the community, track record, and the unique characteristics of the local market, for example—rather than rely on a single computer-generated credit score like the big banks do. That level of personal knowledge and consideration helps explain why the loan portfolios of small banks under $1 billion outperform those of their bigger rivals.[2]

The same could be said for the nation's nearly 8,000 credit unions, which, as member-owned not-for-profits, are managed for and by their member-customers.

These community-based financial institutions have been the chief ally of small business. Loans to small business make up 27 percent of the overall loan portfolios of banks with less than $500 million in assets, compared to just 5 percent for banks with more than $50 billion in total assets.[3] While financial institutions of all sizes cut back lending in the aftermath of the subprime meltdown, none did so as drastically as the large banks. Community banks and credit unions offered the only lifeline for many borrowers.

Overall, community banks increased their total loans by about 2 percent, compared to a 6 percent decline for larger banks. Small business lending dipped by 3 percent at community banks, compared to 21 percent for larger banks.[4] Credit unions, meanwhile, increased their small business lending by 10 percent in 2009.[5] (The amount credit unions can lend to small business is capped by federal law at 12.25 percent of their total assets. Credit unions argue that raising the limit to 27.5 percent for well-capitalized institutions, as some congressional members favor, could spur $10 billion in new small business lending, at no cost to the government).

"It is said that a community with a local bank can better control its destiny," Thomas Hoenig, the outspoken head of the Kansas City Federal Reserve, noted at a hearing of the House Subcommittee on Oversight and Investigations in late August 2010. "Local deposits provide funds for local loans. Community banks are often locally owned and managed—through several generations of family ownership. This vested interest in the success of their local communities is a powerful incentive to support local initiatives. It is the very 'skin in the game' incentive that regulators are trying to reintroduce into the largest banks."

The community bank business model has held up well compared to the megabank model that had to be propped up by taxpayers, Hoenig added. Community banks had higher capital ratios, for example, and have better served their communities. "If allowed to compete on a fair and level playing field, the community bank model is a winner," he concluded.[6]

That's a big "if." In an age of megabank efficiency and power, the traditional community bank model is under threat. Decades of consolidation and other changes in the banking industry have taken a toll on our hometown financial institutions.

The number of single-branch banks in the United States has plummeted from more than 10,000 in 1966 to about 2,000 today. Banks with less than $1 billion in assets today hold just 15 percent of national deposits, down from 28 percent in 1995. The top four largest banks—each with greater than $100 billion in assets—have grown in the same timeframe from 7 percent of all deposits to 44 percent. And those Too Big to Fail banks have emerged from the crisis even bigger: The top four banks added as much market share in 2009 as they had in the previous decade, according to the New Rules Project.[7]

Community Bank

Community banks are typically defined as banks with less than $1 billion in assets, although many have less than $250 million in assets. The real distinction is that they are locally owned and focused on serving the businesses and families in their geographic region. Small business lending has traditionally been the bread and butter of many community banks.

That doesn't bode well for small businesses that rely on bank loans. As a 2007 study noted, "Credit access in markets dominated by big banks tends to be lower for small businesses than in markets with a relatively larger share of small banks."[8]

If You're Served a Lousy Burger, You Don't Have to Eat It

That's why the simplest thing you can do to support your community and its independent businesses is to put your savings in a local financial institution. By banking locally, whether with a community bank or a credit union, the chances are far greater that your deposits will end up being lent to a business or family in your community—rather than plowed into speculative trading or some fat cat's bonus.

Besides, it feels good. Many Americans are still rightfully indignant over the behavior of big banks that, after accepting billions of dollars of taxpayer money intended to encourage them to lend, did the opposite, cutting back on loans and credit lines as entrepreneurs faced the worse credit crisis in recent history.

As customers, we've felt the squeeze of big banks, too. The rationale for much of the deregulation that has taken place since the 1970s was that bigger banks enjoy economies of scale that would trickle down to consumers in the form of lower fees. Instead, credit card interest rates and fees have soared, and hefty bank fees have been slapped on everything from overdrafts to ATM withdrawals. In 2009, with the recession at its peak and many consumers struggling to make ends meet, big banks raised overdraft fees, which are triggered when customers go over their limits. The average overdraft fee for debit card transactions in 2009 was $34, while the average transaction that triggered the fee was just $20.[9] What's more, many customers were charged multiple fees for a single overdraft, helping banks rake in almost $40 billion in such fees.[10] Banks also raised credit card interest rates an average 2 percent in the first half of 2009, according to Pew Charitable Trusts.

At the same time, interest rates on savings accounts have sunk to less than 1 percent, barely keeping pace with even ultralow inflation. Add in creeping fees and it's a losing proposition. One media outlet was moved to ask: "Are savings accounts worth it anymore?"[11]

The big banks may have rebounded from the bubble-induced crisis they helped create, but millions of Americans have lost their homes to foreclosure, and neighborhoods fallen into blight. Rather than work with homeowners, as the government urged, big banks such as Bank of America and JPMorgan Chase contracted with so-called foreclosure mills to speed through the process—often illegally or without proper documentation (more or less the same way the loans were originated). A government oversight report warned that the sloppy handling could potentially call into question the validity of 33 million mortgage loans.[12]

Adding insult to injury, the biggest banks spent heavily throughout 2009 and 2010 to fend off or weaken regulations intended to reign in risky or abusive behavior. Despite those efforts, various reforms were passed, including the Credit Card Accountability, Responsibility, and Disclosure (CARD) Act of 2009, which requires more transparency and disclosure, including an opt-in requirement for overdraft protection, and the Dodd-Frank bill in July 2010, which created the Consumer Financial Protection Bureau to oversee mortgages, credit cards, and other financial products.

But don't expect banking fees to come down as a result. In the famous words of JPMorgan chief Jamie Dimon: "If you're a restaurant and you can't charge for the soda, you're going to charge more for the burger."

Well, if you're a customer and you are served a lousy burger, you don't have to eat it.

Credit Union

Credit unions are nonprofit financial institutions owned by and operated on behalf of their members, who typically share an affiliation, such as an employer or trade. Like other cooperative businesses (see Chapter 11), any excess revenue that does not go back into the business is distributed to members in the form of better rates and fewer fees—one reason they represent a good deal for consumers.

Move Your Money

That's the idea behind the Move Your Money campaign, launched at the end of 2009 by the Huffington Post, with a clever video that interspersed scenes from the Frank Capra classic movie *It's a Wonderful Life* with clips from congressional hearings on the subprime crisis. The grassroots campaign urges people to move their money from the megabanks that brought us to the brink of economic disaster into community banks and credit unions in an effort to "re-rig the financial system so that it becomes again the productive, stable engine for growth it is meant to be."

Can such a small act be anything more than symbolic? Yes. Deposits are a core source of funding for community banks and especially credit unions, allowing them to make more loans. And because local lending is what they do, your deposits get invested back into your community—just as George Bailey explained to restive depositors of the Building & Loan.

As with any local establishment, local banks have a greater multiplier effect on the immediate economy. In Sonoma County, California, for example, more than half of the area's $11.5 billion in deposits are held at local banks and credit unions. Still, if 10 percent of the money currently in nonlocal banks ($534 million) were shifted to locally owned institutions, it could generate up to $4.8 billion in new local lending, figures Derek Huntington, president of Sonoma County GoLocal Cooperative, a business alliance.[13]

Moving your money is also good for your bottom line. Community banks and credit unions typically offer better interest rates on savings and checking accounts, while charging lower and fewer fees than their megapeers. According to a Federal Reserve report in November 2010, banks with less than $10 billion in assets paid an average 1.29 percent interest on deposits, compared to 0.8 percent paid by large banks.[14]

Credit unions, in particular, offer a good deal. Since they are nonprofit cooperatives, their 'profits' flow back to members in the form of better rates and services. A recent analysis by the Pew Charitable Trust found that large credit unions offered significantly lower annual percentage rates (APRs) on credit cards and cash advances than large banks. In addition, they charged lower annual fees, penalty fees, over-limit fees, and late fees—when they charged them at all.[15]

And you don't have to give anything up: Credit unions and community banks generally provide a full range of competitive financial products, from checking and savings accounts to credit cards, mortgages, auto loans, and CDs.

The campaign seems to be striking a chord. In a Zogby Interactive poll conducted in February 2010, nearly one-third of respondents (32 percent) said they had considered moving some or all of their banking from a large national bank to a community bank or credit union. Fourteen percent had actually done so in the past year—the bulk of them (9 percent) as an act of protest. And the nation's nearly 8,000 credit unions added 1.2 million members in 2009, for a total of 92 million members.

Perhaps that's why the big banks are now eager to cast themselves as local. Wells Fargo and HSBC are billing themselves as, respectively, "the nation's leading community bank" and "the world's local bank." Never mind that they are more than 1,000 times the size of the largest community banks.[16]

A Threatened Model

For all of their appeal, our true hometown banks may be an endangered species. Community banks, for the most part, did not participate in the shoddy lending, speculative bets, and off-the-books shenanigans of their Wall Street brethren. Nonetheless, they were hit particularly hard by the recession, in part because they held so many small business and commercial real estate loans. The FDIC shuttered 157 banks in 2010, most of them small and clearly not too big to fail. That's the highest number of failures since the savings-and-loan crisis in 1992, and up from 140 bank failures in 2009.[17] The FDIC has another 860 "problem banks" on its watch list. Credit unions have fared better: Just 28 credit unions were shuttered out of a total 7,965 at the start of the year.[18] (For this reason, it is wise to check the health of a community bank or credit union before you open an account—there is a handy tool for doing so on the Move Your Money site.)

Many small banks are struggling to raise capital—the underlying equity that is distinct from depository funds—to meet stricter regulatory requirements. Unlike their bigger counterparts, community banks are typically privately or closely held, so they can't just issue more shares on the market to raise funds. Credit unions, on the other hand, are barred by law from raising public equity, so they can build funds only through deposits and retained earnings.

Regulations aimed at safeguarding the financial system pose a greater burden for smaller banks, too. Community bankers worry that the more stringent lending standards will disproportionately hurt them. "Banks are being forced to take more of a cookie cutter approach with both residential and small business lending. You fit within this mold, and that's it," says Donald Frain, president and chief operating officer of Quontic Bank in Great Neck, Long Island. "The element of truly knowing your customer is being taken away from community banks—which was the one advantage they had over big banks."

Those concerns were echoed by Thomas Hoenig, the head of the Kansas City Fed. After praising community banks at the August 2010 congressional hearing, he questioned their continued viability in a Too Big to Fail age. In particular, Hoeing said, the perception that the government will again swoop in to save the biggest banks in the event of another crisis gives them an unfair edge. That implicit guarantee allows the biggest banks to run their businesses with greater leverage and a lower cost of capital and debt. The comparatively higher cost of capital for smaller banks, along with the increased expense of regulatory compliance, will encourage even more consolidation, he said.

That pressures smaller banks to adopt big bank practices. Community banks used to hold their loans on their books, for example, giving them the accountability and "skin in the game" that regulators so prize. But no lender wants to hold a 30-year mortgage when they can sell it off to investors, who then package it up with other loans into a security. Today, many smaller banks routinely sell mortgages, auto loans, and even SBA-backed commercial loans into the great securitization machine.

Eli Moulton, the Vermont attorney, says banking has fundamentally changed from the days of Dudley Davis. "The whole principle of banks was to support community local investing, right?

As depositors, we'd all go put our money in the bank, and the bank would turn around and loan that to our local business and entrepreneurs, reinvest it in the community. So it was a circle. And once you started repackaging and securitizing the loans, that's gone away."

Wall Street on the Missouri

Millions of fed up individuals have moved their money into local financial institutions. But what if that idea could be implemented on a larger level? As state governments grapple with the worst budget shortfalls in years, some are taking a closer look at North Dakota, a rural red state, as a model for public banking and a way to lessen their dependence on Wall Street. The Bank of North Dakota, based in Bismarck, is the country's only state-owned and -operated bank. It doesn't take consumer deposits, but all state government agencies are required to place their funds in the bank, for which they receive interest.

"We take those funds and then, really what separates us, is that we plow those deposits back into the state of North Dakota in the form of loans. We invest back into the state in economic development type of activities. We grow our state through that mechanism," Bank of North Dakota president Eric Hardmeyer explained to *Mother Jones*.[19]

The idea has caught the attention of many state and local agencies, which often deposit their money in out-of-state banks, some of the very same ones that were bailed out with taxpayer money and have been hoarding cash since.

The Bank of North Dakota was ushered in on a wave of populism almost a hundred years ago. Farmers in the agrarian state were tired of grain prices and loan terms being dictated back East. The nostalgic-sounding Non Partisan League (if only!) took control of the legislature and, in 1919, created the Bank of North Dakota (as well as the North Dakota Mill and Elevator Association to regain control over grain marketing and financing).

Today, the bank acts as sort of a mini-Federal Reserve clearinghouse for the state, but it is also an important source of funding for the region. The bank uses its capital to fund agriculture, energy, and education in the state, including student loan financing—all in partnership with local banks. It guarantees some small business loans in the state, similar to the Small Business Association, and provides venture capital and assists higher risk startups and existing businesses in obtaining loans of up to $500,000.

After a flood in 1997 ravaged the state's Red River Valley, encompassing Fargo and Grand Forks, the bank set up a disaster loan program to assist businesses. It also turns over half of its profits each year to the state, adding a third of a billion dollars to state coffers in the past 10 or so years.[20]

That, along with a booming oil business in the state, may explain why there is no credit crisis in North Dakota. In 2009, when many commercial banks were struggling, the Bank of North Dakota celebrated its 90th birthday with record profits, assets approaching $4 billion, and an outstanding loan portfolio of $2.7 billion. And, while many states are slashing services, pensions, and jobs to reduce their multi-billion-dollar budget gaps, North Dakota was eyeing a surplus of $1 billion for its budget cycle ending in June 2011. The state's unemployment rate, at 4 percent, is the lowest in the nation.[21]

That's caught the attention of state and local officials from Massachusetts to Oregon. Virg Bernero, the mayor of Lansing, Michigan, has talked up the idea of a "Main Street Bank" modeled on the Bank of North Dakota that would help create jobs in the hard-hit state.[22] He figures the bank could be capitalized with the interest the state earns on tax revenues, about $350 million, and could partner with banks doing business in the state as well as make some loans directly. "Wall Street banks are not lending to Michigan's small businesses, and reports show that is the No. 1 problem blocking job creation here," Bernero told the *Detroit Free Press*. "If we invest in our small businesses rather than Wall Street banks, we can finally break the credit-crunch logjam and unleash Michigan's entrepreneurs to create hundreds of thousands of new jobs." The idea has even won support from some in the banking industry.[23]

In the state of Washington, a bill that would establish a state bank modeled on North Dakota's was introduced in January 2011.

The Washington Investment Trust, as the bank is being called, would increase access to capital for businesses and farms, provide financing for education, public works infrastructure, and other projects, support the local financial sector, reduce costs paid by the state for banking services, and return earnings to the state, according to the bill. A study conducted by Washington's Center for State Innovation notes that North Dakota's loan to asset ratio, a measure of lending activity, is an average 7 percentage points higher than the neighboring states of Montana, South Dakota, and Wyoming. North Dakota's loans per capita are 175 percent higher than the U.S. average. And its bank sector is flourishing: North Dakota has more bank offices per capita and less market concentration than neighboring states or the U.S. average.[24]

The analysis concluded that a state-owned Washington Investment Trust could generate 8.2 percent more in new lending activity, or $2.6 billion, creating or retaining more than 8,000 jobs, and return $70 million in dividends to the state after 10 years.

There are very real issues with state-owned banks, most notably the tricky mix of money and politics. The Bank of North Dakota is basically controlled by the governor, who acts as its chairman and appoints a seven-member advisory board. Its funds are not federally guaranteed, but are backed instead by the state (a pro or a con, depending on the state and your outlook for the Fed). And despite their populist pitch, state-owned banks would likely face loud opposition in the rancorous, antigovernment political atmosphere.

Still, if political motive could be kept separate from the banks' operations, a public-interest bank is an interesting model for keeping capital local, and one for which there is growing grassroots support. Ellen Brown, the author of *Web of Debt* and an advocate for state banks, argues that moving your money to a community bank, while a good first step, is not enough to get credit flowing, since the real problem facing local banks is insufficient capital (as opposed to deposits) to support lending. Perhaps someday soon, community banks and credit unions will have new state-based allies that help them remain viable and put our savings to good use.

Game Plan for Locavestors

Community banks and credit unions are the last vestige of the old-fashioned relationship-based banking system that once ruled the land—think George Bailey's Building & Loan. These institutions are small (with less than $1 billion in assets), locally owned, and rooted in their communities. Their business is making loans to local families and businesses, so the dollars you deposit with one of these institutions are much more likely to support your local economy than, say, be plowed into speculative trading. That local bank model is under threat, however. Community banks are being squeezed by increasing consolidation in the banking sector and disproportionately higher capital and regulatory costs.

Pros:

- Banking locally is the simplest, least risky way to support your community. Community banks and credit unions offer a wide range of financial products and services, from savings and checking accounts and CDs to credit cards and mortgage loans.
- Typically, locally owned institutions offer lower fees and higher interest rates on savings and checking accounts than large banks, as well as better rates and fewer fees on credit card and loan products.
- Unlike big banks, their main business is lending to individuals and companies in the area. So, by doing business with a community bank or credit union, you are investing in your community while saving yourself money.

Cons:

- The smallest banks and credit unions may have limited ATM networks, although this is not always the case.
- Small banks do not have the deep balance sheets and access to cheap capital that big banks have, and many are struggling in the wake of the financial crisis.
- Community bank and credit union deposits are FDIC insured, but it is a good idea to check out the financial health of a bank or credit union before you switch. The Move Your Money campaign has a tool that allows you to screen out underperforming financial institutions (see the following page for more information).

The Bottom Line: A no-brainer.

For More Information:

- The Move Your Money site offers an easy way to search for a community bank or credit union near you. The campaign has partnered with Institutional Risk Analytics (IRA) to provide a level of vetting. Only banks that IRA ranks "B" or better, based on government data, are included in the database: www.moveyourmoney.info.
- The Credit Union National Association (CUNA) has a web site for consumers, www.creditunion.coop, that offers a credit union locator and other helpful info. Many credit unions also offer "switch kits" that make switching your bank account easier.
- The Independent Community Bankers of America (ICBA) offers a similar tool to find a community bank, at www.icba.org/consumer/BankLocator.cfm.
- You can read more about the advantages of community banks and credit unions at www.newrules.org/banking. The New Rules Project also offers a checklist for moving your money at www.newrules.org/banking/seven-simple-steps-move-your-checking-account.
- The Center for Responsible Lending is another good resource for consumer banking and loan information, including a shopper's guide to better banking: www.responsiblelending.org.
- For more on state banks, see Ellen Brown's book, *Web of Debt* (Third Millennium Press, 2007) and related web site, www.webofdebt.com.

6

The Biggest-Impact Financial Sector You've Never Heard Of

Community Development Loan Funds Reach Out to Individual Investors

When Kym Ramsey wanted to open a child-care center in 1999, she knew she was not the ideal bank candidate. Then 33, she had no experience running her own business and no collateral to speak of. What she did have was guts and passion. Ramsey, who got her economics degree at Georgetown University on an ROTC scholarship, had jumped out of airplanes and fired tanks in Iraq during Operation Desert Storm. Returning home to the Philadelphia suburbs, she earned a graduate degree in human resources and worked in that field for a couple of large companies, teaching business as an adjunct professor on the side. With her daughter in day care, Ramsey began to think about starting her own day-care center, combining a love of learning and her business background.

After studying the field, she decided that her best bet was to open a franchise of a national day-care school, like the one that

her daughter was enrolled in. To do so, however, would cost
$600,000, with 20 percent down. Then there was rent to pay, sup-
plies to buy, and teachers to hire. "I have no rich family or uncle
or anything like that," said Ramsey. She made the rounds of banks
but was rejected again and again. She had just won $25,000 in
a business plan competition when someone told her about The
Reinvestment Fund (TRF), a lender based in Philadelphia. "I told
them if they would take a risk on me, I know I can make it work,"
she recalls. The Reinvestment Fund agreed to lend her about
$300,000 (with her father as cosigner) over a 10-year term. The
interest was a reasonable 2.75 percent over prime. She scraped
together additional funds by selling her car and moving with her
family into her mother's townhouse.

In 2001, Ramsey opened her day-care center in Skippack, Pennsylvania, an affluent suburb 20 miles north of Philadelphia. She
marketed it at community events and within a year turned a
profit—well ahead of the school's national benchmarks. A few
years later, with more demand than she could handle, Ramsey
returned to The Reinvestment Fund for another loan, this time
for $95,000 to expand into a neighboring space.

Not bad for a first-time entrepreneur that banks wouldn't
touch. But that was just Act I. Ramsey eventually began to think
about opening a school in the city, where there were fewer high-
quality day-care options available. She put her school up for sale
and, after a bidding war, sold it for a million dollars, leaving a tidy
profit even after repaying her loans to TRF.

The Reinvestment Fund is what is known as a Community
Development Financial Institution, or CDFI. These organizations
may be banks, credit unions, venture capital funds, or loan funds,
but they all share a mission of providing financing to underserved
or economically challenged communities. There are 800 or so of
these entities across the country, each specializing in its region.
Although they've been around for years—TRF just celebrated its
25th anniversary in 2010—they have operated somewhat under
the radar. Indeed, community development finance may be the
biggest-impact financial sector you've never heard of.

Community Development Finance Institution

The Community Development Finance Institution (CDFI) is a class of financial institution that serves underserved and often low-income communities. CDFIs, which are certified by the Treasury Department, can be banks, credit unions, venture capital funds, or loan funds. They typically focus on a specific geographic region, making them a good option for local investors. Community development loan funds, in particular, allow individuals to put money to work in their communities in return for a modest, fixed rate of return.

In its quarter-century, TRF, a loan fund, has invested $840 million in more than 2,400 projects like Ramsey's that have served to rebuild and revitalize neighborhoods in Philadelphia and, more recently, the broader mid-Atlantic region. Its Fresh Food Financing Initiative, aimed at funding grocery stores in so-called food deserts, has won national acclaim.

The Opportunity Finance Network, a network of more than 170 CDFIs, reports that in 2008 alone, its members collectively made $2.3 billion in loans, including to more than 51,400 small and microbusinesses that created or maintained 223,738 jobs. [1]

Individuals can open an account at a CDFI bank or credit union just as they can with any bank, with their money being lent in their area. Community development loan funds, on the other hand, raise money primarily through low-cost loans and grants from commercial banks, foundations, and the government. But a growing number of loan funds allow individuals to invest as well, typically for a fixed rate of return. The money goes to consumer lending (often the only alternative to predatory loans in an area), locally active nonprofits, affordable housing, first-time entrepreneurs, microbusinesses, and established Main Street businesses—"everything that goes into building a healthy community," as Donna Fabiani, an executive at Opportunity Finance Network (OFN), puts it.

CDFIs are the last line of defense—or the first line of opportunity, as OFN prefers to frame it—for entrepreneurs like Ramsey, for whom traditional financing is out of reach. Unlike the big banks, they don't have rigid formulas, but take a high-touch approach to financing. And because their business models are built around a mission to help underserved populations, they have more flexibility than banks to make riskier loans. With traditional community banking on the endangered list, CDFIs will play an even more critical role.

"I had been turned down by every bank, but no one ever came to see me," recalls Ramsey. "They just looked at my package and said they'd get back to me, and then I'd get a letter declining the loan." Her experience at TRF was different. She met with her loan officer face to face. "They could see my passion and commitment, and they took a chance," she says.

This fall, Ramsey plans to open a day-care center in the heart of Philadelphia that will put to use all she has learned in her eight years running a center for a national chain—her way of "bringing it back to the community." The center will serve children aged six weeks to six years, with financial assistance for lower income attendees. It will also offer training for teachers and parents to help them better understand children and manage stress. She plans to call it Kimberly Academy. And once again, TRF is backing her. "I really thank God for them," she says.

Helping Entrepreneurs "Buy the Pond"

Small business lending can be tricky, time consuming, and inefficient, so many CDFIs shy away from it. TRF, for example, has decided it is more effective focusing on a few areas, such as education, grocery stores, and housing. For others, such as Accion Texas-Louisiana, small business is their sole mission. Accion Texas-Louisiana, a member of the Accion International network, is the largest microfinance lender in the United States.

Since it was established in 1994, the organization has made more than 10,000 small business loans to more than 4,500 borrowers in Texas and Louisiana who were unable to obtain financing from traditional sources. Most of the loans are small—the average is $7,900, although they can reach $100,000—and have helped entrepreneurs start or grow businesses ranging from tortilla making to medical supplies. While international microfinance agencies have been criticized for exceedingly high interest rates, Accion charges an average 12.5 percent.

Credit scores are of limited value in this market segment. "FICO comes into play and collateral comes into play, but what we really go after is trying to understand first, how much experience the borrower has in the business, how long have they been at the business," explains Cristian Sandoval, vice president for external affairs and marketing at Accion in San Antonio. "Then we can make an assessment of whether you have the passion, the character, whether your business is going to be successful, and then we can give you the money and support you." Many entrepreneurs return for additional loans as their business grows.

Accion views microbusiness lending as the most effective way to help people become more self-sufficient. "We not only want to teach them how to fish, we want to help them buy the pond," says Sandoval. "That way they can go out there and start creating more jobs for other people, bringing opportunities for their kids, and build a stronger community."

Like other community development loan funds, Accion meticulously tracks the impact its loans have on borrowers and their communities. And it is considerable. From 1994 through 2009, Accion Texas-Louisiana's $93.6 million in loans have created almost 2,200 jobs and preserved another 4,000. They have also generated an additional $55 million in payroll spending, or 60 cents for every dollar lent. These loans have transformed many lives for the better. Often, borrowers come to Accion with no bank relationships and poor or nonexistent credit histories. An Accion loan allows them to build up their credit scores and become "bankable." Accion clients, on average, have increased their business equity by 22 percent and their business profits by 67 percent after three small loans. As borrowers are able to raise their standard of living, their children tend to remain in school, graduating from high school and even going on to college.

Taking the Middle Path in New Hampshire

Micro-enterprises are just one part of the equation.

In Concord, New Hampshire, not far from Main Street, is a modest stretch called Wall Street. It has little in common with its more famous namesake in New York. Concord's Wall Street is just two blocks long and its low-rises are mainly populated by dentists. But at the eastern end of the street, some promising financial innovation is underway at the offices of the New Hampshire Community Loan Fund.

In its nearly three decades of existence, the loan fund has mainly supported community-owned housing and micro-enterprises in the state. In its fiscal 2009, for example, the fund's microcredit program loaned more than $213,000 to 66 businesses with up to five employees, increasing their gross sales by an average of $13,249 and helping to create or retain 1,934 full-time equivalent jobs. Individual investors in the fund, meanwhile, get a steady 5 percent return for a 10-year investment in the fund.

For the past several years, the organization has been devising new ways to help established small and midsized businesses—from $2 million and $15 million in revenues and 10 to 150 employees—obtain much-needed expansion capital. That's been the mission of John Hamilton, vice president of economic opportunity at the fund and managing director of its Vested for Growth program. Hamilton sees a financing gap for established businesses that are too risky for banks' lending models but that either can't attract or don't want equity financing. Vested for Growth is designed to address these high-growth, high-margin businesses that fall through the cracks of the financial market.

"The market thinks in bipolar ways—either bankable debt or equity, as if those are the two choices that are out there," says Hamilton. And yet, he says, there is a giant gap between the two. "Think of all the businesses that fall in between."

In New Hampshire, businesses with $2 million to $15 million in revenue and up to 150 employees make up the backbone of the state's economy, he says. These businesses tend to create good jobs that stay local. Yet if they don't have a perfect track record or sufficient collateral, they have little chance of getting a bank loan. The other option—equity—means ceding control. "Particularly here in 'Live Free or Die' New Hampshire, the idea of giving up your independence is not taken easily," says Hamilton. "And what if you just want to grow the business sustainably and long term? An equity investor is going to want to get paid out generally three to five years later. That means being forced to sell the business in the next few years—not everyone is ready to do that." Not to mention, in today's environment, there's no guarantee you'll even find a buyer.

His solution is a royalty financing model, under which borrowers pay a fixed percent of revenue each month until the initial investment, times a negotiated multiple, has been paid off. That provides a degree of flexibility and independence missing in straight debt or equity deals. On months when business is slow, for example, the payments are less. When business is booming, they are more. The interests of investors and borrower are aligned: The better the business does, the better the investor does. And no "exit" is required. Royalty financing can be used alongside conventional loans or as a straight royalty structure.

Royalty financing has been used, with mixed results, in the angel investing world, and has been catching on with other investors. Hamilton believes that while it may not be the best solution for startups, royalty financing is a valuable tool for financing established businesses with healthy profit margins.

For CEPS, Inc., a manufacturer of plastic injection-molded medical devices in Lebanon, New Hampshire, Vested for Growth's royalty model helped it acquire a larger rival, Johnson Precision, whose founder was retiring. James Umland, president of CEPS, saw an opportunity to combine the two companies and keep Johnson Precision in the hands of a strategic, rather than financial, buyer, preserving jobs in the region. In the spring of 2009, however, credit markets were barely functioning and anything with a whiff of risk was hard to fund. The company's local bank was willing to put up $2 million, but Umland still needed to raise another $1 million to pull it off.

Angel investors politely declined. Even though CEPS has been growing at a 17 percent annual clip and the acquisition would position it for even greater growth, they didn't see a clear payoff or exit. That's when Umland's banker brought the deal to Hamilton, who thought it was a perfect candidate for royalty financing. "John took the time," says Umland. "He wants to know not only does the business make sense, but does the person have the personal attributes he's looking for in a partner—because he views this as a partnership."

Since Vested for Growth caps its investments at $500,000, there was still a financing shortfall. When Hamilton and Umland went back to some of the same angel investors with the new royalty structure, this time they bit, and the acquisition was completed in January 2010. The royalty funding concept, says Umland, "provides the kind of return that a mezzanine (high yield debt) investor would want, but with the patience of an equity investor. I like it because we get to keep all the equity, yet if you did this with just traditional debt, you could have all kinds of bad things happen if you miss your numbers."

Out of 13 such deals Hamilton has done over the years, he's seen it all: big success, losses, and the "living dead." But Vested for Growth's internal rate of return has averaged out to a respectable 13.6 percent.

"People are talking about relying on our small businesses to get us out of this recession," says Hamilton, "but they've just taken it on the chin for the last couple of years. Many of them don't have the ability to get additional credit from banks, because they're not creditworthy from the way the bank looks at it. I understand why a bank whose focus is on least cost debt cannot help them, but then we have to answer the question, 'How are we getting growth capital to our established businesses? I think this is a major step in the right direction."

Big Opportunities, Less Capital

Across the CDFI field, demand has spiked as the credit vice has tightened around many businesses and communities. Mark Pinsky,

CEO of Opportunity Finance Network, likes to describe CDFIs as "working outside the margins of conventional finance." When the economy is booming, the margins of conventional finance expand and cover more markets. When the economy is bad, the margins shrink. "It's like a tide, and right now the tide is way out," says Pinsky. "There's just this massive amount of opportunity."

But just as their services are most needed, CDFIs are facing their own challenges.

Community development banks, like most of their banking peers, had to scramble to raise capital as the economy deteriorated starting in 2007 and their loans were marked down, throwing off their capital-to-debt ratios. CDFIs did not engage in reckless lending. Nor were they as highly leveraged as, say, Bear Stearns, which borrowed $43 for every $1 it invested. But even at modest leverage rates, the economic disruption was enough to take down institutions such as ShoreBank Financial in Chicago, the largest and best-known community development bank.[2] Most CDFI banks survived, but many will have to focus on raising capital levels before they can resume normal lending levels, notes Pinsky.

Community loan funds, on the other hand, raise the bulk of their money from foundations as well as banks, which view the low-interest loans and grants as a way to fulfill their mandates under the Community Reinvestment Act (CRA), a law established in 1977 to end the practice of discriminatory "redlining" by banks in neighborhoods they operate in. Since 1994, the Treasury Department has also supported community development entities with financing and tax credits through its CDFI Fund. (It also certifies such entities.) Community development loan funds typically take these loans and grants and lend the money out at a higher, but still modest, interest rate, with the spread supporting their operations.

The community loan fund model generally held up very well throughout the crisis. For one, the funds operate with much higher capital cushions—double, triple, or even quadruple that of conventional banks. During the boom, they might have looked underleveraged and boring, but that conservatism allowed the funds to take an honest look at their portfolios and quickly write off nonperforming loans. Despite that, their net charge-off rates were lower than those at FDIC-insured banks. While the loan funds themselves were in good shape, the entities that supply much of their funding were reeling. In 2008, funding from banks cratered along with the housing market. In New York City, the largest banks cut their community development lending by 20 percent in 2008—despite a 10 percent jump in deposits. A study by the Association for Neighborhood and Housing Development said the decline was part of a longer term and worrisome decline in the "quantity and quality" of Community Reinvestment Act activity. As banks consolidate, there are simply fewer to go around.

That's been partially offset by the conversion of several financial firms into bank holding companies in order to participate in the government bailout assistance. These new banks, including Goldman Sachs, American Express, Morgan Stanley, and GMAC, the financing arm of General Motors, are now subject to the CRA. In addition, with much fanfare, some of the biggest banks have made fresh commitments to small business lending through CDFIs—about $1 billion worth between Citigroup, Goldman, JPMorgan Chase, Bank of America, and Wells Fargo from the fall of 2009 through the summer of 2010 (roughly coinciding with the nadir of their public images). On the surface, these commitments are admirable. But in reality, the loan terms in many cases are too expensive or too short term for many community development loan funds. "They're tailored for maximum PR," one loan fund executive told me.

Indeed, these efforts only underscore how far the big banks have gotten from community-level lending. Writing on the web site JustMeans.com, blogger Michael Hasset observed the irony in one such program, Citigroup's elaborate $200 million Communities at Work Fund, in which it partnered with the Calvert Foundation and OFN:

> Genuine cheers notwithstanding, hold on a minute. In order to do neighborhood level lending, Citi now needs to set up a special fund, in which it is a limited partner with

two general partners who do all the work. This special fund then lends only to other funds. The other funds then actually make loans to real small businesses and charitable organizations. This seems like a fairly complex reinvention of an ancient wheel once known as banking. Remember institutions like Farmers Loan & Trust, Citizens Building & Loan, Bowery National Bank, Richmond Borough National Bank? They all sound like the bank manager was George Bailey from a *It's a Wonderful Life,* don't they. Bet these banks knew how to "make loans . . . rooted in local communities." They have something else in common too, all these banks, by acquisition, merger, etc. are part of today's Citi.[3]

But we digress.

Foundations, the other major funding pillar for loan funds, have seen their asset values plummet, and many are focused on rebuilding their endowments rather than giving. The only true bright spot for loan funds and CDFIs in general has been an increased level of support by the Obama administration.

Individual Investors Play a Bigger Role

With CDFIs scrambling to keep pace with demand, many are reassessing the role of individual investors. Today, individuals make up a tiny slice of overall community development loan fund investment. It is easier to collect large investments rather than chase hundreds of individuals, so most loan funds don't market themselves to the public.

In fact, it can be downright hard to find one in your area. "We are not well known and we know it," says Donna Fabiani of the Opportunity Finance Network. "We need to do a much better job of getting the word out. Micro-enterprise is a household word, but people don't know what community development finance is."

That's one reason that so many individual investors have turned to the Calvert Foundation, a Bethesda, Maryland–based nonprofit that acts as an intermediary between CDFIs and individual investors. The foundation's Community Investment Notes can be bought from most major brokers for a minimum investment of $1,000. The notes allow individuals to choose from one of eight regions in the United States, and then Calvert funnels their investment to a loan fund it has partnered with in the region.

Sounds simple enough, but Calvert spent years doing the behind the scenes work to make its notes—square pegs that didn't fit neatly into the round holes of the financial world—conform with the financial regulatory framework. Today, you just call up your broker or go to MicroPlace, a microfinance site owned by eBay, and place your order. About two-thirds of Calvert Foundation's 7,000 individual investors come through MicroPlace, where investments can be made in increments as low as $20. These days, the foundation sells about a million dollars' worth of notes to individuals every week. (Currently, the notes are paying in the low single digits, depending on the term. But the foundation has a cumulative default rate of less than 1 percent.)

There may soon be another easy alternative for individual investors who want to support CDFIs. A new CDFI bond program, proposed by OFN and included in the 2010 Jobs Act, authorized $3 billion in government guaranteed bonds over a three year period, providing a source of long-term, low-cost capital for CDFIs and a new investment platform for individuals. The tax-exempt bonds could be available by the end of 2011.

As individuals increasingly seek to invest their money in more meaningful and less volatile ways, community loan funds are trying to make themselves more accessible. Some, such as Accion, are listing their loans on microfinance lending sites, such as MicroPlace. "CDFIs are a great channel for individuals to get money into a community," says Fabiani. "Everybody wants to tap into this."

At the New Hampshire Community Loan Fund, based in a tiny New England state that has neither a big budget nor large foundations, "We've always scratched by on a lot of small investors," says Alan Cantor, vice president of philanthropy at the fund. Lately, though, there's been a surge of investments from individuals, who now number more than 350. In the fiscal year ending mid-2010, individuals poured $4.5 million into the loan fund, double the amount from the prior year. That's all the more remarkable given that, like most loan funds, NHCLF does no marketing. Individuals hear about it through word of mouth or from financial advisors.

The NHCLF recently won a prestigious award, which may account for some of the surge, but Cantor believes there is more going on. "People are tired of finding out about collateralized debt obligations and tranches and all this chicanery that was happening with their supposedly traditionally invested money," he says. The idea of investing locally, as well as the security of knowing that your principal will not be lost, is appealing, he believes. And with interest rates on savings accounts at rock bottom, "suddenly our very modest interest rates are very attractive." A lot of the investments coming in, he says, are from Baby Boomers coming into wealth through inheritance and seeking alternatives.

"Would you rather put your money in this or the stock market?" asks Laura Kind McKenna, who has invested personally and through a family foundation in a community loan fund. "Putting capital to work in our communities is just so important."

A CD—With Benefits

So, how do community loan funds work? Typically, individuals can make an investment—usually a minimum of $1,000, but sometimes lower—for a period of one to several years. The loan fund lends the money out to targeted borrowers, and pays the investor a modest, guaranteed fixed-rate return—typically 2 percent to 3 percent for a short-term loan and up to 5 percent or more for a 10-year or longer loan. The New Hampshire Community Loan Fund, for example, currently pays 2 percent interest for 1-year loans and up to 5 percent for loans of 10 or more years. Principal is returned at the end of the loan term.

The rates are similar to a certificate of deposit (although at this writing, loan fund rates far surpass those of CDs). Unlike CDs, the loans are not insured by the FDIC, unless the CDFI is a community bank. Still, community loan funds have an enviable track record, and it is rare a fund does not return capital and keep to its guaranteed rate. Most community loan funds maintain reserve funds that absorb any losses. Even today, while the recession has weakened many portfolios, CDFIs compare favorably to banks in terms of delinquencies and charge-offs.

As a general rule, community loan funds tend to have higher delinquency rates and lower charge-offs than banks. That's because banks, which are closely regulated, have rigorous require- ments for writing off bad loans. Community development entities, in contrast, have more flexibility to keep loans on their books. More importantly, they tend to work more closely with their bor- rowers to help them succeed and avoid default.

As the economy soured, CDFIs proactively wrote off loans in 2008 and 2009. Net charge-off rates were 1.78 percent in 2009, up from 0.93 percent in 2008, according to OFN. That compares favorably to net charge-offs at FDIC-insured banks and finan- cial institutions of 2.49 percent in 2009, up from 1.28 percent in 2008.[4] And although CDFIs have higher delinquency, or "at risk," rates than banks as a rule, their delinquencies have grown at a much slower pace than banks'.

Loan funds are the first to remind you that their investments carry risk. "We are not FDIC insured, we are illiquid, we are what is called alternative risk—all the things financial advisors warn against," cautions Margaret Berger Bradley, director of communi- cations and investor development at The Reinvestment Fund in Philadelphia. "But we have never failed to pay back someone who has lent us money."

Many investors seem perfectly comfortable with the level of risk and return they are getting. Judy Wicks, the founder of the White Dog Café in Philadelphia, known for its sustainable opera- tions and community support, has invested her entire retirement account with The Reinvestment Fund at a mid-to-high single digit rate. Joe McQuillan, a Philadelphia developer, is more typical. He and his wife have invested 5 percent of their retirement fund, at 2.5 percent interest, in the fund. "I've got more confidence that TRF is sound than I do in some of the stocks of blue chip compa- nies that I've invested in in the past," he says. "I lose no sleep on my TRF investment."

Game Plan for Locavestors

There are more than 800 certified CDFIs in the United States with more than $30 billion in total assets. They can be community banks, credit unions, loan funds, or venture capital funds, but they must be certified by the Treasury Department as such. They typically operate in underserved markets and make loans to small business owners and individuals who don't qualify for traditional bank loans. Community development loan funds, in particular, present a little known but interesting investment alternative. The loan funds get the bulk of their funding from low-interest loans or grants from banks, endowments, and the government, but many allow individuals to invest as well, for a modest, fixed rate of return. Think of a community development loan fund as a CD-like investment that gets put to productive use in your region.

Pros:

- Community loan funds are geographically focused, so you can put your money directly to work in your region.
- They typically pay investors a fixed return, currently in the low to mid- single digits. While returns are modest, the risks are also very low, as loan funds have an excellent track record of returning lenders' money and typically absorb any losses themselves.
- As with a CD, you'll be able to lock in better interest rates with a longer-term loan.
- CDFIs experience very low charge-off rates, in part because they are willing to work with their borrowers to help them succeed. In fact, CDFIs help borrowers build credit and go on to be successful banking clients.
- In addition to individual loan funds, investors can put money in Calvert Foundation's Community Investment Notes, which are in turn invested in CDFIs. The minimum investment is $1,000, and the notes are available from major brokerage houses.

Cons:

- Interest rates are low and, while funds deposited or invested with CDFI community banks are FDIC insured, nonbank community loan funds are not.

- Many CDFIs do not actively promote their loan funds to individuals, so they can be hard to find.

The Bottom Line: A good place to park savings or retirement funds that you might otherwise put in a CD.

For More Information:
- The Opportunity Finance Network has a CDFI locator on its web site, www.opportunityfinance.net, where you can search for CDFIs in your state. Look for a community development loan fund, which is the most suitable investment for nonaccredited individuals. The search engine lets you refine your search and presents profiles and contact information as well as CARS that was ratings. CARS, short-hand for the CDFI Assessment and Ratings System, is a comprehensive assessment of the financial strength and impact of CDFIs that was created by the Calvert Foundation.
- For helpful information on community investing and how to get started, the Community Investment Center, a joint effort of the Social Investment Forum and Green America, is a good source. You can search for community development options in your area and calculate the social impact your investment can bring, at www.communityinvest.org.
- The CDFI Coalition, an industry group, also has a search tool, at www.cdfi.org.
- Information on Calvert Foundation Community Investment Notes can be found at www.calvertfoundation.org/invest/how-to-invest/community-investment-note. If you don't have a broker, you can contact the foundation's sales desk directly at 800-248-0337, or open an account with Microplace.com.

CHAPTER

7

A Model to LIONize

How One Pacific Northwest Town
Engineered a Quiet Revival

F orty miles northwest of Seattle, perched at the tip of the Olympic Peninsula, lies Port Townsend, Washington. Its advantageous location, at the junction of Puget Sound and a strait leading to the Pacific Ocean, was considered so strategic that three forts were built around it in the late 1800s. The town was a major shipping hub in those days, home to ship captains and customs officials, and its port bustled with vessels carrying timber from the area's rich forests and other goods. Already prosperous, the town really took off when it was poised to become the northwest terminus for the Union Pacific Railroad. Grand homes were built and investments made in anticipation of the "Key City's" glorious future. But when the money ran out and the railroads stopped east of Puget Sound, the economic rewards fell to Seattle and Tacoma. Port Townsend, isolated on the western side of the Sound, began a steady decline.

In a twist of fate, Port Townsend's missed opportunity in the 19th century has led to a modern-day revival. Many of the town's Victorian-era buildings, which might have been torn down in a more robust economy to make room for new ones, were spared. Restoration efforts began in the 1970s, and Port Townsend is now listed on the National Register of Historic Places as one of just three Victorian seaports. Those stately houses, along with the town's postcard-perfect setting between the Olympic Mountains and the Port Townsend Bay, have lately drawn flocks of newcomers who covet the beautiful architecture and quality of life.

These new residents, many of them retired doctors, professors, and executives who have relocated here over the past couple of decades, have led an economic revitalization of the town. Rather than relying on railroads or outside investment, this is a homegrown effort that aims to create a resilient local economy less likely to be buffeted by the larger economic forces blowing across the Sound.

Today, Port Townsend boasts a thriving farmers market and a local food co-op. The historic Rose theatre, which operated from 1907 to 1958, was reopened in 1992 with the help of local residents, who put up around $85,000 and became shareholders in the theatre. And new businesses are popping up all over town.

Keeping Money Local

The quiet force behind many of these developments has been the Local Investment Opportunity Network, or LION, a group of residents who banded together to connect local investors with small businesses in Port Townsend and surrounding areas. The idea is to help to local enterprises flourish and keep more dollars circulating locally—money invested in and spent at local businesses tends to stay in the area, benefiting the local economy.

"That's the way you keep profits local," says Kees (pronounced Case) Kolff, a retired pediatrician with a neatly trimmed silver beard who's been a LION member from the start. "We have so much profit going out of small communities to corporate headquarters—it's pitiful."

LION members are like angel investors but with a hyperlocal focus. James Frazier, a former options trader and hedge fund manager who moved to Port Townsend with his family in 2006, is the group's unofficial spokesperson. He became disillusioned with "in your face" capitalism, and now works as a financial advisor, when he's not hiking, DJ-ing, or fielding calls about LION. The group's members, he explains, "place a very high value on putting investment dollars back into the community and helping the multiplier effect really benefit our community. It's the same thing with spending local, it's just investing local. So money comes back as a return and the principal, when loans are paid off, gets reinvested back in the economy for another business. You can literally watch the money multiply, helping one person and then another and another."

The group's impact can be seen all over town. On Upper Sims Way, the Mt. Townsend Creamery churns out cheese made from local cows' milk. Visitors to the shop can watch the cheese makers at work behind a glass wall. Nearby on Water Street is the Broken Spoke, a full-service bike rental, retail, and repair shop that opened in 2009. At the northern edge of town near Fort Warden State Park and overlooking the sound is Olympic Hostel, a youth hostel that draws families and backpackers for its agreeable accommodations and access to kayaking and hiking. In the historic Uptown district, a developer is finishing up small-scale cottages that blend in with the area's low-key aesthetic and eco-friendly culture. And 12 miles south of Port Townsend in a rural area known as Chimacum is Finnriver Farm, a family-run organic farm and cidery that produces sparkling cider and fruit wines. All of these enterprises contribute to the vitality of the area, but few would be as successful, or perhaps exist at all, had it not been for the financial backing of LION members.

Their work has inspired other efforts as well. A group of 10 residents, including Kolff, has invested a total of $160,000 to install a solar array at the airport through a new state law that encourages public/private partnerships to promote solar energy. The 10 investors formed a limited liability company called Jefferson Solar to undertake the investment. Another grassroots organization, Citizens for Local Power, unshackled the town from its high-cost private electric company by creating the first new public utility in Washington in 40 years.

LION began humbly enough. When the local food co-op wanted to move to a bigger space in 2000, a number of residents and co-op members raised $490,000 in loans to fund the move. Then, another opportunity would arise, and another group would come together to raise funding and then disband. LION was created, as one investor explains it, "to bring together the individuals that kept bumping into each other trying to piece together these things in an informal way, and to streamline the connection between potential investors and lenders and opportunities." For a couple of years, they discussed what structure the group should take and began drawing up agreements and other documents. By October 2008 they were nearly ready to launch, when the financial crisis gave them a shot of urgency. "We just said, we need to get going on this right now and step in as banks were pulling back," recalls Frazier.

No Defaults, but Plenty of Cheese

The system is as simple and straightforward as you can get. Local companies can fill out an application on LION's web site. Then they make a presentation in person to potential investors. LION members don't make investment decisions as a group. Rather, investment opportunities are shared among the members, and individuals are free to make their own deals—although quite often several will invest together.

LION has grown from 8 charter members to about 20 today, including retired techies, small business owners, and other professionals. They are not poor, by any means, but neither are they necessarily in the rarified realm of accredited investors. When LION was officially established, members had already informally made well over a million dollars in local investments in about 15 companies. Since then, group members have made another 8 to 10 investments totaling more than $500,000. While there are some equity investments, most deals have been in the form of loans, with interest rates averaging from about 5 percent to 7 percent. To date, there have been no defaults.

Some members set aside just a small amount of their overall portfolio for local investments, say 5 percent or 10 percent, and view it as another asset class to diversify their holdings. Others, such as Kolff and his wife, Helen, have invested 20 percent of their retirement assets in local business and land. "It's a significant part of our investment strategy," says Kolff, who served as mayor of Port Townsend from 2001 to 2003.

Kolff says one of his borrowers, a candlemaking company, had to extend the term of its loan for a couple of years when the once-successful operation began to struggle. The business eventually folded, but the owners honored the loan and paid it back in full. "We knew them personally and we understood the situation," says Kolff. His loan didn't save the business, "but it at least allowed them to shut it down in an orderly way." (Try that with Bank of America.)

That kind of personal connection and understanding is at the heart of local investing. It's the kind of lending that banks used to do, when they were small and community-rooted.

Kolff has even made a zero-interest loan. When Chauncey Tudhope-Locklear, a 20-something born and raised in Port Townsend, had an idea to start a nonprofit bike collective, it resonated with Kolff. The Recyclery, as it is called, rebuilds and repairs bikes and holds free workshops. It also sells affordable, rebuilt bikes and runs an adopt-a-bike program for Port Washington youths. On the other hand, Kolff gets 7 percent interest on his loan to the Broken Spoke, the decidedly for-profit bike shop on Water Street.

But of all Kolff's investments, the Mt. Townsend Creamery may be his favorite—and not just because he has elected to take part of his dividends in cheese. The creamery's founders, Matt Day and Ryan Trail, set out to revive the area's vanishing dairy tradition. At the time, there was just one local cheese maker, who made a small amount of goat cheese mainly for herself. The partners found a location in town to build their plant and a farmer who would supply milk, but the endeavor required a significant amount of capital. They mustered about $180,000 in personal equity, presented their business plan to LION, and raised $150,000 in equity (for a 25 percent stake).

"The numbers weren't knocking anything out of the park," says Day of the business plan. "But there was a reasonable rate of return. It's not like investing in Google."

Still, the venture was successful from the start. The partners made their debut at the farmers market in April 2005 with their soft-ripened and home-style cheese. In the course of two hours, they sold out of everything they had. They made two trips back to the creamery and, by the end of the day, had sold out their entire inventory. While they are still a popular draw at the farmers market, about 65 percent of their business now is selling wholesale to restaurants and stores. The Creamery's sales have grown around 30 percent each year. In 2009, sales approached $1 million. In 2010, the company was on track to hit $1.2 million. "We're building value over time," says Day.

In more ways than one, as Kolff sees it. "You have a small local creamery that hires local people and the profits stay local. They use milk from local dairies and guarantee them a good price so they have assured sales of their milk. That also reduces shipping and transportation-related greenhouse gas. The used whey from the cheese-making process goes back to local farms to feed the pigs—it's a closed loop!" he exclaims. "I feel great about my investment with the creamery on about 10 different levels."

Day and Trail went back to LION in 2008 for a $70,000 loan, at 8 percent interest, to install a bulk tank. That allowed them to store milk, rather than rising each morning to clean the tank in the truck and drive to the dairy farm 25 miles away—all before the dairy farmer got going in the morning.

Now, the 3,000-square-foot facility on Sherman Street is beginning to feel tight. The partners would like to find a bigger space that would allow them to increase capacity, expand the variety of products they offer, and sell to a broader swath of the northwest. "We're building a sound financial case to go back out" to investors, says Day.

Small Is Beautiful

LION has inspired similar groups in Madison, Wisconsin, and elsewhere, and Frazier spends much of his time fielding calls from other communities interested in setting up LION-like investment groups. It's not hard to do. LION makes available on its web site its three key documents: a membership application for prospective investors, a membership agreement that lays out policies and procedures, and an investment opportunity submission form.

But, Frazier warns, the model is not easily scalable. Each investment requires a lot of work; potential borrowers must be interviewed and their businesses vetted. And the investments aren't very liquid—they can't be flipped for quick profit. "It really takes it back to the original model of investing. It's all handshakes and getting to know someone and building trust before you invest," says Frazier. "It's not really efficient so it's forced to be small, to be person to person and to create community. That's the beauty of it, in a way."

Kolff believes the LION model can work for any group of people who share a focused interest. These days, he says, "More and more people are saying, 'We need to preserve our local small businesses.' If you took every single person in this county and said, let's put 20 percent of your investments into local businesses, my god, the local wealth would be incredible."

Still, for all of its potential, LION operates in a sort of gray area, as far as securities laws are concerned. Unlike most private and angel investors, LION's members are not necessarily accredited investors, who have the SEC's blessing to wade into small, private deals that the agency considers risky. "We're more going on the concept of the securities law exemption for non-public offerings," explains Frazier, who is a registered investment advisor.

By that, he means the "private offering exemption" under Section 4(1) of the Securities Act. But what exactly constitutes a nonpublic offering is open to debate. Frazier points me to a 1962 SEC ruling that attempts to clarify when such exemptions from registration are allowed. Traditionally, the private offering exemption has been available for "bank loans, private placements of securities with institutions and the promotion of a business venture to a few closely related persons," the ruling explains. So, as long as the potential investors have a preexisting relationship and familiarity with the offerer of the securities, it can be considered a nonpublic offering. "In a community like ours," says Frazier, "that's usually if not always the case."

Frazier is comfortable with his interpretation of the SEC rules, but concedes that it does entail risk. "We have not had a securities lawyer charging $550 an hour go over the whole concept," he says. "While I think that our idea works well in principal, if there is someone that doesn't know someone else and there is an investment made when they're not really fully educated on what's going on, (the SEC) would have grounds to say that there was a violation of the law. It's something that we're really careful about, to keep it small and in the family of the community of people who know each other."

That's one reason the group holds regular social events so people can get to know each other. And they keep a low profile, just to be safe.

Game Plan for Locavestors

The Local Investment Opportunity Network (LION) is a group of investors in Port Townsend, Washington, formed to promote local investment. LION doesn't invest as a group, but facilitates investment by bringing together local investors with local businesses in need of loans or equity. LION members are not necessarily accredited investors, so companies rely on a private offering exemption for preexisting relationships.

Pros:
- The level of familiarity and knowledge that comes with a local investment can provide investors with greater insight into the business.
- Interest rates on loans generally reflect the higher risk premium.
- Dividends and repayment may also take the form of in-kind payment—for example, cheese in the case of the Mt. Townsend Creamery.
- The rewards are more than financial; by investing in local enterprises you support your local economy and increase the local quality of life.

Cons:

- Private transactions carry risk. There is no regulatory oversight or recourse, and investors must conduct their own due diligence.
- If loans are unsecured, the investment could potentially be lost if the business fails.
- Equity investments are likely to be illiquid and long term, with no easy way to cash out.

The Bottom Line: For patient investors who are comfortable vetting investments and taking some risk.

For More Information:

- LION's web site contains useful information and documents including a membership application; membership agreement, policies, and procedures form; and an Investing Opportunity Submission form, at www.l2020.org/index.php?page=investing-opportunities.

CHAPTER 8

Community Capital

It Takes a Village, or a Police Force, or Perhaps Some Farmers

On a warm spring morning in early May 2009, Greg Rynearson, a police officer in Clare, Michigan, was on a coffee run when he received some disturbing news. It wasn't a robbery or a homicide—this sleepy, Midwestern town of 3,300 hasn't seen either in years. Rather, the alarm bells were set off by a rumor that the 111-year-old Clare City Bakery was planning to call it quits in July. Back at the department, in a stark interrogation room that doubles as a lunch-room, Rynearson shared the news with fellow officer Al White. For the two cops—burly men with matching bushy mustaches who were born and raised in Clare—it was more than the loss of a nostalgic fixture of their youth. If the bakery closed, it would be yet another shuttered storefront on North McEwan, a three-block stretch that makes up the main drag of downtown Clare. Like many Michigan towns, Clare was feeling the impact of a foundering auto industry and severe recession. There were already five vacancies on McEwan, including the former site of Mills End, a Western-wear shop that, like the bakery, had served residents for generations. "We said, boy, if we could get all of the boys in the department to pitch in, we could probably save the bakery," recalls Rynearson.

The officers called the owner of the bakery and asked for a price. She thought they were crazy—it wasn't the kind of business that's going to make anyone rich, but gave them a figure. Scribbling on the pizza box that held their congealing lunch, they worked out the numbers. And that was how the entire nine-member Clare police force came to own a bakery.

The new owners put up a fresh coat of paint, hung some police memorabilia, and tinkered with the bakery's menu, swelling the size of the cookies and adding "the squealer," a maple-frosted doughnut topped with two strips of bacon. Three weeks later, the new bakery—rechristened Cops & Doughnuts—opened its doors. The plucky cops and their doughnut shop quickly became a media sensation.

By August, business was so brisk, the cops expanded into an adjacent historic building that had been empty. They used it to house their growing line of merchandise, including t-shirts emblazoned with slogans like *'D.W.I.' Doughnuts Were Involved* and *Don't Glaze Me Bro*. There are also coffee mugs and a new line of Cops-branded coffee in blends such as Midnight Shift and Off Duty Decaf. Who thinks up these clever gimmicks? "We've all worked the midnight shift at one time or another," explains Rynearson, who is partial to the bakery's oatmeal raisin cookie. "In small-town America, you get time to drive around and think about things, and you come up with stuff."

The cops clearly relish their new roles as protectors of the carbohydrates. They can usually be found at the shop on their days off, chatting with customers and pitching in. Sometimes there is intrigue, as when Rynearson, while removing some old trim in the prep room, discovered a smattering of dried blood. Sure that he had stumbled onto a "cold case"—after all, Clare was a hangout for the notorious bootleggers known as the Purple Gang in the 1920s—he excitedly called in the department's crime investigator, Dave Saad, only to find that the blood was, in fact, raspberry filling. The seeds, noted Saad, should have been a dead giveaway.

For all the jokes, the bakery has become a serious success. Instead of another empty storefront, Cops & Doughnuts now employs 19 people full time, including the former bakery's lone employee. That's more people than the entire Clare Police Department employs. The new owners put up billboards on nearby highways, pulling throngs of tourists into Clare. In the summer, an average of 2,000 people flow through the bakery's doors each Saturday. The bakery's success has spilled over to other merchants, helping to revitalize downtown Clare. "With all the people coming through, nearly every restaurant in town has said this is the best summer they've ever had," says a clearly pleased Rynearson.

There are no hard numbers to measure the impact that Cops & Doughnuts has had. But then, they aren't really needed. "I see it happening," says Lori Schuh, a historic preservation and economic development official with the Clare Downtown Development Authority whose office overlooks McEwan. "People with Cops & Doughnuts bags in Coffee Talk buying lattes and then going into the hardware store." The formerly vacant storefronts are slowly refilling, too: A student-run art gallery opened a few doors down from the bakery, and an antique store is preparing to open.

Like most typical small businesses, Cops & Doughnuts supports other local merchants. Baking supplies come from Dawn Food Products, a large family-run company in Jackson, Michigan. The coffee is roasted by an employee-owned company in Lansing. And the T-shirts are made in neighboring Mount Pleasant, even though a Florida supplier offered a cheaper price. "We buy everything we can locally," says White.

The bakery is also active with local charities and sponsors a T-ball team, called the Little Doughnut Holes, and a girls' soccer team. It recently purchased a drum for the high school marching band.

For all that, the policemen's greatest achievement may be something harder to pin down, something more symbolic. "The biggest thing they did for the community was to say, 'You, too, can do this. You can save your community,'" says Schuh. "Nobody else is going to swoop in. The government is not going to come in and dump buckets of money on the street. Corporate America is not going to come in and save our town. It's our town and our responsibility to make sure that we continue to exist."

Bookworms in Shining Armor

Sure, cops love their doughnuts. But many of us feel just as strongly about our own favorite neighborhood spots—those quirky cafes and shops that give our communities their unique identities. And when those beloved businesses run into trouble, customers have often rallied to save them.

I've seen it a number of times in my own area. Bread-Stuy, a coffee shop in the gentrifying brownstone-filled neighborhood of Bed-Stuy, Brooklyn, fell behind in taxes in 2008 after the recession ate away at sales, and was seized by tax authorities. Neighbors organized fundraisers, collecting enough for the owners to reopen the shop. In August 2010, the *New York Times* reported on an 80-year-old family-run grocery store in Point Lookout, New York, that was similarly struggling in the recession. More than 150 customers wrote checks to help the owners pay $100,000 owed to a supplier.[1]

But, like the officers of Clare, some local residents have gone further, extending loans or becoming part owners in a venture. Vox Pop, a café and performance space with a populist bent ("Books, Coffee, Democracy," its sign reads) in Ditmas Park, another emerging Brooklyn neighborhood, was credited with sparking a culinary revival along a stretch once dominated by dollar stores. When it hit a rough patch, the owners sold shares to loyal customers, turning it into a sort of community collective in keeping with its Marxist spirit. (More on that later.)

Perhaps nowhere do passions run as deep as among book lovers and their local bookstores. You know the kind of place— a cozy, well-curated bookstore where you can browse and bump into neighbors. Every good neighborhood once had one. But independent booksellers have been brutally squeezed by megachains, online retailers, and now the Kindle and its digital ilk. The American Booksellers Association, a 110-year-old trade association for independent bookstores, has seen its membership shrink by more than half since 1990, to about 1,800 members.[2]

So it is especially rankling when another indie favorite is teetering on the brink. In the literary equivalent of cops saving a doughnut shop, a group of professors from the local university stepped up to invest in Tsunami Books in Eugene, Oregon, when they heard of its impending demise in 2005.[3]

In Brooklyn, we've had our share of bookworms in shining armor. In 2007, Catherine Bohne was distraught over the thought that The Community Bookstore, a neighborhood institution she bought from its founder in 2001, might go under. When a regular customer got wind of the situation, she alerted other loyal customers and they rallied to Bohne's defense. One helped Bohne work up a business plan and renegotiate a bank loan, while 12 other locals, including actor John Turturro, kicked in $10,000 apiece for a stake in the store.[4] One investor of modest means even took out a loan to invest. A year later, with shelves again fully stocked, sales were up 40 percent.[5]

The Community Bookstore continues to provide the kinds of services that have made it indispensable to the neighborhood. It sponsors book clubs and a mystery-book swap, and it offers free delivery. Its resident felines, Tiny and Marjorie, roam the aisles. Once a month, the bookstore hosts a Community Forum night to explore an issue or topic of interest to the neighborhood, whether green energy for the home, composting, or bat houses (before you snicker, consider that a single brown bat can eat up to 1,000 mosquitoes per hour!). Bohne also helped organize a "buy local" campaign, hosting a party for merchants to kick it off.

Last year, when Bohne decided to move to a remote valley in Albania to run a guest house (bookstore owners tend to be quirky that way), another longtime customer, a writer named Ezra Goldstein, stepped up with his wife to buy the shop. "The investors have been really wonderful," he says. "Their main concern is that the bookstore stay open." For now, the store is barely breaking even, says Goldstein. But investors will see the value of their stakes rise modestly with the transaction. He is also cooking up new amenities to attract customers, including adding new book clubs and a film series, offering free tea and coffee, and sprucing up the bookstore's garden (thanks to a neighborhood landscaper who refused payment aside from two books).

A Rich Community

A similar scenario unfolded in Fort Greene, a vibrant neighborhood of stately old brownstones that is home to the Brooklyn Academy of Music (BAM), a popular weekend market known as the Brooklyn Flea, and a ton of bibliophiles. Many restaurants and cafes have popped up in the past several years, but one of the amenities the neighborhood was sorely lacking was a good local bookstore. When the Fort Greene Association surveyed residents about what type of retail options they would like to see, the number one answer, with 75 percent of responses, was a bookstore. So it was kismet when the neighborhood association discovered that Jessica Stockton-Bagnulo and Rebecca Fitting, two young book-obsessed women, were hoping to do just that. Three hundred people showed up for a party thrown by the association at BAM to welcome them, before they even had secured a location or financing. The bookstore plans, alas, were set back after the failure of Lehman Brothers in the fall of 2008, which precipitated a deep a credit freeze. Suddenly, the prospects for securing a loan seemed dim.

Even before the financial crisis, Stockton-Bagnulo knew it wouldn't be easy. In a July 2008 entry on her blog chronicling the efforts to open the bookstore, she wrote:

> Most of the folks I know who have opened up independent bookstores in the last 10 years or so have had one of two things:
>
> 1) a mortgage
> 2) a well-off relative or friend.
>
> These are traditional and time-honored means of securing capital for an independent business, especially one as high-risk as a bookstore (it also works with restaurants, bars, and other retail businesses).
>
> I have neither of those things.

Facing up to the fact that there would be no "magical millionaire" riding in to save her, Stockton-Bagnulo came to appreciate what she did have: "Instead of a wealthy individual, a rich community," she wrote. "That's pretty magical to me."[6]

So she and Fitting floated an idea: Would the residents that welcomed them so warmly consider investing in the bookstore to make it a reality? The answer was a resounding yes. The duo raised a total of $70,000 from more than two dozen friends, neighbors, and book lovers.

Lenders were issued promissory notes and were allowed to choose their own interest rate between 2.5 percent and 4 percent—a little above prime. Interest payments would kick in after one year and would be paid in quarterly installments for five years. Two people lent $10,000 or more and are part of the bookstore's advisory council. In addition, all community lenders receive a 30 percent discount on purchases for the life of the loan as well as other perks, which has kept them coming back. As with the LION group in Port Townsend, Washington, the Greenlight deal was predicated on the pre-existing relationships that characterize a community. Such small, private friends and family investments are generally allowed, although interpretation of the laws varies. Other community investments may qualify for in-state or other federal securities exemptions.

Along with their own savings and a $150,000 small business loan from a fund set up to help local businesses after 9/11, the partners gathered the nearly $350,000 needed to open the bookstore. A local architecture team created a bright, welcoming space, and neighbors pitched in to paint, stain shelves, and unpack boxes. As a torrential rain fell on October 16, 2009, Greenlight Bookstore opened its doors to the public, and it has thrived ever since. Defying the gloomy outlook for bookselling, the store was turning a profit and beating expectations after just one year. "The support from this community has been amazing," says Stockton-Bagnulo.

A big part of its success is the way she and Fitting cater to their very diverse and eclectic community. They hold readings and events, usually two or three a week, with an emphasis on local and literary authors. A table is devoted to Brooklyn writers, many from right there in the neighborhood. "It's always groaning and overflowing, that table," laughs Stockton-Bagnulo. "We have to rotate things through to give everyone a moment." They also stock a large number of African American–interest books, interspersed throughout the store. "Being small, we can turn on a dime," she says. When customers started asking about *For Colored Girls Who Have Considered Suicide When the Rainbow Is Enuf,* a play and book that had just been made into a movie, the owners ordered a big stack of them and placed them up front.

Greenlight's children's story time on weekends has become a community affair for the area's many young families, who linger after the hour is over to chat with neighbors. It has become so popular the store is adding another story hour. And like many small businesses, Greenlight supports local charities and is actively involved in the business improvement district.

The financial support of the community, born out of necessity, has only contributed to the success and special appeal of the store. "They've become regular customers," says Stockton-Bagnulo. "They shop at the store now because it's their store."

That's the case for Josh Rutner, a 29-year-old jazz musician who lives in the neighborhood with his wife, Jen, a librarian. After hearing about the efforts to raise money for the store on a local blog, he invested $1,500. "Since I've lived in Fort Greene, it's been a dream to have an independent bookstore around the corner," says Rutner. "If they had set it up as a donation I would have given the same, so the fact that I get my money back and all the perks and discounts—it was an easy decision for me." He regularly pops in for events, like a recent talk by music critic Alex Ross, who had just released a collection of essays called *Listen to This.* "I love the community appeal of the store," he says. "It's a great addition to the neighborhood."

That spirit was on full display one brisk evening in mid-October 2010. Greenlight bookstore's broad windows shined like a beacon onto Fulton Street. The store was mobbed with regulars and well-wishers gathered to celebrate its one-year birthday (the day before, investors had their own celebration, where they were handed their first dividend checks). Champagne popped, toasts were made, and a speech sent by best-selling author Gary Shteyngart was read by three young employees in a mock Russian accent. Stockton-Bagnulo beamed. Then she ran off to find a customer a book.

Indie Revival

Community capital can take many forms. And, while it is not a substitute for a well functioning banking system, it can help plug a funding gap for many small-scale Main Street businesses in both rural and urban areas. This is not risk-free investing, however. Bookstores, in particular, can be dicey propositions. Given their slim margins, they are never going to be big money makers. And the march of digital media has clouded the future of the printed word. Even those bookstores with a passionate following may not be able to survive the competitive pressures. Big Table Books in Ames, Iowa, for example, was famously funded several years back by customer-investors, including author Jane Smiley. But after 13 years of operation, and the opening of a Borders nearby in 2003, the store, with its blue tin roof and colored tiles, shut its doors in August 2006. "It was never a commercial venture. It was a citizenship venture," one investor told the *Des Moines Register*.[7]

In addition, like any enterprise, a community-funded business is vulnerable to sloppy management. Despite its iconic presence and community support, Vox Pop, the Brooklyn coffee shop and café, was shuttered for good in September 2010. Its founder, Sander Hicks, a political radical, author, publisher, and former punk rocker, apparently didn't care much for regulatory regimes like tax collection and health codes. Even under new management, the café wrestled with the debt and fines left behind by Hicks. In mid-September, the café's assets were quietly auctioned off.

Still, those seem to be the exception rather than the rule. In many cases, community financing imposes management discipline that was missing. Often, advisory boards are formed and customer-investors with business experience work with the founder to craft a more viable business plan. They're all in it together, after all.

What seems clear is that the outpouring of community support across the nation signals a thirst among consumers for independent merchants and businesses.

In New York City, Greenlight and The Community Bookstore are just two examples of a surprisingly vibrant indie book scene. "I feel like there's an increasing sense among people who love books that there's a value to an independent bookstore, that there's something you can get there that you can't get from clicking on a button on the Internet—and that's great for us," says Greenlight's Stockton-Bagnulo. "But the story is not that independent bookstores are dying. Independent bookstores are evolving and are still a piece of the picture."[8]

In the last couple of years, more than a dozen indie bookstores have opened in Manhattan and Brooklyn, even as behemoths like Borders and Barnes & Noble have struggled. Barnes & Noble, for example, announced the closing of about 50 stores across the country in 2010. Most were B. Dalton outlets, but the company's four-story Manhattan flagship across from Lincoln Center was a notable casualty. Borders Group closed hundreds of stores before filing for Chapter 11 bankruptcy protection in February 2011. It's not just books. Blockbuster, the video megachain owned by Viacom that put many independents out of business, filed for Chapter 11 the previous fall. It may turn out that the operating model of the big chains—massive cookie-cutter scale and corporate cost structures predicated on generating ever-greater growth and profits—is simply unsustainable, especially as more sales go online. As these behemoths slowly dismantle their vast retail networks, the independents will be left standing, providing their neighborhoods with that modest but inimitable mix of service and community.

A Store to Call Your Own

As we've seen, many community-funded businesses are born out of crisis. But lately, entrepreneurs are designing community support into their business models in a more proactive way.

Saranac Lake is a picturesque town in the New York Adirondacks with a history dating back to the early 1800s. Over the decades, its mountains, lakes, and clean air have drawn summer residents such as Albert Einstein, Theodore Roosevelt, and composer Béla Bartók. This quiet town, whose year-round population of 5,000 triples every summer, is the unlikely center for a radical experiment in community self-sufficiency.

It all started when the local Ames department store went bust. Its closing had little to do with the location. The Saranac Lake store was profitable, but the parent organization, saddled with debt after an extended acquisition spree, was unable to survive an economic downturn and went bankrupt in 2002. Area residents were left with no option but to drive an hour to buy basics like underwear. That prompted some community members to form a group to examine retail alternatives. At first they courted big retailers, but few were interested. That is, except Walmart, which had been trying to open a superstore in the tri-lake region for years. Local activists, fearing that a giant supercenter would destroy their community, had thwarted it so far. But without other retail options, it wasn't clear how long they could hold out.

That's when the group learned of the Powell Mercantile, a community-owned store in Powell, Wyoming, a rural town about the same size as Saranac Lake. The Merc, as it is known, was established in 2002 by a group of citizen-investors after the town's only department store, a chain called Stage, shut down, forcing shoppers to make a 50-mile round-trip drive to the nearest big-box store, in Cody. Powell officials feared that that would set in motion a downward spiral, hurting the remaining merchants as locals did more and more shopping outside the town. A group of residents and town officials raised money in $500 shares from residents and opened their own store in the 7,000-square-foot space formerly occupied by Stage. It may not be fancy, but it carries a wide selection of items, from shoes to luggage, often at a lower price than at the mall. Fashion brands like Tommy Hilfiger share space with rancher-appropriate Wranglers.

The Merc has been hugely successful, turning a profit every year except 2009, thanks to a recessionary dip. Since its sixth year in operation, it has paid healthy annual dividends of around 15 percent to its owners. It has also expanded into an adjacent building, doubling its size. Rather than the downward spiral that town officials once feared, Powell's Main Street is now thriving. "It makes a town feel good about themselves. People can say, 'I'm part of this,'" Merc general manager Paul Ramos told a regional newspaper.[9]

It feels so good that dozens of western towns that have been abandoned by their anchor stores have followed suit.

Saranac Lake will be among the first such examples on the more densely populated and retail-served east coast. When town organizers invited a representative from the Powell Mercantile to come talk at a June 2006 town hall meeting, about 200 residents turned up. "People were excited," says Melinda Little, president of the interim board of directors for Saranac Lake Community Store. And they were enthusiastic about investing, she says. Little, who runs a business camp for girls called Camp Startup as her day job, put together a business plan. As fate would have it, a securities lawyer who grew up in the area, Charles Noth, had just moved back to town and agreed to work on the project pro bono. He put together a prospectus and filed it with New York state authorities, allowing the group to raise money from state residents. Noth, the brother of actor Chris Noth (aka Mr. Big in *Sex in the City*), is also an investor. The prospectus can also be downloaded by potential investors from the group's web site, www.community-store.org.

In an effort to make participation broadly accessible, the organizers kept the price of shares at $100. They also instituted an investment ceiling of $10,000 so that no one person could amass a controlling interest (but also making fundraising more diffi- cult). Shares are open to any New York state resident, but, as Little says, "our investors will be our main customers."

Given the recession, it has taken much longer than hoped to raise the $500,000 needed to open the store. The deadline has been extended several times, but in early 2011, after a final fundraising push, the organization reached its goal. Lease negotiations were underway for a 5,000-square foot former restaurant space, and bids were being solicited from local contractors to renovate it. The orga- nizers had begun interviewing store managers, and were drawing up inventory lists, in preparation for an anticipated July opening

For investors, there is no guarantee of a return, Little says. And initially, any profits will be plowed back into the running of the store. There is also no secondary market to sell shares, so the investment is fairly illiquid. But if successful, like the Powell Merc, the Saranac Lake store could generate healthy dividends someday. More importantly, the more than 600 investors who have chipped in an average $800 each will have the satisfaction of knowing that they will never be at the mercy of a remotely owned corporation that can pull out on a whim. Money spent at the store, meanwhile, will circulate within the community, rather than flying right back out to a distant, faceless headquarters.

A Community Revitalization Project Masquerading as a Diner

There are now community-owned energy utilities, forests, theatres, sports teams (hello Green Bay Packers)—you name it. And it's a global phenomenon. Small-scale, community-owned wind power is commonplace in Denmark and Germany. In England, where 400 pubs and shops closed in rural villages in 2009, victims of modern-day urbanization and an economic slowdown, community-owned shops are flourishing. In the past 25 years, 254 community-owned shops have opened, including 40 in 2010 alone, according to the Plunkett Foundation, an organization that helps set up such shops. In all that time, the foundation notes, only eight of the community-owned stores have closed.[10] Saving the local shop with a community-owned store even figured in the plot line of a popular British radio soap opera, *The Archers,* about the fictional village of Ambridge.

In the United States, many community capital initiatives are an outgrowth of the locavore movement. Community-supported agriculture, in which customers prepay for vegetables and other produce, provides farmers with capital they need to operate until they are ready to harvest. The idea of preselling as a way to manage cash flow has spread to fisheries, restaurants, and dairies. Taking that a step further, some food entrepreneurs are inviting their future customers to invest in the business up front, as lenders or equity owners.

Community-supported and financed restaurants, for example, are a growing trend. One of the pioneers is Tod Murphy, a

Vermont farmer and the founder of Farmers Diner. When Murphy opened his first diner in Barre, Vermont, it was an experiment for both him and his well-heeled investors. Murphy's idea, fairly radical back in 2002, was to serve great tasting, locally sourced food at diner prices. Oh, and expand the concept into a franchise.

The Farmers Diner model centers on creating "pods" of several diners in a region, supported by shared back-end services and a commissary for central purchasing, delivery, and basic food prep. By Murphy's reckoning, each pod will spend more than $1 million annually on food, generating $6 million in additional economic activity and helping support 10 to 40 local farms—like Gleason Grains in Bridport, which supplies the whole-wheat flour for the diner's acclaimed buttermilk pancakes (served with pure Vermont maple syrup, of course). The idea is to take that model and replicate it all across the country. "We like to call it an agricultural community revitalization project masquerading as a diner," says Denise Perras, Farmers Diner's operations director.

Murphy closed the original diner, which had proven out the model but was too small, and opened a new Farmers Diner in 2005 in Quechee, Vermont. That was followed by another diner in Middlebury in 2008. For Middlebury, Murphy decided to invite the community to participate. He threw a free dinner at a church so people could hear about the plans and taste the food for themselves. More than 150 people showed up, and many were interested in investing. But (you guessed it) the deteriorating economy in the fall of 2008 scared many away. Still, Murphy handily raised $150,000 in two weeks from 15 investors, spanning the gamut from a dairy farmer to a retired Morgan Stanley director. Investors earn 9 percent interest on the original investment, with interest payments to begin in year three. After seven years, they can get their original investment back or convert it to a bond. In addition, another dozen or so people prepaid $1,000 apiece for $1,200 worth of meals.

"People were looking for alternative methods of investing after the fiasco on Wall Street," says Perras. There is a quarterly investor meeting, but local investors often drop by to talk about concerns or ideas for the menu. There is also an open-door policy under which they can come in anytime and look at the books.

Farmers Diner is still building up, but it has already begun to fulfill some of the lofty ambitions it has set for itself. The Middlebury diner, which also serves as the commissary, sources 83 percent of its food within a 70-mile radius. It turned profitable in August 2010. Together, the Middlebury and Quechee diners employ about 50 people and generate annual sales of about $1.2 million—all of which benefit the area's farmers and economy. A sister company, Vermont Smoke and Cure, turns locally raised pork into bacon, sausage, and ham.

Now, Murphy and Perras are getting ready for their first foray outside of Vermont: They plan to open a Farmers Diner in Lafayette, California, just outside of San Francisco, in May 2011. In keeping with the pod model, the Lafayette diner will be followed with a second one in the vicinity, along with a commissary to share costs and prep work. Rumors of a Brooklyn diner had local foodies buzzing last summer, and a prospectus was circulating. Although that is still being considered, Perras says, the lure of a nine-month growing season in the Bay Area was just too much to resist. In the meantime, Brooklynites will have to content themselves with *The Farmers Diner Cookbook*, to be published in late 2011.

Community-Supported Everything

The community-owned and -supported ethos has been taken to perhaps its most ambitious lengths in Hardwick, Vermont, where an entire ecosystem revolving around sustainable agriculture and food has taken root, sparking an economic and cultural revival in the area. You might call it community-supported everything.

Over the past three years, Hardwick has created 100 jobs in value-added agriculture. To put it in context, that's one-fifth of the area's total employment. The Hardwick "miracle" has been well-chronicled: It has been the subject of features in the *New York Times* and *Gourmet*, as well as a book, *The Town That Food Saved*, by farmer and area resident Ben Hewitt. But less attention has been paid to the creative financing that made it all possible.

Like any story about Hardwick, it all seems to begin with Tom Stearns, the red-bearded, charismatic founder of High Mowing

Seeds, a purveyor of organic and heirloom seeds. (A "high mowing," in case you are wondering, is an old agricultural term that refers to the mowed hilltop hayfields that were common in the area a century ago.) Stearns started growing seeds as a hobby and turned it into a thriving business. From 2000 to 2005, his sales grew by an average 80 percent a year, and he began to contract with other farmers to grow additional seeds. He was soon at what he calls a critical juncture, faced with a decision of either slowing down the breakneck pace of growth, or embracing it. Like any entrepreneur worth his salt, Stearns chose the latter. But that required investments in new facilities, equipment, technology, and staff to support the additional business.

Stearns knew he couldn't service more debt during this period of capital investment. Yet equity posed a challenge, too, since he wanted to retain control of his company and couldn't exactly offer the kinds of huge returns that angel or venture capital investors typically expect for their money. Ultimately, he decided on a convertible debt offering that would provide reasonable returns and liquidity to investors, but on favorable terms to the company. Stearns proposed a 6 percent interest rate. The interest would start accruing immediately, but no interest would be paid out for the first five years. At the five-year mark, investors could either convert some or all of their principal into equity and receive a lump sum payment of accrued interest, or elect to be paid back principal and accrued interest in quarterly payments over another five year period.

In less than five months, Stearns had raised roughly $1.1 million from 17 investors—all within 50 miles.

The investors were all accredited, meaning they met the SEC's definition of a wealthy, and by implication sophisticated, investor. Stearns needed to raise large sums, and he didn't want to have to communicate with an unwieldy number of investors, so limiting it to accredited investors made sense. And, as noted in Chapter 2, it's easier from a legal standpoint to deal with such investors. Still, says Stearns, "We need vehicles to allow smaller investors and smaller amounts of money to go into these things so on an aggregated basis it could total hundreds of thousands."

That's where Eli Moulton comes in. Moulton was born and raised in Huntington, Vermont, just outside of Burlington. After law school, he worked at a big law firm in Boston, doing corporate deals for Fortune 500 clients, before returning home to Vermont to join the husband-and-wife team of Merritt & Merritt (now Merritt & Merritt & Moulton), which had carved out a niche in early stage funding and private equity. Moulton has become the go-to guy for area entrepreneurs in need of solutions—a sort of Dudley Davis for creative financing. It doesn't hurt that he's a home brewer and outdoorsman, which his largely food and agricultural clients can relate to. "One of the things we run into every day is trying to reconcile this whole movement for slow money and local investing and supporting these early stage investments with the regulatory regime that exists," says Moulton. "It was created in the Great Depression to protect investors from risky investments, and there is this constant tension between those two things."

Moulton helped Stearns structure the High Mowing Seeds deal, though he admits he was skeptical at first. "The market rate for such a loan was more like 7 or 8 percent," he explains, with a maturity date closer to five years. "Tom was a little bit ahead of the curve in recognizing that there are a lot of investors out there that want to get some social return on their capital."

Since then, Moulton has helped several other Hardwick-area entrepreneurs raise money, including Claire's Restaurant, a favorite gathering spot in Hardwick that gets its ingredients from local farmers (its motto: *Local ingredients, Open to the World*). Moulton is fond of tiered offerings that target different investment structures for different investor groups. Claire's, for example, raised a big chunk of equity from accredited investors in a private offering, while 50 smaller investors bought prepaid "food coupons" at $1,000 a piece, entitling them to $25 off a meal once a month for four years. Sometimes Moulton adds a middle tier of debt or notes, issued in smaller denominations to a wide group of community investors.

Another main hub of Hardwick's economic activity, and its heart and soul, is the monthly gathering of a dozen or so local business owners who began meeting many years ago to socialize and help one another work through business issues. "It's through this group that many of the creative financing models have been shared," says Stearns. One problem common to many of the young companies—a soy milk producer, a vegetable grower, a cheese maker, among others—was how to manage rapid growth. Like High Mowing Seeds, some of them were doubling sales every year. The business owners began making informal bridge loans to each other, to help make necessary investments to support the growth.

That works especially well when they happened to have opposite cash flow cycles—or, "when my fat time is your lean time," says Stearns. High Mowing Seeds, for example, is flush in the winter and early spring months, when it sells most of its seeds. Its lean time is October through December, when Stearn is putting together the next season's catalogue, buying seeds, and staffing up for the busy season.

On the other hand, for Pete Johnson of Pete's Greens, spring and early summer are the lean months. It's a year-round organic farm, thanks to the hand-built greenhouses, but that's when Pete's is ramping up for the main growing season. Come late summer and fall, "he's selling colossal amounts, and is more than paid up for any borrowing he's done for spring," explains Stearns. The two friends have lent money back and forth 8 or 10 times over the past five years, says Stearns.

The Hardwick model, as it has been called, comes down to the close relationships and collaboration of its new-breed entrepreneurs. The success of local cheese makers like Jasper Hill and Cabot Creamery has opened up a vital market for local dairy farmers who supply them with their raw material. Claire's Restaurant showcases the produce of local farmers, while unused crops get composted by local enterprises and turned into fertilizer to nourish the fields of local farms. Andrew Meyer, the clean cut founder of Vermont Soy, which produces small-batch tofu, and Vermont Natural Coatings, which makes nontoxic wood finishes from the leftover whey, created the nonprofit Center for an Agricultural Economy to further marshal the community's resources.

The spirit of mutual support has created a thriving economy in a former quarry town that not long ago was slowly dying. And its success is attracting more talented and ambitious entrepreneurs to the area. Honey Gardens, a winery that makes mead wine, relocated to Hardwick from Burlington to be part of the scene, opening a tasting room in town.

The Vermont Food Venture Center, a $1 million shared-use facility, plans to open its doors in spring 2011, right next to Claire's. The center will make its dairy, meat, and specialty food processing equipment and expertise available to local food businesses and startups—replicating, in a sense, the village canneries and creameries that once dotted the landscape here. "That building," says Stearns, "will jumpstart a whole new generation of food entrepreneurs.

Game Plan for Locavestors

Community capital is sort of a catch-all term for investments that bring together local residents with a local enterprise to fill a need—be it a café or a department store. These enterprises are typically supported or owned by the people they serve. There is no one model. Transactions can take the form of low risk community-supported agriculture and prepaid shares, interest-paying loans, or equity shares for those with a higher appetite for risk. The financial returns may vary, but the feeling of being part of a local institution is, as the famous ad says, priceless.

Pros:
- There is perhaps no better feel-good investment than putting your money into a beloved local enterprise, whether a bookstore, café, or shop.
- Although the monetary returns may be modest, such investments often carry perks, like discounted products and services.
- For some communities, it is a pragmatic way to bring in a critical service or business that is lacking in the neighborhood (like those British villages that lost their local pubs and shops, or a Brooklyn neighborhood that wants a bookstore to call its own). The arrangements can involve equity, debt, or prepaid shares, allowing business owners to tailor the investments to investors' appetite for risk.

- If you want to play it safe, prepaid shares are an easy, low cost way to support a local establishment. Those with more disposable investment capital might be comfortable becoming an equity investor. For small businesses, community capital is a great way to engage customers and literally get them invested in their success.

Cons:
- These are high-risk propositions. Small businesses, especially those without a track record, can fail. Good management is critical.
- Most community capital deals are ad hoc. There is, as yet, no formal way for investors to find out about such opportunities. Typically information is spread informally through word of mouth or from the business itself.
- Interest rates on loans to a community-supported business may not be commensurate with risk.
- The downside of equity investments, in addition to risk, is that such investments in privately held businesses are typically illiquid.
- Finally, community capital deals should involve an experienced professional, since they can easily run afoul of SEC laws.

The Bottom Line: Community capital can be a wonderful way to support a business that you care about, and it makes great sense if you are already a regular customer. For communities, it can build a sense of belonging and shared purpose. Prepaid shares are an easy, low-risk way to support a local establishment.

For More Information:
- General information on community capital and public policy can be found at the Institute for Local Self Reliance's New Rules Project, at www.newrules.org. The Institute's The Big Box Toolkit, at www.bigboxtoolkit.com, is chock-a-block with advice and practical strategies for communities that want to protect and enliven their own downtowns or organize their own community-owned stores.
- The Plunkett Foundation tracks news and issues relating to rural cooperatives and social enterprise at www.plunkett.co.uk.
- The Democracy Collaborative maintains a comprehensive site devoted to community wealth-building at www.community-wealth.org.
- For information on creating community-owned energy production, see www.cooppower.coop.
- For Saranac Lake Community Store, see www.community-store.org.

CHAPTER 9

Pennies from Many

When Social Networking Met Finance

Like many startups, Trampoline Systems, a British software maker, raised its initial funds from friends and family. It followed that with an infusion from angel investors. The company had a potential winner on its hands: Its software promised to plumb the sea of online data and communication to discern patterns in social networks—exactly the kind of things that big corporations obsessed with brand image salivate over. (Trampoline famously demonstrated its visualization software in 2006 by running it against a public database of e-mail messages from Enron.) But more capital was needed to commercialize it.

In 2007, Trampoline lined up roughly $5 million from a U.S.-based hedge fund. All was well—until the financial system nearly collapsed in the fall of 2008 and the hedge fund, like so many investors, retreated from the market. "The options were pretty stark. It was either close the business or do a kind of fire sale," says Trampoline's cofounder and CEO, Charles Armstrong, a 39-year-old ethnographer with a wild mane and a penchant for loud suits. Armstrong began exploring alternatives. He knew firsthand the power of online social networks, and figured he'd try raising funds over the Internet. Heck, he had nothing to lose. "We didn't know if it would work out or not, and we knew that it was going to be hard work, but it was better than the conventional options," he says.

Armstrong and his team worked with securities lawyers to navigate the regulatory thicket of the Financial Services Authority (FSA)—Britain's equivalent of our SEC—and set out to raise £1 million in equity financing from up to 100 high-net-worth investors, in a sort of Internet-enabled private placement. Trampoline closed its first tranche of £250,000 in October 2009. A second round hit a snag when an investor who promised a lucrative stake turned out to be blowing smoke. But a year later, Trampoline lined up another £300,000 from a roster of A-list investors affiliated with major technology and finance companies.

Banking with Neighbors

As credit and venture capital have been harder to come by, entrepreneurs are beginning to look past traditional sources of capital to a broader range of potential investors. Increasingly, that means tapping into their online networks through crowdfunding. The idea is to collect lots of small sums—whether loans, equity investments, or donations—from lots of folks, bypassing banks, venture capitalists, and other middlemen. This pennies-from-many model is opening up a new way of investing for entrepreneurs and investors.

Crowdfunding is a natural evolution of crowdsourcing, the collaborative Internet ethos that gave us Wikipedia and the open-source Linux operating system. Just as the contributions of many individuals have created free or low-cost alternatives to expensive commercial products, crowdfunding allows hundreds or thousands of investors to take the place of traditional financial gatekeepers. By cutting out the middlemen, companies can raise money without hefty fees and investors can access lucrative investment alternatives, giving crowdfunding a distinct populist appeal.

Crowdfunding

Crowdfunding is an approach to raising money that aggregates small sums from many individuals via the Internet. Think social networking meets finance. This sort of person-to-person finance (P2P) was popularized by sites such as Kiva.com, a microlender, and Kickstarter, which lets people donate to creative projects. More recently the focus is on profit-making P2P consumer lending, small business lending, and small business equity investing. By eliminating the middleman, borrowers pay less interest and investors get higher returns. What could be more democratic than that?

Crowdfunding is attracting both sophisticated and amateur investors who are looking for alternatives to the volatile stock market and the anemic interest rates for savings, bonds, and CDs. For entrepreneurs, it is a potentially critical new source of funding at a time when venture capital and bank lending are on the wane. "The question is, what's going to fill the gap?" says Armstrong. "Crowdfunding is one of the few emerging models that could."

This sort of direct, person-to-person lending harkens back to the way transactions were handled for millennia, before our mediated, securitized financial system took hold. It's family lending to family, neighbor to neighbor. Tom Stearns of High Mowing Seeds lending to Pete Johnson of Pete's Greens.

The Internet and social networking have supercharged such P2P financing with new power, scale, and potential. The concept, in its modern incarnation, was first popularized by Kiva, the microlending web site created in 2005 by Matt Flannery and Jessica Jackley, to let people make small loans to goat herders, street vendors, and fishmongers in developing countries.

The Kiva founders took their inspiration from Nobel Prize winner Muhammad Yunus and his Bangladesh-based Grameen Bank, which, in the late 1970s, pioneered the idea of making microloans to the poor. Grameen showed that lending to those considered unbankable could be profitable and, in fact, a better risk than many wealthy borrowers in the developed world.

Although Grameen's loans are modest—typically just a few hundred dollars—they have helped millions of people, mostly women, invest in sewing machines, milk cows, or looms to start micro-enterprises. Defaults have been surprisingly low, historically ranging between 1 percent and 5 percent. Grameen's success had a lot to do with its reliance on peer pressure, or "social collateral," to encourage repayment. Borrowers are required to form a small group of five entrepreneurs, who are each responsible if another member misses a payment. To date, the bank has made $9.4 billion in loans to 8.3 million borrowers, at interest rates of 20 percent or less. These borrowers also own 95 percent of Grameen's shares.

The need for microfinance is not limited to the developing world. As the recession wore on, another 4 million Americans slid into poverty in 2009, according to the U.S. Census Bureau, raising the number of Americans living below the poverty line to 44 million, the highest in 15 years.[1] In recent years, the gap between rich and poor in the United States has widened. In the five-year period from 2001 to 2006, the wealthiest 1 percent of Americans pocketed more than half of total income gains.[2] Indeed, the top 1 percent owns more than a third of the country's private wealth—more than the entire wealth owned by the bottom 90 percent. So it is no small irony that, in 2008, Grameen America opened its first branches in New York and Omaha, Nebraska, the homes of Wall Street and billionaire Warren Buffet, respectively.

At the opening of the Manhattan branch, Professor Yunus was pointed in his remarks. "In these skyscrapers that New York built, they control world finance. . . . They do the banking with the world but they don't do the banking with their neighbors. We are here to show that there is nothing wrong with doing banking with neighbors."[3]

From Patronage to Profits

Kiva brought microfinance to the masses by tapping the power of the Internet and appealing to people's humanitarian instincts. From the start, Kiva's founders sought to put a human face on their borrowers, posting photos and a story for each—whether a 27-year-old woman in Tanzania who wants to open a café, or a taxi driver in Mongolia who needs a bigger vehicle to expand his business. Average loans requests are under $400. The human connection resonated with lenders, and the site made it easy for them to act with the click of a mouse. By all measures, Kiva has been a phenomenal success. In its first five years, almost 500,000 people have lent more than $160 million to individuals in 54 countries to help them start self-sustaining businesses. Kiva doesn't make the loans directly, relying instead on a network of microfinance institutions based locally to vet and make the loans. Like Grameen, its default rates are teeny, around 1 percent.

The loans can be very lucrative: Microfinance institutions often charge interest rates of 40 percent or more (Kiva's partners charge an average of 38 percent). A high rate is necessary to cover the considerable costs of vetting far-flung borrowers, but many organizations are making cushy profits—one reason the microfinance sector has gotten a black eye. In a sign of investor appetite for such firms, SKS Microfinance, an Indian company, raised more than $350 million in a public stock offering in August 2010.[4]

Kiva's individual lenders see none of that bounty, however. They get their principal back (assuming no default), but nothing more. That's because if Kiva were to promise a profit, suddenly those microfinance loans would become securities in the eyes of the SEC. Jackley and Flannery originally envisioned a site that would allow lenders to earn interest, but the SEC regulations proved too daunting given their limited resources. So Kiva became much more about philanthropy. Profits are kept solely by the microfinance institutions that vet and handle the loans. (On the other hand, MicroPlace, a similar microfinance site launched by eBay, had the deep pockets to fully register and therefore can offer interest to lenders.)

Still, at least Kiva lenders get their principal returned. That's more than the people flocking to popular funding sites like Kickstarter and IndieGoGo get. On those sites, which raise money for music, film, and other creative ventures, it's strictly donations. Donors are often rewarded with perks—a film credit, a copy of a CD, a *tchotchke*, or simply bragging rights. In perhaps the most successful example to date, in June 2010, four New York University students raised $200,000 on Kickstarter from 6,500 small donors to build a Facebook-like social networking site with better privacy.[5] In its first year of operation, Kickstarter members pledged a total of nearly $15 million in donations.

Building on the natural connection between artists, film-makers, musicians, and their audiences, crowdfunding has established a strong foothold in the arts. Sellaband, a Dutch site, lets music fans help fund new albums. The rap duo Public Enemy raised $75,000 from donors on the site. And new sites are cropping up weekly, it seems. Indie filmmaker Harmony Korine is behind Cinema Reloaded, the latest entrant to the crowded film-funding field. "Be a co-producer!" the site beckons. In return, it promises access to private forums, updates from the filmmaker and perks such as a ticket to the film's premier—"depending on availability."

The modest perks have not deterred donors. Today you can fund fashion designers, photojournalists, and football clubs. Even the Louvre raised $1.3 million from thousands of online donors to help buy "The Three Graces," a Renaissance masterpiece by the painter Lucas Cranach the Elder depicting three saucy nudes.

These efforts are essentially micro-patronage, but their success raises an interesting question: If people are willing to lend hundreds of millions of dollars on Kiva without any expectation of profit, and to donate millions more on sites like Kickstarter for projects they admire, what would they be willing to dish out if they could expect a decent return? Profit-producing P2P is the focus of the latest wave of startups. "If you are going to really turn crowd-funding into something meaningful and large scale, it only makes sense that investors get returns," says Jeff Lynn, the founder of one such site in London.

That's happening with consumer lending. Sites such as Prosper.com and LendingClub.com allow individuals to earn interest by lending to other individuals, who may be looking to pay down expensive credit card debt or finance home improvements. Lenders can earn enviable rates averaging 10 percent, while borrowers pay lower rates than those charged by banks.

It's a win-win. By the end of 2010, more than $400 million in loans had been originated on the two sites alone. Next up: small business funding. As Trampoline Systems showed, crowdfunding—that potent combination of social networking and financial technology—has the potential to revolutionize the way we invest. The latest sites—such as Funding Circle in London, ProFounder in California, and Grow VC in Hong Kong—provide a platform for bringing together investors and entrepreneurs. As with consumer P2P lending, both parties benefit. By cutting out the middlemen, entrepreneurs can obtain funding at more attractive rates and terms than offered by banks or VCs, while individuals gain access to potentially lucrative investment opportunities and businesses they care about.

There's another major benefit. By design, crowdfunding is the antithesis of Too Big to Fail finance, where a handful of powerful financial institutions can bring the economy to the brink of collapse and send the credit markets into a deep freeze. In a P2P network, there are no systemically important points of failure: Funding is dispersed across many individuals, who spread their investments in small increments over many borrowers to mitigate risk. It's the same principal that makes a distributed electricity grid less vulnerable to blackouts, or a distributed computing system less likely to be taken down by the failure of one server.

Who could argue with that?

The Securities and Exchange Commission, for one. The watchdog agency, for now, regulates the nascent crowdfunding industry. This emerging field requires close supervision, but there is the danger of going to the other extreme. The fact is, our 1930s-era regulations are woefully unsuited for the Facebook age.

Growing Pains

Prosper.com provides a cautionary tale. When it launched in 2006, it was hailed as an eBay-like marketplace for loans, where any American could lend to any other American. Underscoring that promise, the San Francisco–based startup raised an initial $20 million from eBay founder Pierre Omidyar's social investment fund, early eBay backer Benchmark Capital, and other blue-chip Silicon Valley investors.

Borrowers can list loan requests for up to $25,000 on the site, along with the interest rate they are willing to pay. Their credit scores, ratings, payment history, and personal story are also posted, as well as any affiliations or endorsements. (The actual identity of the borrower and sensitive data are not publicly revealed.) Many Prosper borrowers are looking to consolidate high-interest bank loans, while others are raising money for college or for business purposes. Investors can browse the requests and make loans to individuals in increments as low as $25. Borrowers with excellent credit can get loans with APRs as low as 6 percent, while higher risk borrowers pay an average 16 percent, still far below what they would pay to a bank.

Prosper relies on credit scores to screen borrowers, whose loans are unsecured by collateral. To spread their risk, many lenders make a number of small loans—say, $25 or $50—to a large number of borrowers, perhaps of varying credit levels. So, a $5,000 investment could be spread among 100 loans of $50 each. That way, if a few loans default, an investor's losses are minimized. Lenders can also buy and sell loan notes from one another, aiding in liquidity.

Prosper makes its money by charging borrowers a fee, ranging from .5 percent to 3 percent of the loan amount, depending on their credit rating. Lenders pay an annual servicing fee of 1 percent of the outstanding principle balance of their loans.

Chris Larsen, Prosper's founder and CEO, calls it a "third way of banking"—something between the Wall Street model of securitizing loans and spinning them off, and the banking model, where customers earn low interest on their savings while the bank profits handsomely by lending their money out at double-digit rates.

Prosper had been operating for two and a half years, with $174 million in loans initiated and 650,000 members, when in 2008 the SEC took a sudden interest. Prosper, the SEC charged, was selling unregistered securities to the public.

Larsen says he was taken by surprise. Before launching the site, his company hired top lawyers to engage the SEC to make sure the company was complying with regulations. In Larsen's view, Prosper was dealing with a banking product, pure and simple— although some securities experts say it clearly meets the definition of a security, with its promise of a profit.[6] "They basically said, 'We trust your attorney's interpretation of this so go ahead, we haven't made a decision on this space but we'll watch it,'" recalls Larsen. "That was as much of a green light as you're going to get from the SEC."

With the company's fate in the balance, Larsen and his team worked with the SEC for months on a solution, with the commission demanding that the site shut down first before it would negotiate. Prosper argued that shutting down would irreparably harm its business. In the meantime, it tried to get a bank charter, which would give it legal cover to offer securities, but new charters were not being issued. Having no other choice, the company stopped making new loans in November 2008. A week later, it received a cease-and-desist order from the SEC. The letter, dated November 24, 2008, stated that Prosper had violated sections 5(a) and (c) of the Securities Act, which prohibits the offer or sale of securities without registration or a valid exemption from registration.

It took Prosper nine months and $4 million to register its securities with the SEC as well as with each state's regulators. Today, the company is regulated like a public company issuing securities, although it is privately held. It must file a prospectus with the SEC for every $25 loan. "We're going to have more Edgar filings than any company in America at this rate," sighs Larsen, referring to the SEC database. "They have morphed this thing from a direct, people-to-people lending thing to basically a Wall Street special interest entity."

The SEC wasn't Prosper's only problem. As the economy deteriorated, so did many of its loans. Like the broader credit market, Prosper's risk model turned out to understate risk. Default rates, particularly among borrowers with lower credit scores, skyrocketed to as high as 36 percent on some loan types, according to one report.[7] From 2006 to 2008, investors averaged a negative 4 percent return, Larsen says. So he took advantage of the downtime to make some changes to the service. Larsen concedes that his company's great experiment in market libertarianism didn't pan out. Today, the company takes a more paternalistic view. It has tightened its lending standards, instituting a minimum FICO credit score of 640, up from 520 (rendering a broad swath of its former borrowers ineligible). And it has added more credit analysts to its staff. Default rates are back in check—around 6.5 percent averaged across all categories, according to the web site (although most outstanding loans are still early into their loan terms and could still go bad).

As Prosper scrambled to regroup, Lending Club, a rival peer lender based in Redwood City, California, gained on it. The site, which started out as a Facebook page, completed its SEC registration in 2008, just before Prosper was shut down. From the start, it employed higher credit screening standards. It also debuted a number of innovations, such as affinity-matching technology to connect investors and borrowers based on factors such as where they went to school, where they grew up, or their professions. That's intended to help investors find borrowers with which they share some sort of social bond, on the theory that such social connections promote repayment. In August, 2010, The Lending Club issued more than $12 million in loans, a record monthly amount for the P2P industry.

Larsen argues that his company and other P2P lenders should be overseen by banking regulators or the new Consumer Financial Protection Bureau headed by Elizabeth Warren. His lawyers lobbied for such an arrangement, and a bill passed in the House of Representatives. The Senate, meanwhile, ordered up a study of P2P lending and how it should be regulated. A report, along with recommendations, is expected to be completed by the Government Accountability Office sometime in 2011.

The saga has cast a pall over the burgeoning P2P market. "I don't think people realize the damage that's being done by what's not being allowed or the uncertainty that's being created—it just stops ideas cold," says Larsen, who also cofounded mortgage-lending site E-Loan.com in 1997. "You have a situation now where VCs have shied away from financial technology because of that tremendous uncertainty, even though there's a greater need than ever for these types of companies. This tidal wave of social networking just hit the world in the last couple of years, fundamentally changing all things having to do with communication, entertainment, and interaction. It could easily spill into equity, credit and finance, but it's not being allowed to. There is a firewall that's being built for no good reason. No one has thought it through. If that wall was lifted, you'd have a tidal wave of Kickstarters that would be spreading into the raising of credit and equity that I think would fundamentally rewire Wall Street and the big banks in a very positive, low cost, and open way. The whole thing with P2P was that any American could be a granter of credit, so you'd have millions of competitors providing credit rather than a handful of Too Big to Fail folks."

Larsen pauses and adds dryly: "Not that I'm bitter or anything."

You could understand if he is. The SEC's cease-and-desist letter to Prosper came less than two weeks before Bernie Madoff confessed to his sons that his multi-billion-dollar money management operation was nothing more than a Ponzi scheme—the biggest Ponzi scheme the world had ever seen. Although red flags had been raised with regulators for years, the SEC was caught completely off guard. Madoff's clients were largely wiped out.

P2P Goes Global

For all the uncertainty and early missteps, P2P lending shows no signs of slowing. Analysts at the Gartner Group project that P2P lending will expand 66 percent by 2013, to $5 billion in loans worldwide. The brisk growth, says Gartner, will be driven by "investors seeking higher returns and borrowers shunning (or being shunned by) banks."

There are dozens of P2P funding sites around the world, and new ones seem to pop up every day. And, with 2 billion Internet users and growing around the globe, the crowd of potential investors is vast. Often, the sites play on consumer and business disenchantment with big banks. "Where everyone wins, except the fat cats," crows the website of Zopa, a British P2P lending pioneer similar to Prosper. "I think people are also coming to us because they are fed up with the banks. People feel their money is disappearing into some sort of weird casino which bears no relation to the real world," Zopa cofounder and CEO Giles Andrews told *The Independent*.[8] Since it launched in March 2005, Zopa's half-million members have lent more than £100 million at an average 8.3 percent rate (after Zopa's 1 percent fee). CurrencyFair, a web site based in Ireland and regulated by Irish and European Union authorities, lets individuals exchange currency with each other rather than banks—"avoid being fleeced," the site exhorts.

And in a sign of investor support, Prosper in April 2010 raised another $14.7 million in financing—its fourth round of funding—from existing investors and newcomers such as Google executive chairman Eric Schmidt's venture fund. Lending Club raised $24.5 million the same month. And the sites have lately attracted some big money investors and hedge funds in pursuit of higher yields.

For now, P2P sites that can't afford to undertake the onerous process of registering with the SEC are carefully tiptoeing around securities regulations—especially when it comes to investing money in small business. Sites such as Grow VC, Virginia-based WealthForge, and Austin, Texas-based MicroVentures are only open to accredited investors—those wealthy angels that the SEC deems sophisticated enough to not need protection. Others are bypassing the United States altogether. Zopa, for example, briefly entered the U.S. market but pulled out in 2008, shortly after Prosper was shut down.

Indeed, the action in crowdfunding at the moment is taking place in the United Kingdom, where the combination of a developed financial and legal system and more accommodating securities laws are providing fertile ground for exploration. It is here that the new models for small business funding are being invented and tested. And they are finding an eager audience.

Small businesses employ 60 percent of the United Kingdom's private sector workforce and account for half of its GDP. Yet their lending options are even more constrained than in the United States. The banking industry in Britain is extremely consolidated, with the top banks providing 92 percent of small business loans.[9] With little competition, interest rates for small business loans hover in the range of 11 percent to 12 percent.

That's where Funding Circle comes in. The company, launched in August 2010 by a trio of Oxford University chums and backed by high-profile private equity players, aims to do for business lending what Zopa has done for consumer loans. Its online marketplace gives small businesses access to more affordable loans, while providing everyday investors with stable, higher yielding investments and a chance to support small, independent enterprises. In its first 10 weeks, Funding Circle, which has no net worth requirement for lenders, signed up more than 1,600 people, who made £1 million in small business loans. The average amount invested was £2,000, at an average interest rate of 8.2 percent.

"You have to accept some risk in order to get a decent interest rate," explains Geoff Chapman, a director at a London-based financial firm and a Funding Circle lender. "But if I put my cash in a bank, they are the only ones making anything from it."

Crowdfunding is not necessarily local investing—in fact, it can often lead to the opposite. But at its best, it can mobilize the desire of investors to support their communities, whether those communities are defined by physical or philosophical parameters.

One of the motivations driving investors on Funding Circle has been a desire to support local companies, says Samir Desai, the site's cofounder and director. The site encourages members to form "circles" of lenders who share a common interest. Some of the first circles were created to lend to companies in specific geographic locations, including Edinburgh, Hertfordshire, and Bristol. Other lenders have focused on particular sectors. For example, one circle was set up to support UK manufacturing and engineering businesses. "UK manufacturing companies are a core part of British history. Help us lend to and support companies that produce real things," the group's page urges. It attracted 146 members in just several weeks. Another circle supports small businesses in London.

Funding Circle uses industry-tested credit models and established data sources to vet borrowers. And its own underwriter looks at every application, explains Desai. In addition, like most good P2P lending sites, Funding Circle has made contingency plans to service its loans should the site cease to exist for any reason.

Desai believes crowdfunding's potential is huge, and figures that his company can capture 1 percent to 2 percent—or more—of total small business lending in the United Kingdom. At least one local government agency has expressed interest in investing a large amount of funds through Funding Circle as a way to support the local economy. For now, the site doesn't have the volume of deals to support a large infusion of capital, but, Desai says, when it does, that kind of institutional participation could give the site, and the concept, an enormous boost. Indeed, he muses, in the event of another financial crisis, sites like Funding Circle could potentially provide a more effective way for governments to inject capital into small businesses than another big bank bailout.

A "Kiva for Equity"

While Funding Circle was making its first loans in the late summer of 2010, elsewhere in London two other Oxford grads, Jeff Lynn and Carlos Silva, were putting together their own plans for a startup. It will follow the script for P2P marketplaces, only this time, for equity investments in startups. Called Seedrs, it aims to be a sort of "Kiva for equity." At the time of my conversation in September with Lynn, the CEO of Seedrs, he was preparing to register with Britain's FSA.

Lynn, an American-born ex-pat living in London, and Silva, who is Portuguese, first considered launching in the United States. "The U.S. is the Holy Grail for everything startup and financial, so the obvious idea would have been to do it in the U.S.," explains Lynn. "But the one fatal flaw is, it can't be done there."

Securities regulations in the United States and United Kingdom are actually pretty similar. Both are mainly concerned with disclosure. If a company is going to offer shares in either country, it needs to file a comprehensive prospectus as part of the registration process. That process can cost tens of thousands of dollars. Both countries make exceptions for very small offerings for which registration would be too costly; the difference, explains Lynn, is how those exemptions are structured.

UK regulators say that as long as an intermediary they have recognized, such as Seedrs, takes responsibility for a financial offering and vouches that the promotional material is fair, clear, and not misleading, it can be marketed relatively broadly. Under U.S. law, the burden is on the company raising the money. Exempt companies can communicate whatever they like about the offering, but only to people they know (aka friends and family). There can be no general solicitation or advertising in most cases. That, says, Lynn, is bound to be tested. "I can imagine there will be litigation someday over what general solicitation and advertising means in a connected world," he says, noting that the last time the SEC comprehensively addressed the issue was in 1989. In those days, the social networks that regulators were concerned about revolved around the golf club, not the Web, and Facebook founder Mark Zuckerberg was just five years old.

Lynn, a former lawyer for Sullivan & Cromwell, says he and Silva looked very closely at SEC regulations. "The fundamental problem, and somebody may prove us wrong, is that the only way you can come close to doing this in the U.S. would require you to limit the number of nonaccredited investors to 35." That posed a problem for two reasons, he explained. "The accredited investors have plenty of deal flow and are not as likely to use a platform like this. And to limit each project to 35 nonaccredited investors we think is very tough. You can't crowdfund a project with that few investors."[10]

So Seedrs will launch in the United Kingdom in the first half of 2011. It will have company. Another British crowdfunding startup, Crowdcube, is aiming at the same space. In Germany, Seedmatch raises equity for startups in that country. And Grow VC, a site based in Hong Kong that bills itself as a virtual Silicon Valley, already had more than 7,000 registered members from 100 countries and $20 million in active funding rounds by early 2011.

Once Seedrs is established, Lynn hopes to expand into Europe—a fairly simple process once the site is approved in the United Kingdom. And he's excited about the prospects. "It used to be you came up with a good idea over here and the first thing you did was hop on a plane to the U.S. to get it funded. We think there is every reason to believe that London and Berlin and Milan and Sofia should be real innovation centers," he said, citing a new entrepreneurial-minded generation. "Platforms like ours make the possibility of greater innovation in Europe a reality."

Can You Create the Next Google in Increments of $100?

Are we stifling innovation in financial technology and social networking in the United States and, more important, impeding the development of potential solutions to our social and economic ills? I asked Kevin Lawton, a serial entrepreneur based in Silicon Valley and an expert on crowdfunding, for his perspective. Lawton, who has a degree in computer science and started his career at MIT's Lincoln Laboratory in space-based radar and satellite communication, is a self-described trend spotter, idea creator, author of multiple patents, and news and business book junkie. "Absolutely, the answer is yes," he says, without hesitation. Lawton, who considered starting a crowdfunding startup himself, said many entrepreneurs start off thinking, "Wow, this awesome future thing could be huge!" But once they begin delving more deeply into various approaches and the regulatory hurdles that must be surmounted, they invariably end up with a scaled-down, less potent model.

Like others who have studied the problem, Lawton believes that as long as these funding models are limited to accredited investors—a tiny portion of the population—they'll never reach critical mass. "We'll never really get the power out of crowdfunding until we get the entire spectrum of people to participate," he says. For what it's worth, he thinks he has a solution figured out, but he's been busy finishing up a self-published book about crowdfunding.

Jouko Ahvenainen, the Finnish chairman of Grow VC, observes that complexity begets complexity. "When you have very complex regulations, one outcome is that you have very complex investment instruments. It is more and more difficult for anybody to understand how these instruments work and what the consequences are if something happens, as we saw with Lehman Brothers." Like most P2P companies, Grow VC's aim, he said, is to make the market more transparent. He readily acknowledges that investing in a startup carries risk, but at least you can see what you are investing in—all the relevant information is posted on the web site and investors and entrepreneurs are encouraged to communicate directly. Grow VC's system also aims to harness the wisdom of the crowd to identify potential winners. "We believe that in the future, financial services will be more transparent, so it will be easier for people to understand exactly where they make their investments. That could be a better solution than making it so that you must be a sophisticated professional before you understand how these instruments work."

There have been attempts to change the securities laws as they pertain to crowdfunding, or at least loosen them a bit. The Coalition for New Credit Models, a group initiated by Prosper, is lobbying for change. Other efforts have focused on petitioning the SEC to make allowances for P2P funding.

Paul Spinrad, a San Francisco–based editor with a longtime interest in micropayments, raised $1,099—through crowdfunding, naturally—to pay for a lawyer at the Sustainable Economies Law Center in Oakland, California, to draft a petition to the SEC for a crowdfunding exemption. The idea is to create an exemption for companies raising up to $100,000 from individuals investing small amounts of money—up to $100 apiece—without the company needing to go through a costly federal and state registration process. One hundred dollars is enough to make a difference in aggregate, if enough investors participated, but hardly enough to bankrupt someone if the venture failed.

"Securities law lets you gamble your retirement on investments conveyed through the all-controlling financial system, but you can't invest $100" to help someone "start a small business, write a book, make a film, build an iPhone app, or develop a new product that you believe has commercial potential," writes Spinrad on his crowdfunding campaign site.[11] While our securities laws served their purpose well for many years, today, he believes, the cost prohibits many small ventures from raising needed capital, and individual investors from investing in companies or artists they would like to support. The result, he says, is "millionaires who can invest freely, and normal people who can only invest in what the big financial companies offer and promote to them—and anything small or local will never appear on the menu."

The petition—filed in July 2010 and officially dubbed File No. 4-605—makes the case that such an exemption would promote capital formation with minimal investor risk. There's been a relative groundswell of support for the proposal on the SEC's site— and Whoopi Goldberg has even thrown her support behind the effort. But not all are pleased.

Lawton, for one, believes a $100 cap is too restrictive. "You can't create the next Google in increments of $100," he says. Besides, an exemption like that, if granted, could dash hopes for any further action for a decade or so, since the SEC would not be likely to revisit the issue, so Lawson is working on his own proposal. "I want crowdfunding to apply to everything," from capital-intensive life sciences and clean-tech ventures to startups with smaller capital needs, says Lawton. "What we need is something different from these little exemptions. Let's prove it out. Let's not put limits on it."

In the meantime, the Dodd-Frank financial reform bill passed by Congress in 2010 actually raised the hurdles for accredited investors, by excluding from the calculation of net worth the value of one's primary residence. "That's really, really stupid," says Trampoline's Charles Armstrong. "That's going to hurt innovation in the U.S. and hurt the enterprise ecosystem."

Shave Ice and Crack Seed

Back in California, Jessica Jackley, the cofounder of Kiva, is working on her next venture, a P2P funding platform called ProFounder, which she started with fellow Stanford University MBA graduate Dana Mauriello. From their vantage point in Silicon Valley, the two women noticed a striking gulf between high-tech startups, which had ready access to venture capital, and entrepreneurs in less glamorous fields who struggled to raise funds. They also saw that for the latter group, the entrepreneurs' community—the friends, family, customers, neighbors, and others that revolve around a business—could be their best source of capital and support, if only they knew how to tap it. As ProFounder's web site explains:

> Why can't anyone just invest a few hundred dollars in a small business they love? We've heard hundreds of stories from entrepreneurs and small business owners who have tried gathering investments (real investments, not just donations) from friends, family, and other members of their community, but have struggled along the way. Unfortunately, the process is unnecessarily confusing, costly, and complicated.[12]

ProFounder, of course, aims to change that. If anyone knows how to do a "Kiva for equity," it should be Jackley. To comply with securities regulations, Jackley and Mauriello came up with a two-tiered investment system, one for friends and family and one for broader social circles. Both employ a revenue-sharing model, which is easier for startups and small companies to deal with than equity.

The first tier helps entrepreneurs manage the often-messy process of raising money from friends and family. ProFounder hosts a private site for the entrepreneur, who can invite a close circle of friends and kin to view details of the offering and financial information. This focused capital raising is conducted under the Reg D, rule 504 exemption for restricted offerings under $1 million.

Reaching out to broader communities—social networks, alumni groups, or customers, for example—posed a trickier challenge, because the public nature of the offering raises the SEC hurdles. Jackley and Mauriello wanted to be able to tap into a wide audience without requiring securities registration, which would be prohibitively costly for a small firm. Their solution was to fall back on the Kiva model: Members of the public can make a loan to the startup, which will be repaid, but the revenue-sharing portion, or profit, gets donated to charity.

"Money on its own is one thing," says Jackley, who likes to surf in her off-hours. "But money plus a supportive community is a whole different thing. I saw that happen on Kiva and I think that is the most powerful tool to catalyze entrepreneurs."

ProFounder's first client, a Hawaiian treat shop called Uncle Clay's House of Pure Aloha, epitomizes the type of entrepreneur that ProFounder seeks to help. Uncle Clay's is beloved in east Honolulu, where many traditional "shave ice" shops like this have given way to chain stores. (Shave ice is sort of like a Slurpee.) The shop's official name is Doe Fang, but everyone knows it as Uncle Clay's, for its wide-grinned owner. It's the kind of place where the walls are lined with photos and postcards from friends near and far. Everyone is treated as *ohana,* or family. "If you come to Uncle Clay's alone, you'll leave with 10 friends," says Bronson Chang, Uncle Clay's nephew.

Friendly, yes. But hardly the type of thing a VC would be interested in.

Like other Hawaiian mom & pops, Uncle Clay's has been struggling lately with the encroachment of national chains and the sluggish economy. So Chang, fresh out of University of Southern California's MBA program, has jumped in to help. The strip mall where the shop is located is being renovated, so the pair are taking the opportunity to launch a new and improved Uncle Chang's that will reinvent the iconic shave ice with natural flavorings made from island-sourced ingredients, like lychee. The shop will also feature other locally made specialties, such as taro chips, and nostalgic items like "crack seed," a traditional preserved fruit. Once they demonstrate the store's success, Chang and his uncle hope to open more Uncle Clay's in other communities, spreading what Chang calls "the spirit of pure aloha."

To help open the new store, they turned to ProFounder. In September 2010, they raised $54,000 from 19 friends and family investors, offering two percent of the store's revenues over four years in a first-tier financing round. They followed that up with a public fundraising effort, complete with a Facebook campaign and a splashy web site, where their simple 64-page investment agreement could be downloaded. In six weeks, the pair raised another $7,500 in loans from 49 individuals—albeit less than they were initially seeking—to be paid back over three years. (The 1 percent of revenue that will be shared gets donated to charity.)

"Crowdfunding completely appealed to me," says Chang. "Uncle Clay's is such a community-centric business ... that we could actually connect with the community to literally build a new store, it was hard to think of a better way."

Will Jackley be able to pull off a Kiva-style success? "Even within existing laws and limitations there are ways to be creative and make really good things happen, so I'm hopeful," she says brightly. "Although it will be really exciting when there's more freedom someday to have an unlimited number of people invest in your business in a way that's a lot less onerous for entrepreneurs."

Game Plan for Locavestors

Crowdfunding represents a potentially revolutionary new model of finance that cuts out middlemen and lets individuals directly lend to, or invest in, other individuals and businesses, typically in small increments. Person-to-person lending sites have flourished in recent years as an alternative to expensive bank credit. Small business lending and equity investing is trickier, at least in the United States, due to securities regulations. For a glimpse of the possible future, keep an eye on the innovative experiments in P2P business financing taking place in the United Kingdom and Hong Kong.

Pros:

- For now, most crowdfunding opportunities that offer financial returns on your investment (as opposed to *tchochkes*) are focused on consumer borrowing. By cutting out the middlemen, lenders get higher returns and borrowers pay lower rates—a win-win. And you're not lining some fat cat's pockets.
- P2P lenders can typically choose their level of risk and return, and average returns of 10 percent are possible—nothing to sneeze at. You can (and should) mitigate your exposure to any one borrower or risk category by distributing your investments across many borrowers.

- Crowdfunding sites aim for a high level of transparency, and most provide aggregate performance data for loans they have facilitated. Research any site and its track record before you lend money.
- Sites such as ProFounder in the United States and Funding Circle and Seedrs in the United Kingdom are bringing the P2P to model to business investing. That could open up new avenues of funding for entrepreneurs and the ability to tap into their social networks. However, U.S. securities regulations limit the opportunity here.

Cons:

- Most P2P loans are unsecured and subject to default, so there is real risk. As mentioned, it is wise to spread your investments out over multiple loans to mitigate risk.
- In addition, many crowdfunding platforms are startups themselves without long track records. Before signing on with a P2P marketplace, make sure it has contingency plans to service its loans in the event that it ceases operations.

The Bottom Line: Crowdfunding has great potential to democratize lending and investing, and open up new sources of capital for entrepreneurs.

For More Information:

- Kevin Lawton's book can be found at www.thecrowdfundingrevolution .com.
- To view the crowdfunding exemption (file no. 4-605) or leave a comment, go to www.sec.gov/rules/petitions.shtml
- Further commentary can be found at www.crowdfundinglaw.com and www.sustainableeconomieslawcenter.org.
- Microfinance sites: Kiva.com, MicroPlace.com.
- P2P consumer lending sites: Prosper.com, TheLendingClub.com, Zopa.com, Loanio.com.
- P2P student loan funding: www.fynanz.com
- P2P currency exchange: www.currencyfair.com
- P2P business lending sites: FundingCircle.com, ProFounder.com, Cofundit.com.
- P2P equity investment sites: Seedrs.com, GrowVC.com,*Crowdcube. com, Seedmatch.de, WealthForge.com,* MicroVentures.com.

* For accredited investors only.

CHAPTER 10

Slow Money

Finance for Foodsheds

Hi. My name is Terry, and I work for Morgan Stanley.

The introduction, made in the confessional tone usually reserved for alcoholics and overeaters, sent a murmur rippling through the small room. But this was no Alcoholics Anonymous meeting or Jenny Craig weigh-in. Terry was one of a couple of dozen New Yorkers who had gathered in a dimly lit East Village bar one evening in the fall of 2010 to launch the New York chapter of Slow Money. It was a diverse group—lawyers, entrepreneurs, a chef, artists, students, and corporate journeymen—few with any particular financial or investment expertise. But what they all shared was a desire to create an alternative to Wall Street, right here in its very shadow.

Slow Money is the brainchild of Woody Tasch, a former venture capitalist and foundation money guy turned financial revolutionary. Inspired in equal parts by Fritz Schumacher's *Small Is Beautiful* and Carlo Petrini's Slow Food movement, Tasch, from his New Mexico base, is on a mission to change the way we think about investing.

Through Slow Money, a nonprofit organization, he aims to create new pathways for investing in local, sustainable food and agriculture enterprises, the kinds of businesses that are passed over by conventional finance. To bring finance *back down to earth*. Slow Money is the pragmatic cousin of Slow Food, which celebrates food diversity, taste, and tradition and from which Tasch liberally (and literally) borrows. Petrini has called attention to the question of where our food comes from. Now Tasch is urging us to ask, where does our money go?

As Tasch tells it, it goes flying around the globe at a mind-boggling pace in pursuit of profit and usually ends up in a smoke-stack in China. Our voracious financial system has enabled an industrial food system that consumes vast amounts of fossil fuels and water and spits out cheap, fast food. As we have seen, that system is taking a terrible toll on our health, our environment, our food security, our communities, and, especially, our small-scale farmers and food production.

Slow Money

Slow Money is a national organization made up of semi-autonomous local chapters dedicated to creating financing solutions for small-scale food and agricultural producers.

In the 1950s, there were 25 million farmers in the United States. Today there are fewer than 2 million.[1] We lose two acres of farmland per minute.[2] Industrial-scale megafarms farms supply the bulk of our food. Four companies control 85 percent of the nation's beef production, 70 percent of pork, and 60 percent of poultry, according to Slow Food. One company (Dean Foods) controls 40 percent of the milk supply. These concentrated animal feeding operations routinely feed antibiotics to their livestock, contributing to dangerous levels of resistance among pathogens. Industrial farming is also heavily dependent on chemical inputs. Each year, 80 million tons of nitrogen-rich fertilizer is spread onto fields, the vast amount of it washed away (along with topsoil) into rivers and waterways, creating algae blooms that snuff out life, like the nearly 8,000-square-mile dead zone in the Gulf of Mexico. There are now 400 identified dead zones worldwide, up from 49 in the 1960s.[3]

Tasch sees a direct connection between the speed of capital and the fertility of soil. Indeed, his description of our "technology-heavy, extractive, intermediation laden food system" could just as easily describe our financial system.

It was against this backdrop that the idea for Slow Money began to take hold in Tasch's overactive brain. Over 2008 and early 2009, he convened several regional gatherings that brought farmers, entrepreneurs, and investors together to discuss local needs. Along the way, he published *Inquiries into the Nature of Slow Money: Investing as if Food, Farms, and Fertility Mattered* (Chelsea Green, 2008), a meandering manifesto of sorts. He might have continued at this leisurely pace, had the financial world not begun to unravel in 2008. Tasch decided to launch his not-yet-fully-baked concept. Slow Money could not wait.

So, in September 2009, almost a year to the day of the Lehman Brothers collapse, more than 400 people from all over the country gathered in a farmers market building in Santa Fe for the inaugural Slow Money gathering. The crowd, a mix of New Age hippies, professional investors, entrepreneurs, and farmers, noshed on locally sourced frittatas as Tasch opened the conference with a rambling but rousing speech. "This is the craziest thing I've ever done," he began.

Tasch, a tall, angular man with an unruly puff of salt-and-pepper hair, is prone to digressions and asides, quoting Thoreau one minute and Tom Robbins the next. *We live in an age where barriers are being shattered—the 6 billion population barrier, the billions of instructions per second barrier, the billions of shares per day barrier. We are disoriented and seduced by speed. Our profit-at-any-cost system has risen to the level of economic violence. We've got to slow money down. And did you know there are billions of organisms in a single gram of topsoil?*

It was a kaleidoscope tour of finance and fertility. In a way, it was hardly necessary. The financial crisis had set the stage more eloquently than words ever could. And Tasch was preaching to the choir.

One Percent for Local Food

Slow Money's vision is to create a new type of entrepreneurial finance, one that respects the land and the farmer, connects investors to their local economies, and enlarges our definition of fiduciary responsibility. The message is as simple as it is urgent: To replenish the soil that our local foodsheds depend upon—and indeed our future health and security depend upon—we must invest in small-scale, sustainable food and agricultural enterprises. Slow Money has facilitated $4 million in investments so far in a dozen enterprises, such as Hometown Farms, which creates urban vertical farms; Greenling, an online store that delivers local, sustainably grown produce to households in central Texas; and Gather, a locavore restaurant in Berkeley, California.

Foodshed

Similar to a watershed—a geographical area's life-sustaining source and flow of water—a *foodshed* refers to a region's food production and distribution system. It encompasses the farm, the table, and everything in between. Like watersheds, foodsheds are vital to the health and security of a region.

As chief instigator, Tasch's job is to rally the troops. To date, more than 12,000 people have signed the Slow Money Principles, a five-point affirmation that starts with "We must bring money back down to earth," and ends with a quote from Paul Newman ("I just happen to think that in life we need to be a little like the farmer who puts back into the soil what he takes out.") The goal is to get a million people to sign, and eventually commit 1 percent of their assets to local food systems.

He hopes Slow Money will spur innovative solutions. "Could there be a local stock exchange? Could there be municipal bonds devoted to local food systems? Could there be funds dedicated to CSAs or buying organic farmland? The answer is yes, there could be all those things," says Tasch. "But it will take serious intellectual and financial horsepower."

Slow Money, however, is simply a catalyst. The movement is being shaped by people on the ground and in the field. It has already spawned at least 16 local chapters, from southeast Georgia to northern California, that are incubating ideas and creating solutions that work for their communities. The goal is that a set of models or templates will arise and be used by other communities.

In Boston, Slow Money members have organized events to showcase sustainable food and agriculture entrepreneurs who are looking for funding. In North Carolina, the Abundance Slow Money Project is promoting what it calls place-based lending by matching local investors and local borrowers. So far, it has made three collateral-backed, low-cost loans to a baker, a Greek restaurant that sources ingredients from local farmers, and a vegan bakery and catering company specializing in southern soul food. The Type-A Wisconsin chapter has held a series of in-depth planning sessions with entrepreneurs and legal experts to determine the gaps in financial and technical resources available to local agricultural entrepreneurs, and to identify potential funding solutions as well as legal and financial roadblocks. In western Massachusetts, Slow Money members raised a $1 million fund that blends venture capital investing with philanthropy. And the-little-chapter-that-could in Austin has spread to the entire state of Texas.

The Slow Money vision is lofty, but down on the ground it is arduous work—as the New York chapter was finding out. But by early 2011, the group had swelled to almost 150 members, and was planning its first official event: an entrepreneur showcase that would give local food businesses a chance to pitch local investors.

A New Generation of Food Entrepreneurs

Slow Money is tapping into a powerful undercurrent of dissatisfaction with the financial establishment as well as a growing desire for local and sustainably grown food.

Farmers markets have increased threefold in the past decade. CSAs—community-supported agriculture, in which customers prepay for a share in the season's harvest—have grown from 60 in 1990 to more than 2,000. The number of small farms is on the rise for the first time in decades. Writers from Wendell Berry to Eric Schlosser and Michael Pollan have raised awareness about food issues, and food blogs are exploding. Sixty-five communities around North America, from Allegheny to Wasatch, have their own *Edible Communities* magazine. The forgotten arts of pickling, canning, microbrewing, and even butchering are enjoying a revival. Locally sourced meats and seafood, locally grown produce and sustainability topped a list of food trends for 2011 in a National Restaurant Association survey of chefs.[4] Sales of locally grown food have grown from $2 billion in 2002 to more than $5 billion in 2007—the same year that the *New Oxford American Dictionary* crowned *locavore* word of the year.

Still, translating that momentum into financial investment is another story. If there is a financing gap for small business, it is even greater for those in the food and agricultural fields. Small-scale farms and sustainable food enterprises are not exactly at the top of most investors' hot list. In fact, they are not on their radar at all.

By nature, these sorts of enterprises—small farms and dairies, artisan producers, ecofriendly pest-management companies, or sustainable-minded restaurants—are not the kind of hockey-stick growth prospects that cause investors or bankers to pull out their checkbooks. Their returns may be modest and their growth, well, slow. They don't promise the mind-boggling profits required by venture capital, yet they are too risky for cookie-cutter bank loans, as Dante Hesse and others have found. According to the Carrot Project, 40 percent of agricultural startups are denied financing. More than half of farmers responding to a National Young Farmers Coalition survey cited lack of capital as their biggest obstacle.[5] What they require is patient capital—what Tasch calls nurture capital.

Sustainable may be an overused word, but what it implies— that a practice such as farming or forestry or finance can replenish as it produces, and nurture not destroy—is vitally important. It recognizes the implicit relationship between farmer and earth, logger and forest; the mutual and measured give and take. Just as sustainable farming does not extract from the soil or earth more than it can reasonably give, sustainable finance does not burden small farmers and entrepreneurs with debt they cannot repay or terms that are destructive. It seeks a common ground, recognizing the connection between investors and entrepreneurs and the fact that we all live on this Earth together. (RSF Social Finance, a financial organization and Slow Money affiliate that invests in food, agriculture, and other social impact ventures, actually brings together representatives from its borrower and lender groups to agree upon a fair interest rate).

We typically think of returns solely in financial terms. But there are other ways to measure return. A safe food system, fewer food miles, increased biodiversity, the pleasures of a great meal— these are all dividends of investing in sustainable food enterprises. Economically, the returns include the creation of stable, local jobs and money that stays in the community.

Food-related businesses in New York's Hudson Valley, for example, have a local multiplier effect of 2.5 to 3.5, according to the Columbia County Agribusiness Corporation, an economic development agency. In a survey of farms in four contiguous towns in the county, the agency found that farmers made the bulk of their purchases, for items like fencing, feed, and the like, within an hour's drive.

A study by the University of Georgia concluded that, if each of the state's 3.7 million households spent $10 per week on produce grown in Georgia, more than $1.9 billion would be pumped into the state's economy. And for every 5 percent increase in local produce sales, the state would gain 345 jobs, $43.7 million in sales, and $13.6 million in farmer income. Today, just a tiny fraction of produce grown in Georgia ends up on its tables.[6]

Similarly, a study of a 16-county region in northeast Ohio found that if local producers could supply 25 percent of the region's food demand, 27,664 jobs could be created, providing work for one in eight unemployed residents. In addition, the region's economic output would see a $4.2 billion boost, generating $126 million for state and local tax collections.[7]

These are among the considerations that drive people like Christopher Lindstrom, a Slow Money board member and cofounder of the Berkshares local currency, to change the way they invest. "I really want to start putting my money where my mouth is," says Lindstrom, who has pledged to invest a large chunk of his wealth in small scale, sustainable agriculture. "My principle desire is to make change. And shifting money towards sustainable enterprise and local business would have a huge impact."

Lindstrom, a grandson of David Rockefeller, has unique motivations as well. When Standard Oil, the source of his family's vast wealth, was broken up in 1911, much of the stock was transferred to the Rockefeller Foundation. The foundation, he says, had a hand in promoting modern petroleum-based agriculture—synthetic fertilizer and pesticides and seeds that were resistant to them—which (not coincidentally, he believes) benefited Standard Oil founder John D. Rockefeller's remaining oil interests. "I'm very aware of my family connection to the oil paradigm," he says. "I've financially benefited from it, but I'm also inheriting a world that is falling apart." That karma, he says, fuels his desire to help move the economy toward renewable energy and sustainable practices. Still, he says, investing in local agriculture takes a huge amount of work. And it can feel like taking a leap into the abyss. "It's always that way when you are taking money from something secure to something more risky."

The economics of food and agriculture may pose special challenges, especially for investors who are not Rockefeller descendants. The wider returns are often a key part of the equation. But that doesn't mean there are not high-growth businesses with the potential to richly reward investors who take a chance. One need look no further than Ben & Jerry's, Stonyfield Farm, Niman Ranch, Whole Foods, or Odwalla, among many other success stories, to see that the food and ag sector can spawn high-growth, high-profit companies.

These enterprises all had clear values. But they were all well positioned for growth and run by management that could execute on the opportunity—with the help of a little creative financing. Amid clamoring demand for everything local, organic, and sustainable, there is fertile ground for a new generation of break out successes.

A Dairy Farmer's Financial Education

I first met Dante Hesse, the subject of this book's introduction, at the Slow Money gathering in Santa Fe. I had the sense that he'd rather be tending to his herd, but there was a determination that overrode that impulse. His operation, Milk Thistle Farm in New York's Hudson Valley, was exactly the sort of enterprise that Slow Money aims to support—a local, sustainable, growing dairy. By now, Hesse was under the protective watch of John Friedman, a chain-smoking lawyer who had recently moved with his wife to the Hudson Valley, leaving behind the cramped studio they had long shared in Greenwich Village.

Freidman had read about how Hesse was trying to raise money from customers and "potentially getting into trouble." In return for learning the dairy business, and perhaps some fresh-raised pork, Friedman offered to help Hesse raise money for a new processing plant and keep him on the right side of the law. "Most farmers don't have the first clue about how to structure a deal, and can't afford someone like John," said a clearly grateful Hesse.

Freidman's first order of business had been to put together an offering memorandum so that Milk Thistle's informal plea to customers for funding complied with securities laws (the offering was permissible under Reg D, rule 504, if they registered with New York State, says Friedman). But soon it became clear that, to raise the $850,000 Hesse required, another approach was needed. So here they were at Slow Money, like everyone else, in search of solutions.

Milk Thistle was in the sweet spot of the fast-growing market for high-end, grass-fed organic milk. It is, by nature, a fragmented market made up of tiny dairies (large brands like Horizon, owned by Dean Foods, are technically organic but use industrial-scale practices). Milk Thistle had been growing at 100 percent a year and was generating profits without the benefit of a large operation to spread costs over. If Hesse could just get funding for a new plant and perhaps a bigger farm, he could take Milk Thistle to the next level.

Hesse and Friedman talked to professional investors and private equity types in Santa Fe and at a series of similar conferences for so-called patient capital. At one event, they met a potential private equity investor in an elevator—which tickled Hesse since Friedman had tutored him on the importance of the short but pithy sales pitch known as the "elevator pitch." After drawn out negotiations, however, the deal fell through. Meanwhile, Hesse was spending so much time away from the farm trying to raise money that his employees teased him that he could no longer identify his cows. But ultimately, Milk Thistle's salvation was to come from a customer after all.

Building A Premier Brand

When their son Finn turned one, Charles Zentay and Clare Sant began researching organic products. Milk was of special concern, given the hormones and antibiotics that mainstream producers regularly feed their factory-confined cows. The more the couple researched, the more they were horrified by industrial dairy practices. That's when they found Milk Thistle Farm milk at a Whole Foods store on the Upper West Side of Manhattan. They were buying three gallons a week when Sant heard about Hesse's efforts to raise money. She mentioned it to her husband, who does angel investing on the side of his job as a management consultant. He has invested in a farm in Brazil and a couple of software companies, among other deals. Zentay contacted Hesse, and they began a dialogue that would result in a novel deal that could point the way for other agricultural investors and entrepreneurs.

For Zentay, Milk Thistle has that rare combination of potential and ability to execute shared by other successful food and ag brands. "Organic has traditionally been seen as small scale, artisanal, and not necessarily driven by a goal towards profitability," he says. But that's not necessarily the case. With Milk Thistle, "We see an opportunity to become the premier brand for ultra-organic in New England."

In late 2010—two years after Hesse first hung out his sign at a farmers market looking for funds—construction began on a processing facility on a 250-acre farm in Stuyvesant, New York, a half-hour northwest of Ghent along the Hudson River. This would be the new home of Milk Thistle Farm. If all goes according to plan, the plant will be completed in May 2011, and Milk Thistle's expanded herd of 150 milkers—a threefold increase—will be contentedly munching away in their spacious new home. With the additional capacity, Milk Thistle should be able to more than double its sales over the next three years, and expand from the New York market into neighboring states, says Zentay.

Zentay put together a group of eight angel investors—all urbanites like himself who care about the environment and protecting their upstate foodshed—who invested $830,000 in equity capital. The investors created a separate limited liability company, Blossom Farms, LLC, that will own the land and processing facilities, which will be leased back to Milk Thistle on favorable terms. The LLC owns a noncontrolling percent of Milk Thistle, and in turn Dante and Kristin Hesse have a stake in Blossom Farms—so goals are aligned. In addition, Milk Thistle and its investors lined up close to $1 million in debt, including a seller-financed mortgage to buy the land, which they plan to convert to a bank loan.

A deal that size—a total of $1.65 million—for a small agricultural operation is unheard of in the Hudson Valley. "I think it's going to be groundbreaking," says Hesse. "I'm hoping it sets a precedent and that we can be agents of change." (Just to drive the point home, Freidman was planning to take out a "tombstone"—the nickname for the ads that firms take out when they've closed a major financing deal—in the *Wall Street Journal.*) With the additional processing capacity, Hesse plans to work with other area farmers who want to process their own milk and dairy products. "We want to help other local businesses," he says.

A central motivating force for Zentay and his fellow angel investors was the ability to make an investment in something that not only provides a financial return, but also reflects their values. "I was impressed by Dante's vision for the company and his balance of what's good for the animals and environment and people and what's profitable," says Zentay. "With so many companies, there is a tension between those things. In the organic space, those values are aligned. I've never been in a deal that the investors are so passionate about."

For now, much of the investment in small-scale food and agriculture is confined to affluent investors such as Zentay and Lindstrom. We still don't have the infrastructure and investment vehicles to facilitate the flow of mainstream capital to these types of businesses. But that is exactly the problem that Slow Money has set out to tackle. It has a long way to go still, but the grassroots army is swelling.

Game Plan for Locavestors

As the local food movement grows, small scale food and agriculture enterprises have an opportunity to expand. But these businesses typically have a difficult time raising capital from banks and traditional investors. Slow Money is creating innovative new funding strategies that connect local investors with local food enterprises.

Pros:

- Local food is a growth business. As demand grows for local and sustainably produced food, the food and agriculture market presents attractive investment opportunities, particularly in high-growth, high-margin segments.
- For people who are already buying locally and sustainably grown products, it is another way to support those producers and share in their growth.
- Investment in sustainable food and ag companies offer added returns in the form of benefits to the environment, health, and local communities. A robust local food system contributes to greater food security and quality, and reduces food miles and reliance on oil.

Cons:

- There are few avenues, at present, for non-accredited investors to participate in this segment, aside from CSAs and prepaid subscriptions.
- Sustainable food and agriculture is often, but not always, characterized by small, artisan producers that cannot easily take advantage of economies of scale.
- Farming and agriculture can be extremely risky, given the vagaries of weather, competition from industrial farms, and slim margins.
- Many farmers lack the business savvy necessary to successfully expand or execute on a growth strategy, so good management is key to any investment.

The Bottom Line

- Grassroots action at its best.

For More Information:

- Learn more about Slow Money at www.slowmoney.org. Or contact the organization at info@slowmoney.org.
- To read and sign the Slow Money principles, visit www.bit.ly/slowprinciples.

CHAPTER

11

From Brown Rice to Biofuels

Co-ops on the Cutting Edge

The opening of a microbrewery in indie-minded Austin, Texas, is always cause for celebration. But there was an added dimension to the revelry at the grand opening of the Black Star Co-op Pub & Brewery. On a mild December evening in 2010, local bands performed on an outdoor stage as attendees munched on Texas pub fare and sampled Black Star's handiwork. Although the pub had quietly opened several weeks earlier, this was the first tap of Black Star's very own brews, an eclectic lineup that includes High Esteem, a pale ale with a touch of rye and local honey, and Double Dee, a malty British-style bitter brewed with brown sugar. The pub's 20 taps also feature offerings from Austin's growing craft beer scene. Anyone bellying up to the locally sourced pecan wood bar that evening could not miss the sign hanging on the bright red wall above the taps: *Welcome to Your Brewpub.*

This is more than a bar where everybody knows your name. Many of the people knocking back Double Dees and bopping to the music were in fact owners of the pub. More than 2,000 people had paid $100 (or made a downpayment) to become lifetime members of Black Star. Two hundred people went even further, investing an average of $3,000 apiece to raise the $600,000 needed to build the brewpub. Blackstar has so many proud owners, that when they assembled for a group portrait on the grand opening weekend, the photographer had to climb a 15-foot ladder and use a wide-angle lens to fit them in.

Steven Yarak, a thirsty young man with a physics degree from the University of Texas in Austin, began dreaming of opening a microbrew pub back in late 2005. At the time, Austin had a lively nightlife scene but surprisingly few brewpubs. Yarak envisioned a community-owned bar along the lines of a neighborhood-owned café he had visited in Belgium. He shared his idea with craft brewer communities online and posted fliers around town, and soon a group of beer enthusiasts assembled —a few fellow math geeks among them—who signed on to the mission. The idea of structuring the microbrewery as a cooperative seemed a natural. "We wanted something that was very community focused," says Mark Wochner, a 31-year-old research scientist studying underwater acoustics at UT who is now president of Black Star's board of directors. "We liked the idea of having a bar where the people that drink there are also the owners."

Besides, they didn't have the money to open a pub themselves.

It helped that one of the members of the group, Johnny Livesay, was on the board of the Wheatsville Food Co-op, a longtime Austin institution. Livesay explained the Texas cooperative statute and described how Wheatsville had raised funds from member-owners to open the initial store in 1976 and, more recently, to complete a major expansion. It was also important to the band of would-be microbrewers that they treat workers fairly and give them a say in the management of the business. The result is what the founders believe is the world's first cooperatively owned and worker self-managed brewpub.

As Yarak, who now heads the Workers' Assembly at Black Star, explained to a local newspaper: "In a pub, you have a natural gathering space in a community, built on a business model of repeat customers. You have a model in which this community is putting their resources into it, and yet a lot of times you have this disconnected or absentee ownership of it, and so the resources of your community really are being funneled out of it. So my vision there was, let's just close the loop. Let's make it so that's being reinvested back into the community in a variety of ways, whether it be better jobs for the work force or investment in expansion or improvement of the current assets you have or refunding excess [profits] back to the membership."[1]

A Natural Loop

Cooperatives—businesses owned by and run for the benefit of their members—were first established in the late 18th and early 19th centuries in the face of disruption brought about by the Industrial Revolution. As people left farms for employment in the fast-growing cities and mechanization threatened the livelihoods of craftsmen, workers were often at the mercy of abusive employers. These marginalized members of society— whether workers, consumers, farmers, or producers—began banding together as a way to protect and promote their mutual interests.

Cooperative (Co-op)

Cooperatives are associations run for the mutual benefit of their member-owners. They generally adhere to the seven Rochdale principles: open membership, democratic member control (one member, one vote), economic participation of members through the distribution of profits, independence and autonomy, community concern, cooperation with other co-ops, and education and training. Co-ops can be worker owned, consumer owned, producer owned, or buyer-owned associations—or sometimes a combination. They range from tiny food and energy co-ops to multi-million- or billion-dollar enterprises such as Organic Valley, Land O' Lakes, and The Co-operative Group of Britain.

(Continued)

The definition I like most, however, comes courtesy of go.coop, which explains on its web site: *We all have childhood memories of parents, teachers, and others encouraging us to work together. A co-op is what "working together" looks like all grown up.*

Often, workers were forced to spend their meager wages at company-owned stores, which overcharged them for basic goods. That's what led a group of 28 weavers and textile mill workers in Rochdale, England, in 1844 to pool their savings and open their own store, where they could buy staples such as butter, sugar, flour, and oatmeal at reasonable prices. The Rochdale Equitable Pioneers Society, as they called themselves, is widely considered the first successful co-op, and its governing principles, known as the Rochdale Principles, are at the heart of the worldwide co-op movement today. The Rochdale store tracked each member's purchases, and at the end of each year it distributed any surplus profits back to the members in proportion to how much they had spent. The weavers welcomed new members, growing to 74 by the end of the first year. As their enterprise thrived, they rented extra space in the building, where they set up a library and held educational lectures for the betterment of their members and community. The cooperative eventually operated bakeries, dairies, painting services, coal delivery, a laundry, and mills.

By the 1860s, the Rochdale pioneers were receiving visitors from all over the world who came to see how a successful cooperative was run. The operating philosophy that allowed the cooperative to thrive boiled down to seven principles that were adopted by the International Cooperative Alliance in 1937 and are adhered to by cooperatives today: Economic participation of members, open and voluntary membership, democratic control, autonomy and independence, education and training, concern for the community, and cooperation with other co-ops. Through these governing ideals, co-ops balance profit-making with a commitment to work in the best interests of their communities.

Members of the Black Star Co-op Pub & Brewery, for example, will receive a patronage rebate each year that the pub operates in the black, the exact percentage to be decided annually by the board. Members participate in the management of the pub by electing board members, attending membership meetings, and bringing concerns and ideas before the board. (While the board sets overall policy, day-to-day operations are run by the Workers' Assembly, a body made up of employees who have completed a one-year apprenticeship period. The Workers' Assembly elects a liaison to the board of directors.) Black Star plans to set aside a small portion of its surplus revenue to create an educational fund to teach people about craft beer and cooperatives. And, demonstrating the principle of supporting other co-ops, the Wheatsville Food Co-op generously invested $50,000 in Black Star.

The spirit of community support is a strong part of the cooperative ethos. In New Mexico, the La Montanita Food Co-op, which has grown from one store in Albuquerque in 1976 to four stores in the area and 14,000 members, has been working to strengthen the local foodshed. Most of New Mexico's 20,000 farms and ranches export their products, from cattle to pecans to chiles. Just 3 percent of food grown in the state is consumed by its residents. At the same time, 17 percent of New Mexican households and a quarter of New Mexican children are food insecure, meaning they are not sure where their next meal will come from.

La Montanita has helped establish a local distribution infrastructure, making its delivery trucks and refrigerated storage available to producers. It has also lent out more than $40,000 to farmers and suppliers in "prepayment" loans in recent years. The demand for such loans is more than it can address on its own. Yet loans to small farmers, value-added food enterprises, and startups are considered high risk by banks, especially in an area without a strong local banking network. So in 2010, the co-op created the La Montanita Fund, or LAM Fund, which provides collateral for farmers, ranchers, and other producers so that they can obtain bank loans. La Montanita's goal is to raise $100,000 for the LAM Fund through investments by the co-op as well as individual members, who can buy "interests" of $250. The funds will be deposited in a New Mexico credit union, where they are federally insured and investors will earn the highest possible money market rate.

A thousand miles north, in Bellingham, Washington, the Community Food Co-op, a popular cooperative whose two stores pull in around $24 million in annual sales, sets aside a small portion of its surplus revenues for its Farm Fund, which makes grants and low-interest loans to local farmers and suppliers. Member and shopper donations at the register contribute an additional $2,000 to $3,000 annually to the fund. A Farm Fund loan allowed the young owners of Osprey Hill Farm, which raises rare breeds of chickens and turkeys that are sold at the co-op, to install a well for irrigation. Another grant went to a group of local, organic farms working to bring back northwestern grain varietals that can thrive in the area's challenging climate. The rewards of the program are widely distributed: Local farmers get a helping hand; co-op members get fresh, delicious food; and the community benefits from increased jobs and food security. "It's a great natural loop," says Jean Rogers, board and Farm Fund administrator for the Community Food Co-op.

A Quiet Force

If you think co-ops are just dusty natural food stores that sell bulk brown rice, think again. Cooperatives have been adopted by just about every sector of the economy, from energy to finance to housing. They can be organized and owned by workers, consumers, or producers, as well as by small businesses that band together for greater purchasing clout.

Today, more than 800 million people worldwide are members of co-ops. Cooperatives employ more than 100 million people around the world—20 percent more than multinational enterprises.[3] Their impact is so potentially transformative that the United Nations has declared 2012 the International Year of Cooperatives.

In the United States, about one in every four people belongs to a co-op of some sort. The country's 29,000 co-ops collectively generate $654 billion in revenue, more than 2 million jobs,

$75 billion in wages and benefits, and $133.5 billion in value-added income, according to a study by the University of Wisconsin Center for Cooperatives.[4]

Co-ops tend to fill a need that the marketplace is ignoring. And often, they are at the forefront of important trends. Those crunchy-granola natural-food co-ops, for example, were instrumental in establishing the organic and natural foods market—well before John Mackey opened his first Whole Foods store in 1980 or Walmart glommed onto the organic trend in 2006.[5] New associations, such as the Seattle Farm Co-op, created in 2009 by urban farmers who needed a source of livestock feed, worm starter kits, and farming supplies suitable for their city environs, are helping establish brand new markets. Similarly, today's energy cooperatives are on the cutting edge of distributed, renewable energy production from solar, wind, and biofuels.

Most co-ops are small, but some have been hugely successful, rivaling the biggest corporations. Italy's Coop Italia, a national retail cooperative, operates the country's largest retail chain and produces more than 1,600 products, from tomatoes to soccer balls. The UK-based Co-operative Group spans finance, travel, food, and even funeral services. With 4.5 million members, it is the world's largest consumer co-op.

In Spain, the Mondragon Cooperative Corporation (MCC) is a prosperous federation of worker-owned cooperatives employing 100,000 workers and generating more than $20 billion in revenue. Mondragon cooperatives manufacture consumer appliances, bicycles, and industrial components. They sell insurance and run a university, whose graduates typically find employment within the cooperative within three months. MCC also operates Eroski, Spain's largest retailer. Like all co-ops, the net revenue that Mondragon generates annually is invested back in the company, with any surplus distributed among the workers and directed to community programs. Compare that to the multinational corporations with their multi-billion dollar cash reserves sitting idle in offshore accounts while domestic workers, capital investment, and communities languish. It is little surprise that a growing number of civic and business leaders are making pilgrimages to the bustling Basque town of Mondragon to divine the secrets of the co-op's success.

In the United States heartland, St. Paul, Minnesota, is home to CHS Inc., an agricultural and energy co-op owned by farmers, ranchers, and individual cooperatives. With around $25 billion in annual sales, it ranks among the Fortune 100 largest companies. In 2009, the top 100 U.S. co-ops generated $175.6 billion in revenue.[6]

Even regular customers may not be aware that household brands such as Land O'Lakes, Ocean Spray, Sunkist, Welch's, and Organic Valley are cooperatives, owned and operated by many small farmers and producers. The hardware "chains" True Value and Ace Hardware are owned by independent retailers that pool their purchases to more effectively compete with giants like Home Depot. True Value's 5,000 retailers rack up around $2 billion annually. Ace's 4,600 stores generate around $12 billion in annual sales. And your news headlines are often brought to you by the Associated Press, a cooperative owned by its American newspaper and broadcast members.

Valley of the Co-ops

Vernon County, Wisconsin, is known for its European and Scandinavian heritage, iconic round barns, and hilly, wooded contours, thanks to its location in the southwestern part of the state, which escaped the massive glaciers that shaped the Great Lakes and much of the Midwest and Northeast. It's a sparsely populated area with about 37 residents per square mile, which accounts for another of the county's distinguishing characteristics: a preponderance of cooperatives. In rural areas like Vernon County, which don't have enough people or potential profit to attract corporations, residents have had to establish their own basic services.

There's the Vernon Electric Cooperative, formed in 1938, which provides power to 11,000 member households, and the Vernon Telephone Cooperative, which offers telephone, cable, Internet, and wireless services to 7,000 subscribers. There's a farm supply co-op, several food co-ops and credit unions, the

Westby Cooperative Creamery, and the big cheese of the area, Organic Valley.

In 1988, a small group of Vernon County farmers, concerned about the threat to family farms, created the Coulee Region Organic Producer Pool (CROPP). The cooperative—better known as Organic Valley for the brand name it sells its products under—has grown to more than 1,600 farmer-owners in 33 states. It is best known for its milk, but the co-op also sells cheese, juice, eggs, produce, soy, and other products—all organic—as well as meat sold under the Organic Prairie brand. CROPP, based in La Farge, is one of the oldest and largest organic farmer-owned cooperatives in North America, with more than $600 million in annual sales. The co-op has offered an economic alternative to hundreds of small family farms, which are organized into regional producer pools. Eighty-five percent of its 1,336 dairy farmers have herds of 100 or fewer cows—such as Scott and Robin Mikitas, fourth-generation farmers in Calhan, Colorado, who have 67 milkers. The average flock of egg-laying hens is 5,000, compared to 100,000 or more for industrial-scale egg operations.

In addition to preserving family farms, Organic Valley has been a champion of high-quality organic standards. Its producers are bound by a membership agreement and quality standards set by the CROPP Board regarding pasture, access to outdoors, and farm materials. Those standards often go beyond U.S. Department of Agriculture (USDA) organic standards, which big agribusinesses constantly attempt to water down. For example, CROPP farmers are required to provide 1.75 square feet of indoor space and 5 square feet of outdoor space for each laying hen. In comparison, the USDA is considering raising its outdoor square footage requirement for organic hens to two or perhaps three square feet—a small move that has already met with fierce opposition from large-scale producers.

Organic Valley's farmer-owners put up equity when they join the co-op, investing the equivalent of 5.5 percent of their annual milk production in Class B preferred stock, which forms the base of the co-op's working capital. Farmers earn 8 percent on their money and can put more into the fund if they choose. But the co-op has also looked beyond its members for capital.

When the cooperative struggled with cash flow in the late 1990s, it couldn't find reasonable terms from banks. Instead, it turned to friends and family. It created a new class of nonvoting preferred shares, dubbed Class C, that paid an 8 percent dividend and raised $3 million. That was followed by the Freedom Fund, a series of short-term loans to a small group of members and nonmembers. The fund raised about $1.7 million and paid lenders up to 14 percent interest. The Freedom Fund, says Eric Newman, Organic Valley's vice president of sales "was critical to our stability and growth."

Organic Valley was growing quickly, and in 2004 it needed to raise more capital. The co-op's first impulse was to try and raise a couple of million dollars from "green" funds that might be attracted to its mission, recalls Diane Gloede, Organic Valley's investor relations manager. The co-op created a new series of nonvoting preferred shares, called Class E and priced at $50, that would pay a 6 percent annual dividend. The mutual funds, however, weren't interested if the shares weren't registered and publicly traded. So Organic Valley turned to another potentially simpatico group: the residents of its hometown, La Farge, a sleepy Kickapoo River town with a population of around 800. The co-op took out ads in local newspapers and, by time the year was out, had sold almost $3 million worth of shares to area investors.

Buoyed by the reception, the co-op broadened its advertising to a radius of 60 or so miles around La Farge and promptly raised another $3 million the next year then $4 million the following year. Reaching out to its core customers, the co-op began advertising the shares in food co-op publications around the country and was inundated with buyers. By the time it closed the offering in January 2010, Organic Valley had raised an impressive $43 million from 1,780 investors in 40 states and the District of Columbia.

The funds were used to position Organic Valley for its next stage of growth. The co-op built its first real headquarters, consolidating eight different leased locations around the area, and erected a state-of-the-art distribution center. It also invested in hardware and software systems. Between 2004, when the Class E shares were introduced, and 2010, when the offering was closed, Organic Valley's sales tripled from $208 million to more than $600 million.

Investors got a steady 6 percent annual dividend over a period when the stock market turned in negative returns. One of them was David Hough, a freelance editor who grew up on a farm near La Farge. After he got laid off from his book publishing job in San Diego in mid-2008, Hough moved back to the family farm to help take care of his parents. The small dairy herd, beef cattle, and pigs were now gone, and his parents rent the land out for hay fields and pasture. But Hough retains a deep appreciation for the life of a family farmer—a big factor in his decision to invest a good chunk of his retirement funds in Organic Valley.

"For me it was a no-brainer. The fact that it supports family farms . . . I grew up on a family farm, I know how hard it is to make a living on a family farm. It's almost as bad as writing books," says Hough, just half-joking. "I think it's important to keep the family farms going. I don't particularly trust corporate or industrialized farming, and we should certainly have alternatives to that kind of food production."

Organic Valley's impact on the local region, where it employs more than 450 people, was another consideration. "The fact that they are local is huge. We live in a very rural area that was always economically disadvantaged—even the Indians were poor and starving around here," says Hough. "Organic Valley has had an enormous impact on the community, economically, socially, you name it."

As with other cooperatives, community support is part of Organic Valley's DNA. Ten percent of its excess revenue, after expenses, goes to a community fund that has supported local schools and athletic programs and helped protect LaFarge's watershed. The cooperative also donates product to schools and food pantries, maintains a disaster relief fund for farmers, and provides grants to organizations promoting organic research and advocacy.

And from a purely financial perspective, the Class E shares perfectly suited Hough's needs. "I'm 53, I'm half retired relying on a freelance income which comes and goes, so a steady 6 percent check every three months worked well for my financial situation. All the pieces of the puzzle fell into place for me. I buy their products. And I really like the idea that it's a co-op. I think this every-man-for-himself economy that we live in is a bad thing for everyone. You know, I believe everyone has to win a little bit, instead of winner take all."

The New Pioneers

Cooperatives have often been formed out of necessity—when workers or farmers or producers needed to band together for greater economic clout. They also rise up to fill unmet market needs, such as the electric and telephone co-ops in rural areas like Vernon County. Co-op activity is especially high in times of economic adversity, as in the United States in the 1930s, when many consumer co-ops, including many credit unions, electric utilities, and food co-ops that continue today, were established.

So it's not surprising that there has been a resurgence of cooperatives since the economy cratered in 2008. On one hand, the number of credit unions and agricultural co-ops has decreased over the years as associations have merged. But their overall impact has grown. For example, there were 22,000 credit unions with 40 million members in 1987. Today there are 7,500 credit unions, but membership has swelled to more than 90 million. And a fresh growth spurt is taking place. "Once again, we are seeing people join together to try and solve the needs of their communities," says Paul Hazen, CEO of the National Cooperative Business Association. One design and urban planning site proclaimed "the reinvention of the co-op" one of its top 10 trends for 2011.[7]

Just how widespread the co-op revival is is hard to gauge—the University of Wisconsin survey is the first comprehensive attempt to tally up the nation's cooperatives in decades. But there are at least 300 food co-ops under development around the country right now, says Hazen. That represents a 60 percent increase over the roughly 500 existing food co-ops. Renewable energy cooperatives are popping up everywhere you look to address demand for community-scale sustainable energy, from Piedmont Biofuels in North Carolina to Co-op Power in Greenfield, Massachusetts. And there is renewed interest in worker-owned cooperatives as a way to combat the dehumanizing effects of unemployment, outsourcing, and concentrated economic power.

One of the most compelling experiments is taking place in Cleveland, where the Evergreen Cooperatives are pioneering new models for creating jobs that protect the environment and build community wealth. A partnership of several institutions, including the Cleveland Foundation, the City of Cleveland, Case Western Reserve University, the Cleveland Clinic, and University Hospital, the cooperative aims to create two to three new worker-owned businesses a year, each generating 40 to 50 jobs in a city with a crippling poverty rate of 30 percent.

Evergreen is thinking big. Its first business, the Evergreen Cooperative Laundry, sets its sights on the huge, and growing, healthcare market by providing commercial laundry services to the area's big hospitals. And its state-of-the-art plant gives it an edge in an increasingly eco-conscious world: it uses just eight-tenths of a gallon of water per pound of laundry, compared to an average three gallons per pound for most industrial laundry facilities. Workers are hired from the co-op's University Circle neighborhood and, after a probationary period, begin earning equity in the business through payroll deductions, which could lead to a $65,000 stake after several years.

Another Evergreen business, Ohio Cooperative Solar, owns and installs solar panel arrays on institutional, government, and commercial buildings—its first installation is on the Cleveland Clinic's roof—and provides weatherization services. Green City Growers is planning a five-acre hydroponic greenhouse that will grow produce in the middle of Cleveland. The greenhouse, which will begin construction in the spring of 2011, expects to grow 5 million heads of lettuce and leafy greens each year. The produce will be marketed to local grocers and foodservice companies. A fourth business being incubated by Evergreen is a free local paper called the *Neighborhood Voice*. In each case, employees learn skills and are paid a living wage as they build equity in the business. And the businesses contribute a portion of their profits back into a main Evergreen fund that helps establish new ventures.

Innovative initiatives like the Evergreen Cooperatives are helping to raise awareness of worker cooperatives and update their hammer and sickle image. A 2009 *CNNMoney* feature highlighted six successful worker-owned businesses, from We Can Do It!, a group formed in 2006 by Latina housekeepers in Brooklyn that has since spun off child-care and cooking co-operatives, to Mushkin Enhanced, an Englewood, Colorado, maker of computer components. "It's a unique model—the worker-owned business. Some say it sounds like socialism, but these six companies say it's helped them tough out the recession," the article led off.[8]

Indeed, the cooperative model could point the way forward for beleaguered labor unions and corporations that are locked in mortal combat over balloooning pension obligations that appear increasingly unsustainable. In late 2009, a potentially far-reaching alliance was formed between the Spanish worker cooperative Mondragon and the United Steel Workers to create manufacturing cooperatives in North America that marry cooperative ideals and governance with union membership. "Too often we have seen Wall Street hollow out companies by draining their cash and assets and hollowing out communities by shedding jobs and shuttering plants," said USW International president Leo W. Gerard, in announcing the pact. "We need a new business model that invests in workers and invests in communities."[9]

A Multi-Stakeholder Approach

Lately, a new type of cooperative has evolved that more closely aligns the interests of all stakeholders, rather than organizing around just one group, such as producers or workers. This new vision of cooperatives is unfolding—where else?—in that cradle of cooperation and collective action, Wisconsin.

One of the first such cooperatives to adopt a multi-stakeholder approach in the United States (multi-stakeholder co-ops already have a foothold in Italy and Canada) is Maple Valley, an organic maple syrup producer in Cashton, 15 miles northwest of La Farge. It had been run as a private venture since 1991, gaining some 6,000 customers, but was restructured as a cooperative in 2007. Its founder, Cecil Wright, knows a thing or two about co-ops: his day job is vice president of sustainability and local operation at Organic Valley. Wright and his fellow syrup makers wanted to create a co-op that drew upon the strengths of all of its stakeholders, so they designated four classes of membership representing producers, customers, employees, and investors. Producers still have a dominant role—they elect four of Maple Valley's seven directors, with the other member groups each electing one—but the cop-op believes that the participation of the other groups makes for a stronger, more resilient organization.

William Neil, a financial planner in LaCrosse, embodies the mutual and overlapping interests of many co-op members. He produces a small amount of syrup from a stand of maples on his property, which is sold by Maple Valley. He's also a customer—although lately he has been cutting down on his sugar intake. And, he is an investor. Like many cooperatives, Maple Valley is tapping its members for capital to expand. Its goal is to raise $300,000 by 2013. It is offering Class B preferred shares, priced at $25, that pay a 6.5 percent annual dividend. Neil, a registered principal with brokerage firm LPL Financial, considers that an excellent investment—the equivalent of a B-rated corporate bond. "As a financial planner, I'm looking for stability and steady returns—that's hard to find these days. The rate of return relative to risk with a cooperative is very good," he says. Co-ops, and local investments in general, he believes, are a good way to diversify. "Co-ops, at their best, develop a level of insulation from global economic volatility."

Neil especially likes the multi-stakeholder approach. "Knowing that the power is fairly equally distributed among the members fosters trust," he says. And input from various groups help the business stay nimble and responsive to market changes, for example, by turning a producer surplus of sap into a product—say, maple candy—that customers are enthusiastic about. That gives Neil confidence as an investor. So much so, he believes that cooperatives "are the investment of the future."

Other cooperatives are taking a similar multi-stakeholder approach. The Producers & Buyers Co-op in Chippewa Valley, Wisconsin, brings together local farms and institutional buyers, such as hospitals and schools. And the Black Star brewpub in Austin combines worker and consumer membership and control. Fifth Season Cooperative, formed in 2010 in Viroqua, Wisconsin, is going further. In order to pursue a broad mission of building a thriving regional food system—the area has many small and mid-sized farms but little of their product is consumed locally—Fifth Season sought to engage the entire food chain. Its member groups include producers of produce, meat, and dairy, value-added processors, distributors, institutional buyers and workers. The goal is to develop long-term relationships that lead to fair pricing for both buyers and producers—and keep money in the local economy.

The various members spent six months hammering out a mission statement and bylaws that articulate the group's vision and values. "Now, we feel like we can solve any conflict or dispute that arises, because we share these values," says Susan Noble, executive director of the Vernon Economic Development Association (VEDA), which was instrumental in the co-op's creation. VEDA obtained a federal grant to help transform a 100,000-square foot facility left empty by NCR, once the area's second largest employer, into a regional food processing and distribution hub with commercial space for local food businesses such as Fifth Season. "We have to rely on our own local businesses, and that's what is happening here," says Noble. "We're growing our own local economy."

As Noble was helping spur new cooperative businesses in northwest Wisconsin in early 2011, a hundred miles away in the state's capital, union members massed to protest governor Scott Walker's attempts to eliminate collective bargaining and weaken public unions—which have a long and proud history in the state (and, not incidentally, represent the last pillar of Democratic fundraising). The need for new models that align the interests of various stakeholders could not have been clearer. The age-old antagonism between labor and management has spilled over to taxpayers and political leaders. No one, it seems, feels they are getting a fair shake.

The issues are complex, to be sure. States and municipalities are grappling with enormous budget gaps and declining revenue. And some union members have gamed the system. But should we be comparing the pay and benefits of teachers and other public servants to the private sector—where wages have stagnated and benefits have been shaved even as productivity (and CEO pay) have soared? If public employees are the "haves" and private workers are "have nots," as the Wisconsin governor suggests, is the intent to make us all "have nots?" Is Walmart really the new gold standard?

Clearly we are in need of some fresh thinking. And we could do worse than to give the cooperative model some serious consideration.

"Co-ops are ready for the mainstream," says Neil. Pointing to another set of protests—by members of the unionized Detroit Symphony Orchestra, which cancelled its 2011 season after contract negotiations failed—Neil, who is an accomplished composer and pianist in addition to a financial planner, says the cooperative model could provide a solution. Why not structure an entity where musicians, management, subscribers and donors are all working together toward a common goal, he muses. "Let's develop a method of cooperation that would allow the organization to float freely amid the turbulent markets."

The Un-Casino

Cooperatives are also filling a need among investors for sustainable investment options and alternatives to the Wall Street casino. As with all small businesses, access to adequate capital is the most pressing challenge for new and established co-ops. Their main sources of capital are membership fees—usually small sums paid once in return for lifetime memberships—and retained earnings. But neither method is very efficient for amassing large amounts of capital necessary for growth. That's why more and more co-ops are turning to their members to raise additional capital in the form of preferred shares or long-term loans.

Black Star Co-op Pub & Brewery, for example, raised the $600,000 it needed to build its brewery from a special class of member-investors. In return for the nonvoting shares, priced at $100 apiece, Black Star intends to pay a 6 percent dividend each year once it begins operating in the black, which it is on track to do very quickly. The board may elect to pay a higher dividend on a good year, and reduce or even eliminate the dividend if the co-op experiences a difficult year.

Cooperatives have an advantage here: They are often (but not always) exempt from federal securities regulations, as long as they keep their fundraising to their membership base and within a single state. State regulations vary widely, but some states exempt them as well. Texas, for example, allows for in-state offerings to members, so co-ops such as Black Star can raise large amounts of capital with minimal red tape. For investors, co-ops present an opportunity to invest in a business they know and trust—after all, they are owners of it—and earn market-rate returns while supporting their broader community. In addition, the growth and success of the co-op flows back to them through better products and services and patronage rebates.

Co-op members have responded enthusiastically. Take the Wheatsville Co-op in Austin. Despite being in the hometown of Whole Foods, the $9 billion natural food retailer, and two miles from the chain's flagship store, the Wheatsville Co-op has thrived. In 2005, it raised over $700,000 from 165 members in just two months to finance a major expansion, which doubled its retail space. The co-op's aisles are no longer cramped, and it can now offer more prepared foods, among other things. The store's sales have doubled every year since 2005.

The Willy Street Co-op, a popular food co-op in Madison, Wisconsin, with 23,000 members and $20 million in sales, has a long history of raising money from members to fund expansion, starting with its original store opened in 1974. In its most recent effort, the co-op set out to raise $600,000 from members for a second Madison store. Members could invest as little as $200 in "owner bonds," zero-coupon bonds that are paid back at their maturity with interest, ranging from 4 percent to 5.2 percent, depending on the length of the loan (three to seven years). In an outpouring of support, co-op members snapped up $1 million in shares in just 39 days, blowing past the co-op's fundraising goal. The new "Willy West" opened its doors in late 2010. "When you see something like this, it really does show how people are thinking today," notes Deborah Mitchell, a lecturer at the University of Wisconsin in Madison. "It's sort of a values choice by consumers."[10]

Casting a Wider Net

Some of the bigger co-ops with greater capital needs have gone outside of their membership base and across multiple states to raise money. Organic Valley's Series E preferred shares are one example. Because these public offerings are subject to multiple state regulations, only the biggest co-ops can usually afford it. (Due to its status as a tax-exempt cooperative under section 521 of the Internal Revenue Code, Organic Valley was exempt from federal securities regulations, but complied with the individual securities laws of the 40 states it offered shares in). The shares are usually nonvoting to preserve the co-op's governing structure and values. And they typically have the characteristics of a bond, with a fixed dividend and nonfluctuating face value set by the co-op board. In addition, the shares are usually illiquid and can be sold only to the co-op itself, subject to terms of the share agreement. Black Star, for example, will repurchase shares at their original $100 value, plus any undistributed dividends, upon request. Members who purchase $5,000 or more worth of shares will get a 5 percent premium per share (or 10 percent for members who purchases $10,000 or more worth of stock). The co-op may also elect to redeem shares at any time, based upon the same repurchase terms.

At Organic Valley, redemption requests for all classes of stock must be approved by the board of directors, which meets once a month. But in 22 years, no request has been denied, says Gloede. The shares are repurchased at their original price.

CHS Inc. is an exception. The giant ag cooperative sold 3.5 million shares of preferred stock, priced at $25, that pay an 8 percent dividend. With its ample resources, CHS fully registered the securities, which are traded on NASDAQ (ticker symbol CHSCP).

Despite the constraints, the steady dividends that these preferred shares generate—typically between 4 percent and 8 percent— and the lack of speculative trading make them very attractive to some investors. Just as the share price does not go up, neither does it lose value. When the Wheatsville Co-op in Austin offered its preferred shares back in 2005, the economy was booming and the shares' 4 percent dividend looked modest indeed. Not so these days. "People tell us we're their best investment right now, which is kind of sad," says Dan Gillotte, Wheatsville's general manager. Only one or two people have exercised their right to sell their shares back to the co-op. And what investor would not have liked to have locked in the 6 percent returns that Organic Valley investors enjoyed over the past several years?

Will the interest in cooperatives fade when the economy is again chugging and investor expectations rise along with the Dow? Gillotte, for one, believes co-ops have staying power. "Co-ops are starting to establish a track record that shows that we are resilient, so even if we run into disasters we get through them and people get their money back. Typically we are more responsible than the average business and people have a lot of trust in their co-ops, which helps," he says. Sure enough, a 2008 study by the Quebec Ministry of Economic Development, Innovation and Export Trade found that the survival rate for cooperatives was twice that of other businesses.[11] And there is tangible benefit, says Gillotte. "Investors can see what happens with their money. People don't often get to build things or really feel connected with something that their money goes into. To see it go into your grocery store that is doing really cool things or your brewpub—that's really gratifying for people, I think."

As head of the National Cooperative Business Association (NCBA), Paul Hazen is, naturally, bullish on co-ops. But his views have an indisputable logic. "If you're interested in creating local jobs and economic activity, it's the perfect model, because the people running the business are from the community and are going to do what's in the best interest of the community," he says. "You don't have to worry about your investment going to China or Mexico with a cooperative."

Preferred share offerings by co-ops, however, are not all that common. "You kind of have to trip over them by luck," says Hazen. What's more, registered financial planners like Neil, who are regulated by the Financial Industry Regulatory Authority (FINRA), are not allowed to recommend co-op offerings or other unregistered securities. (Although Neil's firm, LPL Financial, has recently begun vetting such investments for clients upon request.)

Two developments are worth noting. A new form of cooperative, the limited cooperative association (LCA), has been approved by five states (Wyoming, Tennessee, Iowa, Minnesota, and Wisconsin). Designed to help co-ops raise capital, the LCA allows for a class of investor membership where the interest is purely financial. In an LCA, investors are on more equal footing with patron-members, rather than being subordinate, and dividends can potentially be higher. Critics, however, say the hybrid structure of an LCA undermines the democratic premise and principles of cooperatives. More promising, perhaps, is an initiative underway by the NCBA and the Calvert Foundation. To make co-op investing more accessible, the organizations are exploring the creation of a National Cooperative Capital Investment Fund, which would allow individuals, as well as foundations and institutions, to easily invest in cooperatives around the country. Investors could put money into the fund, which would make investments in the cooperatives in the form of preferred shares or subordinate debt. With the Calvert Foundation acting as fund manager and intermediary, there would be no SEC obligations for the co-ops, and individuals would not have to be co-op members to invest. Hazen hopes the fund will be a real option for investors and cooperatives soon.

Game Plan for Locavestors

Cooperatives are businesses that are owned by their members and run for the mutual benefit of their membership. They generally provide two types of investment opportunities: Members share in the business's surplus revenue (aka profit) through patronage rebates. In addition, co-ops often raise expansion capital from members and sometimes from outside investors by issuing shares that pay a modest but steady dividend.

Pros:
- Although co-op investment terms vary, they generally involve loans or non-voting preferred shares that offer steady bond-like dividends. These investments are the opposite of speculative. When shares are offered, it is typically at a fixed price, with a fixed dividend. Therefore, there is no depreciation or volatility.
- In addition, members of a co-op share in its prosperity through improved products and services, patronage rebates, and other perks.

- As democratically run enterprises, co-ops tend to be very transparent about their operations and the uses of funds.
- In addition to financial gain, an investment in a co-op pays dividends to the community by filling unmet needs and generating jobs and economic activity. Most co-ops set aside a small portion of excess revenue to invest in local initiatives.
- Cooperatives allow small producers, retailers, or buyers to band together for greater economic clout, providing a counterbalance to corporate economic power.
- Any co-op member can run for a seat on the board.

Cons:
- Investments in a cooperative have limitations. Terms, including share price and repurchase policies, are controlled by the co-op board. And dividends are generally capped at 8 percent. As (typically) unregistered securities, the shares cannot be traded, although most co-ops will repurchase shares upon request.
- Most shares offered by co-ops have a fixed price and do not appreciate in value.
- Like any business investment, there is always the risk a cooperative business will fail.

The Bottom Line: Co-ops provide a relatively safe, bond-like investment that will reward beyond dividends.

For More Information:
- The National Cooperative Business Association provides research and advocacy for the co-op sector. www.ncba.coop.
- The International Cooperative Alliance represents co-ops worldwide. www.ica.coop/al-ica.
- For Organic Valley investment information: www.organicvalley.coop/about-us/invest/stock-prospectus/.

CHAPTER 12

The Do-It-Yourself Public Offering

The Allure of Public Venture Capital

So far, we have explored various ways that entrepreneurs can connect with investors. These models hold great promise, but each has its limitations. Sometimes the most effective method of raising capital is to take the leap and go public. Indeed, the initial public offering, or IPO, is the magical moment that many entrepreneurs and their early stage investors dream of, when they can reap the rewards of their risk taking. Nothing says you've arrived like an IPO.

Generations of ambitious companies have chosen this route. Public stock offerings are often the best solution for companies that need a significant capital infusion. Selling shares to the public opens up a huge new pool of growth capital with none of the constraints of private investments. This is long-term capital: no loan to pay back, no interest payments to be made, no pressure to sell the company. And millions of ordinary investors get their first shot at owning shares of an admired company with strong growth prospects.

IPOs, however, come at a cost. For one, they are expensive. Costs for legal, listing, and accounting fees can easily exceed $1 million, so IPOs make sense only for companies seeking to raise large sums, usually $25 million or more. Once public, there is the ongoing expense of managing investors and issuing quarterly audited financial reports. Suddenly, the company is thrust into the harsh glare of the public spotlight, where the demands of Wall Street can make it difficult, if not impossible, to make strategic investments and management decisions that lower earnings in the short term.

More broadly, the public markets have not been welcoming to small companies lately. The minimum thresholds to list on the NYSE or even the traditionally smaller cap NASDAQ rule out companies without a significant market capitalization,[1] but a bigger obstacle is that investment banks these days don't want to waste time on any but the biggest and most lucrative IPOs. The median IPO size 20 years ago was $10 million; by 2009, it was $140 million. In addition, the volatility and short-term demands of the public markets have scared off many promising IPO candidates—one reason the number of IPOs has declined precipitously in recent years.

But there is another twist that is gaining favor among smaller companies: the direct public offering, or DPO. Think of it as an IPO for the do-it-yourself (DIY) crowd.

Direct Public Offering

Like the more familiar initial public offering, or IPO, a direct public offering (DPO) raises capital by selling shares to the public. The difference is that the company raising the money handles the marketing of the offering itself, rather than going through a Wall Street underwriter. Eliminating the middleman reduces costs, making the public markets more accessible to smaller companies for whom a conventional IPO may be out of reach. For investors, DPOs allow them to get in on early stage investments typically reserved for angels and venture capitalists.

In a DPO, a company sells shares to the public, as in a traditional IPO. The main difference is that the company sells the shares directly, rather than going through a Wall Street intermediary—the investment banking underwriters that take a standard 7 percent cut of the offering. As with crowdfunding models that cut out financial middlemen, DPOs reduce the costs of raising capital. DPOs can be cost effective for offerings as small as $50,000, although they typically range from $1 million to $3 million. Moreover, they give ordinary investors an opportunity to participate in the type of high-risk, high-reward investments typically reserved for venture capitalists and accredited investors.

What exactly is entailed? In a traditional IPO, the Wall Street underwriter handles a number of things: It prepares the prospectus and files documents, conducts a road show to promote the deal to institutional investors, and ensures that there is a well-primed market for the securities once they are publicly traded. In the case of a DPO, the company issuing shares takes on these responsibilities itself, usually with the help of an attorney or accountant. The cost savings can put the public offering option within reach of smaller companies that otherwise could not afford it. DPO expenses can range from a few thousand dollars for extreme DIY cases to tens of thousands of dollars with more professional assistance. DPOs fill a significant gap for companies looking to raise tens of thousands of dollars up to several million dollars.

Getting in on the Ground Floor

DPOs are a fairly new phenomenon. They may have been technically feasible, but it wasn't until 1980, when Congress passed the Small Business Investment Incentive Act, that state and federal authorities began to pave the way for many small, private companies to more easily tap the public markets. In response to the Act, the Securities and Exchange Commission and state regulators created a series of exemptions and streamlined options for small business capital-raising that eliminated onerous regulatory requirements. Today, most DPOs are conducted under one of the following federal exemptions:

- The intrastate offering exemption (also known as Rule 147) makes an allowance for securities offerings limited to the state in which the firm is incorporated and does the bulk of its business. An unlimited amount of captial can be raised from in-state residents within a 12-month period.
- Regulation A allows firms to raise up to $5 million in a 12-month period. While documents including an offering circular must be filed with the SEC, simplified forms may be used.
- Under certain circumstances, Regulation D, Rule 504, more commonly associated with private placements, can be used for public offerings of up to $1 million in a 12-month period.[2]

In all of the cases above, there are no restictions on the number of non-accredited investors, public advertising, or secondary trading of securities. Relevant state regulations apply, but for offerings under $1 million, the Small Company Offering Registration (SCOR), a simplified form in question and answer format, may be used in many states. And, if the issuing company has less than $10 million in assets and 500 or fewer shareholders, there is no ongoing public reporting requirement. These direct offerings can be structured as equity, convertible debt, or other forms of financing, such as revenue sharing. Often, DPOs are part of a coordinated capital-raising process that might start with a private placement, proceed to a DPO, and ultimately, an IPO.

DPOs aren't for everybody. But they tend to be a good match for companies with strong affinity groups—such as loyal customers, employees, or the community at large—that may be receptive to the offering. Many early DPOs were conducted by catalog retailers and community banks that had a built-in communication channel with customers and potential investors. Today, a healthy online community or Facebook presence fits the bill. It also helps if the company has an easily understood business—beer versus polymer science, for example. Companies with enthusiastic followings don't necessarily need, or want, an investment banker's

Rolodex to rustle up investors. A DPO allows them to directly reach out to their biggest fans and supporters—that could be you—and save tens or hundreds of thousands of dollars doing it.

When Annie's Homegrown, the maker of the packaged macaroni and cheese that is a staple at natural food stores, directly offered shares in 1996, it advertised the opportunity with a coupon in each box of mac and cheese. When mothers went to fix a quick, healthy meal for their kids, they learned of the opportunity to buy the $6 shares (although more than a few of the coupons ended up in a pot of boiling water). Annie's used the more than $3 million in proceeds to expand its geographic distribution and introduce new products for the fast-growing organic and natural foods market.

Real Goods, a renewable energy pioneer founded in 1978, had built a devoted following among the ecominded customers who subscribed to its catalog featuring solar panels and other green products. In 1991, Real Goods founder John Schaeffer was looking to branch out into new markets, but banks deemed the business too risky. So Schaeffer offered customers a chance to invest in the company, which was generating about $3 million in sales. A mailing to 15,000 customers who had made a recent purchase and lived in one of the 13 states where the offering was registered drew 6,200 requests for the offering documents. More than 10 percent of those, or 674 customers, became shareholders, investing a total of $1 million. Another 175 people had to be turned away after the offering was oversubscribed. Two years later, Real Goods raised an additional $3.6 million in a follow-on DPO.

Even after the second offering, Schaeffer still owned 75 percent of the company (try that with a venture capitalist or private equity investor). To his delight, he discovered that his new shareowners purchased twice the dollar amount of products as nonshareholders. "Your customers become owners of your company, and therefore become very loyal," says Schaeffer. "If you own Coke, you're not going to buy Pepsi." Real Goods's shareholder meetings were more like love-ins, held at campgrounds and wineries and drawing hundreds of customer-shareholders.

For investors, DPOs offer an opportunity to get in on the ground floor of a company that offers exciting growth potential.

It's also a way to support a company whose products they love and whose values they share, while participating in the upside (or downside) of the business. Investors in Annie's Homegrown, for example, were able to share in the growth of a company that went from a home operation to a national brand with the country's number-two selling macaroni and cheese. (Annie's was taken private by new management in 2002).

Real Goods Trading grew from a tiny catalog retailer to a $19 million company with five stores selling everything from organic cotton apparel and gardening tools to rain barrels and small wind turbines. In 2001, after some financial struggles, Real Goods merged with Gaiam, a natural lifestyle products company. In a reminder that this is essentially public venture capital with all the attendant risk, investors were offered slightly less for their shares than they initially paid (although the deal was sweetened with generous discounts on future purchases). But the combined company today is a $60 million leader in its field.

Other small companies with strong followings have had similar success with DPOs, including California Federal Bank, Mendocino Brewing Company, Zap Electric Bikes, and Diamond Organics.

Some are household names. Price Club, which pioneered the member-only warehouse club model of retailing, figured its members knew a deal when they saw one. So, when it struggled with cash flow in 1991, the company offered members the opportunity to invest directly in a Real Estate Investment Trust (REIT) that would purchase Price Club properties and lease them back to the company. Advertising in the Price Club circular, it raised more than $70 million. Price Club later merged with CostCo, which reported revenues of $76 billion in 2010.

And in 1984, when two guys named Ben and Jerry were looking to raise money for their little ice cream operation in Burlington, Vermont, they turned to their biggest fans: their customers. They advertised the Ben & Jerry's shares—priced at $10.50 a piece with a 12 share minimum—in local newspapers and on pints of ice cream with the slogan, "Get a Scoop of the Action." About 1,800 ice cream-loving Vermonters did, raising $750,000. The DPO allowed the founders, Ben Cohen and Jerry Greenfield, to build a new plant and expand their distribution, setting the stage for a $5.8 million national IPO the following year.

In the DPO prospectus, amid the boilerplate risk discussion, the straight-talking founders insisted on adding a line, in plain English and all caps: "If you can't afford to lose it, don't do it." As Cohen and Greenfield recount in their book, *Ben & Jerry's Double Dip: How to Run a Values-Led Business and Make Money, Too*: "It's one thing to fail and lose the capital of a bunch of investors we'd never met. It's anther thing to lose our neighbor's hard-earned $126. So the public offering gave us an extra incentive to do well financially, to make sure our neighbors' investment in us was to their advantage as well as ours."

Safe to say they succeeded.

A Brewing Revolution

No one currently tracks direct public offerings, but as a benchmark, 358 companies raised $454.8 million through DPOs in 1996.[3] Still, DPOs are hardly mainstream. Most investors, entrepreneurs, and even lawyers know little about them, if they've heard of them at all. But why would they? After a spurt of popularity in the latter decades of the 20th century, direct public offerings have fallen off the radar.

What is holding this potentially valuable capital-raising solution back?

If the Small Business Investment Act cleared the way for a wave of direct offerings, the widespread adoption of the Internet in mid-1990s was poised to crack the market wide open. Suddenly, it was much easier and less costly to market shares and distribute investment information.

One of the first people to grasp this fact was a corporate lawyer-turned-microbrewer named Andrew Klein. On a trip to Amsterdam in the early 1990s, Klein became enamored with a traditional Belgian-style wheat beer, or *witbier*, and decided to try his hand at brewing his own back in New York. In 1993, the Spring Street Brewing Company was born. Microbrewing was in its infancy in the United States, and Klein's Wit beer developed a fast following. Soon, however, Klein, an affable guy with a base-ball cap usually pulled low on his head, found himself down to his last $200,000 in working capital. He needed to raise money to keep Spring Street Brewing Company alive.

Frustrated after venture capitalists strung him along for months, Klein decided to put his legal skills to work. As an attorney at Cravath, Swain & Moore, he had worked with companies that had used Reg A, the SEC exemption for offerings under $5 million, to sell shares directly to the public. The Internet was still fairly young—Netscape had just released its Web browser, and Google wouldn't be founded for another three years—but Klein saw that it was a great platform for marketing and disseminating investment information. (It may seem like a no-brainer now, but at the time, investors typically would call an 800 number to request a prospectus, which would be sent via postal service.)

Klein had another ready-made platform: his beer. The Spring Street offering was advertised right on the labels of the company's Wit beer, putting it literally in the hands of his most valuable audience. Klein also distributed postcards about the offering at bars and restaurants where the beer was served, inviting potential investors to his web site, where the prospectus could be downloaded. He had a tailor-made customer base: "young, well-educated, Internet-generation males with a penchant for surfing cyberspace and for drinking gourmet beer—often at the same time," as he described it.[4]

The charismatic founder and his little beer company were perfect fodder, sparking a media frenzy as word of the first "Internet IPO," done without the aid of expensive Wall Street bankers, was picked up by news outlets from the *Wall Street Journal* to CNN. By December 1995, Klein had raised $1.6 million from 3,500 investors, mostly beer enthusiasts.

Long after the offering was closed, Web surfers continued to come to Spring Street's site looking to buy shares, giving Klein the idea to create a bulletin board where would-be buyers and sellers of Spring Street shares could directly trade with one another. The liquidity such trading provided would make the shares more attractive. Spring Street could also post its audited financial statements on the site to help inform buyers and sellers. Klein banged together a simple site he called Wit Trade and, displaying his newfound media savvy, cranked up the promotional machine. A party to launch the "first-ever digital stock trading mechanism" drew scores of journalists and TV crews.

"I didn't anticipate the potential people would see in the idea—how this little company stumbled into a method that, taken to its logical extreme, could radically change the way stocks are sold," Klein told *Inc.* magazine in one of his many press interviews at the time.

Nor did he anticipate the reaction of the SEC, which saw Wit Trade as a dangerous experiment that could disrupt the status quo. The SEC wanted the bulletin board shut down. At the last moment, one technologically inclined commissioner, Steven Wallman, intervened. Wallman saw the potential for digital technology to make markets more efficient and capital more accessible to a wider range of companies, and he viewed Klein's trading system as an innovative experiment that should be allowed to proceed. Spring Street was granted a waiver, called a No Action letter, to operate the electronic exchange.

Klein sensed a bigger opportunity, however, to radically change the way companies and investors interacted. So he launched his second startup, Wit Capital, which would help other businesses follow in his footsteps and use the Internet to directly reach investors hungry for venture-stage investments—without expensive investment bankers. Through its proprietary trading platform, Wit would also let investors directly trade with one another, bypassing fee-charging brokers. It was the age of "disintermediation." The Internet was tearing down barriers and leveling the playing field for the little guys, and Wit Capital would be their champion.

It was a remarkable moment, and one for which I had a front-row seat after leaving my job as an editor at *Business Week* magazine to join Wit Capital as senior vice president of content in the fall of 1998. By then, the Internet was exploding and the first dot-coms were beginning to make their staggering debuts on the public markets. TheGlobe.com, an early social networking site, went public in November that year. Priced at $9 a share, it soared as high as $97 a share before ending its first day of trading at around $63, seven times its initial offering price. The dot-coms had the barest outlines of a business plan and lost tons of money, but they made fortunes for venture capitalists and well-connected investors who got in on the low offering price that inevitably soared when the shares hit the NASDAQ. They were built to flip.

Klein's lofty vision of helping other small companies raise capital soon morphed, for practical and opportunistic reasons, into a platform for channeling a small portion of these coveted pre-IPO shares to a clamoring investor public. There was an element of the original idea: The fledgling dot-coms often wanted their Internet audience and customers to participate in their initial offering, in which case Wit might be allocated a small number of shares to offer to the masses of individual investors at the initial offering price (usually by lottery, since demand far outstripped supply). More often, the dot-coms simply wanted their friends and family to get in on the action. Wit Capital became that conduit, while the blue-chip investment banks kept their lock on the underwriting, the fees, and the bulk of the shares. The market had demonstrated, not for the last time, its preference for fast and easy, if ephemeral, profits, and we were happy to oblige.

Venture capitalists were throwing money at Internet startups with no track record, and Wall Street was eager to take them public. The companies that Wit might have helped raise capital, however, operated in the real bricks-and-mortar world and were bound by its limits. They would probably never deliver 400 percent returns, overnight, like some dot-coms did at the height of the bubble.

The DPO revolution would have to wait.

DPO Revival

Fast-forward 10 years. The dot-com crash is a distant memory, replaced by a more recent and traumatizing lesson in bubble economics. And there is once again fresh interest in direct, DIY offerings. In part, it is driven by necessity, as traditional capital sources have dried up for small companies. Investors, meanwhile, are looking for investment alternatives that fall somewhere between anemic savings accounts and an increasingly volatile stock market, and that perhaps align with their values and interests.

Drew Field is a securities lawyer and DPO trailblazer who handled many of the early direct offerings, including Real Goods and Annie's, and authored a book on DPOs. In his view, the "infectious greed" of the 1990s derailed interest in such deals, and the subsequent dot-com bust scared off many of the small investors who would be inclined to invest in a direct offering. After that, he says, "there never seemed to be the political will to connect individuals with small investors, nor did individuals have the same drive to invest in these firms." Field, who is now retired, believes that a shift in investor sentiment from a Wall Street mentality to "a sense of community, ownership, and common objective," such as we seem to be experiencing in the aftermath of the latest financial calamity, could change that.

Social(ist) Networking

On an early autumn morning, at a low-key coffee shop in Manhattan's Nolita neighborhood, I sat down with Chris Michael, an intense, dark-eyed young man who may just be the next DPO pioneer. Michael tells me about his plan to open a worker-owned diner in central Brooklyn, a gritty, underserved area that has not shared in the prosperity of neighboring brownstone-lined enclaves. The diner is just the first step in a broader worker cooperative empire Michael envisions.

Raised in a New Jersey suburb just over the George Washington Bridge by left-leaning parents, Michael grew up with a keen awareness of social injustice. He wryly tells of boyhood summers spent at a Jewish socialist camp, where activities included singing antiwar songs and role-playing as slaves on "Exodus Day." But he has only recently become passionate about political and economic systems. His goal is to create a worker cooperative model that builds local wealth and can be used by other communities.

In designing his model, Michael had a few requirements. To be easily replicated, it would have to be simple and not require more than $500,000 in capital. And it must be something that regular communities and workers could afford and embrace— in other words, it could not be "bourgie," as he puts it. Add in the fact that the food industry is the largest employer after the government, and a diner seemed the natural solution. Workers Diner, as he is calling his venture, will allow workers to build up ownership equity in the business through accumulation of preferred shares, and to share in the profits. The workers will also have voting rights and a say in the management of the diner. Michael expects the diner to employ about 22 individuals when it opens.

To pursue this vision, Michael and his two partners have created a sort of cooperative business incubator (not unlike Cleveland's Evergreen Cooperatives in philosophy) called Workers Development that will develop the diner concept, create a business plan, get it started, and then move on to develop the next diner. "I'm the fancy guy," he says. "We act the role of the capitalist-entrepreneur, but we don't own the company or exploit it into infinity."

With the details worked out, the only question was how to fund the venture. Michael wasn't keen on taking out a big bank loan, and he decided equity would be a better route. But when he talked to New York lawyers about raising capital, he says, "they laughed us out of the room." (That's one reason he will be starting law school in the fall, after he finishes his master's degree in politics and public policy.) Michael heard about direct public offerings and was referred to Cutting Edge Capital, a recently formed firm that helps small companies explore creative alternatives to raising capital. With Jenny Kassan, a lawyer who is Cutting Edge Capital's CEO, Michael began plotting his capital-raising revolution.

Workers Diner expects to raise money in 2011 through a tri-state direct public offering under Reg D, rule 504 (the exemption for offerings under $1 million) using the simplified SCOR form in New York, New Jersey, and Connecticut. His audience: justice-minded investors. "Not exploiting workers is an intuitively attractive idea," says Michael, and one he believes will resonate beyond Brooklyn. (Workingmen of New York, New Jersey, and Connecticut, unite!)

The shares will be priced at $25, with a four-share minimum, and will pay a fixed annual dividend of 3.75 percent over the prime rate. No voting right is associated with the shares or claims on profits; that is reserved for the employee-owners. To get the word out to potential investors, Michael plans an aggressive online campaign that will lean heavily on Facebook, Twitter, and other social networking tools. "This will be the first Facebook IPO," he says excitedly.

At the very least, you could call it a new form of social(ist) networking.

Other companies have used the Internet to market their direct offerings. For example, the Saranac Lake Community Store, a DPO described in Chapter 8, has a web site and a Facebook page. But to date few direct offerings have really exploited the potential of online social networks. Only time will tell if Michael— or another entrepreneur—will pick up where Andy Klein left off.

In Search of Liquidity

As Cutting Edge Capital's first DPO client, the Workers Diner will be an important test case. The firm—created in 2010 by the local investing brain trust of Kassan, attorney John Katovich, and economist and local advocate Michael Shuman—hopes to streamline the DPO process and bring costs down to a level that is manageable for small enterprises. The legal work for Workers Diner was pro bono, but the firm's principals believe they can get the costs down to as little as $25,000, a modest sum when you consider that a traditional IPO typically costs at least 30 times that amount. Another Cutting Edge Capital client, Tangerine Power, a Seattle-based developer of distributed, community-scale solar power, is also mulling a DPO as a way to reach out to members of communities in which it operates and people who care about renewable energy.

Meanwhile, DPOs are gingerly cropping up across the country. In Buffalo, CityMade, Inc., is directly selling shares to New York residents to raise $1 million to fund growth. The company started out in 1999 selling "made in Buffalo" items—such as Weber's horseradish mustard, made locally for three generations, and Sahlen's hot dogs, a Buffalo tradition since 1869—on the Internet. Today, CityMade sells regional specialties and gift baskets from a dozen cities, from Baltimore to Washington, DC, each with its own branded web site. It plans to use the proceeds to extend its profitable "made in" model to additional cities. According to CityMade's prospectus, its offering expenses, including legal and accounting fees and filing fees, amount to less than 1 percent of the $1 million it plans to raise.[5]

Bissonnette Funding in Boulder, Colorado, is working with three companies pursuing DPOs. And recent seminars conducted by Cutting Edge Capital and Green Ladder Funding drew more than 150 business owners interested in learning about DPOs. "With the inefficiency of capital markets at an all time high, entrepreneurs are looking for ways to approach a broader range of potential investors," says Cutting Edge Capital CEO Jenny Kassan. At the same time, she says, people are looking for ways to support and invest in the local businesses they love. The renewed interest in DPOs could open up opportunities for both. As with any early stage investment, there is a high degree of risk. And with a DPO, there is no underwriter to conduct due diligence on the investment.

The biggest drawback to the DPO model, however, is a glaring one: a lack of liquidity. The shares are not restricted, so they can theoretically be traded in the secondary market. The problem is a lack of robust secondary trading options. Even long-term investors need to know that there is some sort of "exit" that will allow them to cash out their investment eventually and take profits—either through a sale of the company, an IPO, or through secondary trading of the shares. In fact, a lack of liquidity is an obstacle that is shared by many locavesting models.

Some companies that have conducted DPOs have offered to buy back shares under pre-agreed circumstances when their investors want out. In other cases, the issuer may elect to list them on a stock exchange. But because companies choosing the DPO option are typically smaller, an exchange such as the NYSE or NASDAQ is usually out of reach.[6] In lieu of the big exchanges, companies can list their shares on the lightly regulated over-the-counter (OTC) market, but that is the realm of penny stocks and boiler room intrigue, and many companies and investors prefer to steer clear of it. A third option is to operate an alternative trading system, like the one Andy Klein set up for his beer company. Real Goods similarly received a green light from the SEC to run a small trading site for its shares after its 1991 DPO. But SEC approval for such alternative mechanisms is harder to come by these days. And even with approval, not all companies are willing or able to create and maintain a web site capable of matching buyers and sellers.

Regional exchanges used to list their local companies. The Pacific Stock Exchange, for example, until recently carved out a space for regional companies that had conducted SCOR or Reg A offerings to be traded. Shares of Real Goods were listed on the exchange in addition to the company's own bulletin board. But that practice ended after the Pacific Exchange was merged with the NYSE in 2006.

Without a trading mechanism where investors can cash out their shares, DPOs are only half a solution. That's where the local stock exchange comes in.

Game Plan for Locavestors

Direct public offerings are a low-cost way for companies to sell shares directly to the public. In return for capital, investors get in on early stage investments usually reserved for angels and accredited investors. The offerings can include equity, debt, or other forms of financing.

Pros:

- DPOs give investors an opportunity to get in on the ground floor of exciting investment opportunities and participate in high risk/reward venture-stage funding typically limited to wealthy or institutional investors.

- A DPO may serve as an initial fund raising event before a company goes on to a conventional IPO. Companies such as Ben & Jerry's followed their DPOs with successful IPOs, resulting in rich returns for early investors.
- DPOs give individuals a chance to invest in companies with whom they have an affinity or shared values, or whose products they like and admire. As customers, they contribute to the success of their investment.
- Individual investors often have more access to management of DPO companies than they would to management of large publicly traded companies.
- Companies issuing shares directly are required to provide a comprehensive prospectus, so relevant information on the business, its finances, and risk factors is available to potential investors.

Cons:
- Liquidity is an issue. There is often not a way to trade shares on a secondary market, and when there is, volume may be scant. And not all companies will go on to an IPO or sale of the company.
- Any business carries risk, and with DPOs there is no Wall Street underwriter conducting due diligence. Lacking a market mechanism, companies issuing shares directly may arbitrarily set stock price.
- There is not likely to be ongoing coverage of the stock by analysts.

The Bottom Line: If you love the company, this is your chance to own it.

Investor Checklist for DPOs:
- Before you buy shares in a DPO, consider the following:
  - Are you familiar with the company's products or services?
  - What is its financial condition? Does it have outstanding debt or legal issues? Ask to see financials.
  - Are revenues sufficient? Does the company have a good revenue model?
  - What will the proceeds of the offering be used for?
  - How are the securities priced? Do they imply a fair value for the company?
  - Do you have confidence in the management team?

- What are your options for selling the securities?
- Are the securities being offered under a legitimate exemption if they are not registered?

For More Information:

- An explanation of federal securities exemptions for small business can be found at www.sec.gov/info/smallbus/qasbsec.htm#eod6.
- Your state's securities regulator can be a good source of information about the company, its management, and the offering.
- Online social networks can invite fraud. The SEC offers tips on how to avoid Internet scams at www.sec.gov/investor/pubs/cyberfraud.htm.
- Drew Field maintains a web site with comprehensive information on DPOs, including case studies and some interesting commentary at www.dfdpo.com.
- Cutting Edge Capital also has a blog at http://cuttingedgecapital.com

CHAPTER

13

Back to the Future

The Rebirth of the Local Stock Exchange

Can the solution to local investing be found in our past?

It's hard to imagine now, but less than a century ago, the United States was teeming with stock exchanges. Starting in the 1790s, when groups of brokers gathered at the Merchants Coffee House in Philadelphia and under a buttonwood tree on Wall Street, the young nation began piecing together a financial market system that would fuel its breathtaking growth. For several decades, the Philadelphia and New York exchanges served as national markets. As the country grew, so did the number of exchanges. Boston, Baltimore, Milwaukee, and San Francisco established stock exchanges starting in the 1830s. But it wasn't until after the Civil War that regional exchanges really took off. From 1862 to 1930, as America industrialized and expanded westward, at least 24 exchanges debuted, from Wheeling, West Virginia, to Salt Lake City and Honolulu.[1]

The exchanges were important institutions in their communities, both socially and commercially. To purchase shares listed on a regional exchange, investors would have to buy from one of its member-brokers, who were often prominent citizens in the community. Each exchange reflected the unique character and industry of its region. On the Seattle exchange, for example, investors could find hometown favorites such as Olympia Brewing, Alaska Pacific Salmon, and Carnation (acquired by Nestlé in 1985). In Richmond, Virginia, listings tended toward tobacco, local utilities, and southern banks. The Cincinnati Stock Exchange, created in 1885, nurtured young Midwestern companies including a soap maker called Procter & Gamble, a tire maker called Goodyear, and a grocer named Kroger. Its brokers didn't do too badly either. According to one account, the Cincinnati exchange provided "large, deep couches for its members, who spend a large part of their time on the floor playing pinochle."[2]

The history of the early exchanges has been largely forgotten, and few detailed accounts remain. But they were engines of regional growth, facilitating the flow of capital into area business ventures and stoking their local economies. From 1790 through 1930, the number of exchanges rose in tandem with U.S. industrial production, according to researchers at Franklin & Marshall College, who conducted one of the most comprehensive studies of the role of regional exchanges. To better assess the impact the exchanges had on local economies, the researchers compared data before and after the founding of each exchange to measure its effect on manufacturing employment (the dominant employer category at the time) in the area. In almost all cases, the increase in the population engaged in manufacturing was greater in the regions with stock exchanges than for the nation as a whole, leading the authors to conclude that regional stock exchanges are strongly associated with regional economic growth. On average, the regions with newly established exchanges saw a 175 percent increase in manufacturing engagement, compared to 76 percent for the nation as a whole.[3]

The landmark securities regulations of the 1930s, which imposed new registration and reporting requirements on publicly traded companies, began to bleed business away from the regional exchanges. The powerful and politically connected New York Stock Exchange was a key beneficiary. As a *Time* magazine article from 1936 explained: "Because a listing on a small exchange requires the same painful revelations as on the New York Stock Exchange, corporations tended to seek listing there in addition to a listing on a local market. When that happens local trading generally begins to dry up."[4]

The migration to bigger exchanges accelerated with the advent of communications technology that could link the markets. As physical place became less important, the exchanges began to consolidate. The Cleveland, St. Louis, Minneapolis–St. Paul, and New Orleans stock exchanges combined with the Chicago Stock Exchange, which continues today. Others simply folded. The Standard Stock Exchange of Spokane, a mining-heavy market with a colorful, if checkered, history, was among the last of the regionals to close, in 1991.

Today, most public trading takes place on the New York Stock Exchange and NASDAQ. As exchanges go, NASDAQ is a newcomer. A tech-savvy upstart, it became the preferred market for small-cap tech startups like Apple and Microsoft beginning in the 1980s. In recent years, it acquired the Philadelphia and Boston stock exchanges before merging with the Nordic OMX exchange. Today, the NASDAQ OMX Group's services span six continents. The venerable NYSE scrambled to catch up. Starting in 2006, the "Big Board" in quick succession swallowed up Archipelago, an electronic trading network that owned the Pacific Stock Exchange, the pan-European Euronext, and the century-and-a-half-old American Stock Exchange. And in early 2011, the NYSE agreed to be acquired by the Deutsche Börse, which runs the Frankfurt Stock Exchange. As if to eliminate any remaining ties to place, the combined entity would be headquartered in the Netherlands.

The merging of exchanges was a natural evolution that increased transparency and efficiency and lowered costs. But it would also change the nature of the markets in far-reaching ways. As the exchanges consolidated their power and reach, they jettisoned their not-for-profit status and became publicly traded companies themselves, selling shares to fuel their expansion. Over time, they became more focused on large companies and markets that could generate the high trading volumes and profits they craved. Smaller companies fell by the wayside.

The Incredible Shrinking IPO Market

Today, exchanges compete to list global companies from every corner of the Earth. Smaller cap companies have increasingly been pushed off the major exchanges and onto the over-the-counter (OTC) bulletin boards or the Pink Sheets.

Indeed, the New York brokers who gathered under the buttonwood tree in 1792 would hardly recognize what they have wrought. The notion of curbside trading seems positively antique in an age when trading is electronic, impersonal, and more likely to be initiated by a computer algorithm than a person. Wall Street is less a place than a metaphor for a vast, pulsing financial network that, in its pursuit of profits around the globe, has lost its sense of purpose and connection with the communities and regions it once served.

For all of the advances, today's financial markets are a far cry from the efficient market mechanisms they were conceived as. Of the trillions of dollars that flow through our exchanges, perhaps 1 percent goes to productive use—that is, to funding companies through initial and secondary offerings so they can innovate and expand. The other 99 percent is trading and speculation. (And that doesn't factor in the trades conducted on private networks known, rather ominously, as "dark pools," or the trillions of dollars worth of derivative side bets.)

"There is no doubt the trend has moved away from the markets as the mechanism for raising capital," says John Katovich, former general counsel for the Pacific Stock Exchange and founder of Katovich & Associates. "Now it is completely dwarfed by the billions of shares of a speculative nature that are just flying around."

Just look at the NYSE. In 2009, just 17 percent of its revenue was from new companies listing on the exchange. The largest revenue generators were global derivatives trading (28 percent) and cash trading (22 percent).[5]

If initial public offerings are a measure of a vibrant, well-functioning economy, then we are failing miserably. The number of initial public offerings has dropped off steeply in the United States. In 2009, there were just 69 IPOs; in 2010, that number rose to around 130, according to Renaissance Capital in Greenwich, Connecticut. The IPO market is cyclical, and it was already beginning to revive in late 2010, with white-hot tech startups like Facebook and Groupon preparing for possible public debuts. But we're still a long way from the peak of 756 IPOs in 1996. Secondary offerings—when public companies sell additional shares on the market—have also diminished in importance as a source of capital. (Of course, when corporations can lock in long-term interest rates of practically zero, thanks to Fed policy, bonds are an irresistible alternative.)

And who are the lucky few raising public capital these days? They are likely to be mature companies rather than the younger growth firms we typically associate with IPOs. In the past few years, General Motors, Banco Santander, and Visa have made their public debuts (or repeat performance in the case of GM). A good number of IPOs are being brought to market by private equity firms that took the companies private and are looking to cash out. Private equity firms were behind 39 of the 161 companies in the IPO pipeline as of September 2010, according to Renaissance Capital.[6] Those companies include HCA, the largest U.S. hospital operator (owned by KKR, Bain Capital, and Bank of America); Toys "R" Us (KKR, Bain Capital, and Vornado Realty Trust); and AMC Entertainment (Marquee Holdings, an investment company controlled by private-equity investors including JPMorgan Partners and Apollo Global Management).

The market debutantes are also likely to be foreign. For the first nine months of 2010, non-U.S.-based companies represented about a third of activity and capital raised on U.S.-based markets. Over that period, 30 foreign companies, including 19 from China, raised $4.1 billion, according to PricewaterhouseCoopers. "We're seeing smaller, rapidly-growing companies from around the world take advantage of the IPO market for raising capital to fuel growth—and we expect that trend to continue," noted

Scott Gehsmann, capital markets partner with PwC Transaction Services.[7]

Small and mid-sized domestic companies—the engines of job creation and innovation that were once the mainstay of IPO markets—are now as rare as a floor broker.

Our public markets were in decline long before the financial crisis of 2008. In a provocative paper on the state of the IPO market, David Weild and Edward Kim, capital markets advisors at Grant Thornton LLP, trace a dropoff in publicly listed companies back to 1997.[8] The electronic trading that transformed the stock markets around that time also rippled through the broader financial ecosystem. The rise of online discount brokers and new order handling rules reduced commissions and spreads, eroding the profit margins of traditional market specialists and investment banks. As transaction costs plummeted, trading exploded (remember day traders?).

In what Weild and Kim call "an epic case of unintended consequences," the new economics of low-cost transactions favored large cap stocks over small ones and ushered in the age of casino capitalism that thrives on opaqueness and risk. The profits embedded in the spreads and commissions of the old model supported critical functions such as sales, equity research, and market making, where investment banks commit their own capital to ensure a liquid market in a stock. In the new world of cheap transactions, those functions fell away for all but the most profitable stocks. Boutique investment banks that once catered to small companies saw the writing on the wall and sold out to bigger banks. Without those critical support functions, the shares of many small-cap companies have languished in obscurity, and many have delisted from the major exchanges. At the same time fewer small companies can make it to market.

Each year since 2000, more companies have delisted than have gone public. The total number of companies listed on the major U.S. exchanges has slid 22 percent, from nearly 7,000 companies in 1991 to 5,400 in 2008. When adjusted for GDP growth, the decline is a more startling 53 percent, according to Weild and Kim.

That is cause for concern. Without a vibrant IPO market, venture capital investment tends to lag, as VC firms devote more resources to their existing portfolio companies to keep them going. It also dampens job growth. The bulk of jobs at venture-backed companies—up to 92 percent by one estimate—are created *after* they go public. Instead of aiming for an IPO, the exit plan for many VCs these days is to push their startups into the arms of deep-pocketed buyers. (Apple, Microsoft, and Google alone were sitting on $90 billion in cash in late 2010.) Mergers and acquisitions, however, tend to result in job reductions rather than additions. Weild and Kim calculate that, had IPOs kept pace with GDP growth, an additional 22 million jobs might have been created from 1997 to 2008.

The long-term trends don't bode well for American entrepreneurship and innovation. "The whole ecosystem to support small-cap companies has shrunk," Weild, a former vice chairman of NASDAQ and capital markets advisor at Grant Thornton, told the *New York Times*. "This infrastructure is every bit as important as bridges, roads, and tunnels. Without it, you undermine growth."[9]

The Wild, Wild West

The drift toward speculation rather than investment has been underway for decades. Institutions, rather than individuals, now dominate the market. In 1950, individual investors (or retail investors, in industry parlance) owned 90 percent or more of corporate shares; today they own less than 30 percent.[10] Individuals still participate in the market, of course, but they do so largely through institutional intermediaries such as mutual funds and pension funds. As SEC general counsel Brian G. Cartwright noted in a 2007 speech, "Our understanding of financial markets has become far more sophisticated and mathematical. . . . The amateur plays at a disadvantage." It's part of a trend that Cartwright inelegantly terms "deretailization," in which individual investors, or non-accredited ones, in any case, are increasingly marginal players in the stock market, and are cut entirely out of new institution-only markets and alternative asset classes such as venture capital and private equity.[11] Individuals who want a piece of Facebook, for example, will have to wait until the social network company goes public, while venture capital investors and some Goldman Sachs clients were able to buy in beforehand.

The rise of institutional ownership has coincided with the shrinking holding time for stocks and the increasingly speculative nature of the market. Institutions must show quarterly results, so their time horizons and investment decisions are not necessarily geared toward the long term. That, in turn, pressures publicly traded companies to manage their business for the short term and focus on the all-important quarterly earnings. The trading mentality puts little emphasis on the fundamental value—or values—of a company, or its long-term worth.

Today, more than 6 billion shares trade hands on the NYSE every day, up from 100 million in the early 1980s—a 60-fold increase.[12] In 1940, investors held stocks for an average of seven years; by 2007, that was down to seven months, according to NYSE data. Factoring in high-frequency computerized trading, others have pegged the average holding period at more like 11 seconds.[13]

Can we still be called share*holders* when the average length of time a stock is held can be measured in quarterly reporting periods, or even seconds?

As direct public offering expert Drew Field has written:

> We are sold shares that were issued forty years ago. They have nothing to do anymore with supplying capital. We're just buying from someone else who is selling. We're betting that the trading price will go up and the sellers are betting it won't. None of our money will actually get to the business that once issued the shares. It's likely that it isn't even shareownership that we're buying. We may be sold options, futures, swaps or other derivatives, which are even more remote from any business use of capital... . This recycling of gambling symbols, where one side of a trade wins and the other side loses, has become the "capital market."

This cultural shift has been aided and abetted by financial "innovation." Our stock markets have been hijacked lately by one such advance: high-frequency trading, where superfast computers are programmed with sophisticated algorithms to buy and sell stocks in rapid-fire succession. The goal is to take advantage of small price differentials that exist for fractions of a second (think day traders on silicon steroids). These robotrades now account for at least 60 percent of all trading activity—the trading equivalent of spam.

The practice is so lucrative and the trading speeds so fast that high-frequency traders, from Goldman Sachs to privately held GetGo LLC, pay the New York Stock Exchange tens of thousands of dollars a month to "colocate" their black boxes in the exchange's new electronic data center in New Jersey. The couple-of-millisecond advantage that physical proximity buys allows the robotraders to sniff out and act on data before anyone else has a chance to see it. For its part, the NYSE hopes colocation opportunities will help it win back trading business that has shifted to the "dark pools," where institutional investors can anonymously buy and sell large blocks of shares.

The robotraders say they are doing a service by increasing liquidity so that there is always a ready market for stocks. Critics accuse them of "front-running," or jumping ahead of other trades, and distorting the markets by flooding the system with faux buy and sell orders—in other words, cheating. At best, there is little social utility to these high-frequency trades. At worst, the algorithm-based black boxes can behave in unpredictable and dangerous ways. It's one thing to have a computer firing off zillions of trades a second, but multiply that times hundreds of computers, and you're talking serious potential for chaos.

Exhibit A: the flash crash of May 6, 2010. On an otherwise slow afternoon, the market suddenly began an alarming drop. The Dow Jones Industrial Average plunged more than 600 points in a matter of minutes, only to quickly recover. It took months to pinpoint the cause: the sale of $4.1 billion worth of futures contracts by a Kansas mutual fund. As high-frequency trading programs kicked in, the contracts changed hands an astonishing 27,000 times in 14 seconds—or almost 2,000 trades a second.[14] Once again, regulators are scrambling to keep pace with Wall Street "innovations." (And the innovators are trying to buy their way out of regulation: High-frequency trading firms contributed at least $490,000 to the 2010 congressional elections—about five times the amount they gave in 2006.[15])

Meanwhile, mini–flash crashes keep occurring, making market watchers nervous that another big one could happen any time. "It's like seeing cracks in a dam," James J. Angel, a professor at the McDonough School of Business at Georgetown University, told the *Times*. "One day, I don't know when, there will be another earthquake."

Or as Andrew W. Lo, director of the Massachusetts Institute of Technology's Laboratory for Financial Engineering put it: "The U.S. equities markets have become the Wild, Wild West."[16]

No wonder investors are skittish. They have been fleeing stocks in droves for the relative safety of bonds and fixed income. In the wake of the flash crash, investors pulled more than $19 billion from U.S. stock funds in May 2010 alone.[17] And they were poised to plow $300 billion into bond funds in 2010, an amount second only to the previous year's $350 billion infusion. That's quite a statement, considering that bonds are barely keeping pace with even ultralow inflation. In fact, some investors have purchased bonds at *negative* face value.

The big picture is not pretty. Citing two decades worth of advances, including electronic trading, dark pools, flash orders, new trading venues, unregulated derivatives, and high-frequency trading, Thomas Peterffy, an industry veteran and founder of Interactive Brokers Group, told a group assembled in Paris in October for a World Federation of Exchanges conference: "What we've got today is a complete mess."[18]

That is a shame. In its original form and intent—as a mechanism for marshaling passive savings for productive and profitable economic growth—the concept of the stock market is something of a marvel. The markets financed the growth of the nation, supplying the capital that allowed key enterprises from railroads to Silicon Valley startups to grow and prosper. Investors, too, were well served by the markets. "When people started meeting under the buttonwood tree to exchange shares, it was pretty cool, it was working. But that is not our markets today," says Katovich, the attorney. "In so many different ways, we're letting this market control suppress the very thing that it was meant to be supporting in the beginning. So why not come back to our markets? What do we do to engage the market with companies again on a livable scale?"

Reengaging the Market

Those questions are being asked in communities across the country. In Lancaster, Pennsylvania, an area best known for its Amish population, one possible answer is quietly taking shape.

On a sultry, late-summer morning in 2010, I boarded a Keystone corridor train bound for Harrisburg to see for myself. The pastoral scenery gave little hint of the economic carnage visited upon the state; Harrisburg, the capital at the end of the line, was on the verge of bankruptcy. I disembarked in Lancaster, where I was met by Trexler Proffitt, a professor of organization studies at Franklin & Marshall College, a liberal-arts college founded in 1787 with funding from Benjamin Franklin. In describing ourselves so we could identify each other, Proffitt had told me he was "medium in every way." Well, maybe not in name. And certainly not in ambition. Proffitt—who is indeed middling height with neither-here-nor-there brown hair—is on a mission to create a local stock exchange that would serve companies and investors in the eight-county Lancaster region.

The exchange, which he calls LanX, will address a funding gap for companies that have already tapped personal savings, friends and family, and community development capital, but are unable or unwilling to obtain private equity from venture capitalist or angel investors. LanX will help such companies raise between $500,000 and $5 million through direct public offerings of stock or notes (debt), and provide a marketplace where they can be traded. Proffitt figures LanX could inject $10 million annually into the local economy.

Proffitt became captivated with the idea a few years ago after attending a talk by Michael Shuman about local investing, but it took on new resonance after the recession dealt a blow to many communities and small businesses in the region. The need to get capital to small businesses that fall between the cracks has always been there, he says, but in challenging economic times it becomes more urgent. "After a boom-and-bust cycle, people start to question who they can trust. And trust is at the core of all market behavior. If you don't have trust in the people or the system, you can't do anything," says Proffitt. "So how do you restore that trust? I think it comes back to basic human relationships. And where can you get that except at the local level with something you can really understand and get your head around."

Local Stock Exchange

A local stock exchange handles all of the functions of a stock market—listing company shares, providing price information, and facilitating trading—but for a specific region. As the major stock exchanges continue their global consolidation, local exchanges would offer an alternative for a region's companies and investors, much like the small exchanges that once flourished across the United States and other countries.

The Lancaster region already has a strong buy-local program and is developing a local currency. But financing is a critical part of the equation, Proffitt believes. Without adequate funds, local enterprises cannot effectively compete with their larger, national rivals.

The area has many small and midsized companies that could benefit from a localized financial market. One of those is Wolfgang Candy Co., a fourth-generation chocolate maker across the river from Lancaster in York. The Wolfgang family had already been immersed in the art of candy making when, in 1921, Paul C. Wolfgang started his hand-dipped chocolate company. He peddled his chocolates at farmers markets from the back of a pony cart, but the company's main customers were, until recently, churches, schools, and other organizations that sold the candy in fund-raising drives. Today, Wolfgang Candy attracts 17,000 visitors a year to tour its Willy Wonka–like factory, where 150 employees make 120 products, including favorites such as dark chocolate–dipped berries and pretzels.

The family-run company seems to have bucked the old rule that the first generation creates the entrepreneurial success and the third generation runs it into the ground. In this case, the third generation invested heavily in plant and equipment to modernize the chocolate factory, while the fourth generation and current management has continued to modernize while branching out into retail and lucrative private labeling ventures. As Michael Schmid, managing partner of Wolfgang Candy, explains, private label brands were all the rage among retailers, but the trend had barely touched the confection market. Wolfgang's management seized the opportunity, and soon the company was making candy for Walgreens and Giant Eagle, a major regional chain. The company also developed its own brands, including Jungle Jacks chocolate-covered animal crackers and the Eve's line of chocolate-dipped cookies. Today, Wolfgang confections are featured in 140 grocery stores from Pennsylvania to West Virginia, as well as in several national chains. Sales increased 30 percent in 2009 and about 18 percent in 2010, to $12 million, even as the effects of the recession wore on.

Wolfgang's future looks sweet, indeed. The company has an opportunity to develop seven candy products for one of the country's largest drugstore chains. "It takes a lot of investment to make these things happen," says Schmid. And that can temporarily eat into cash flow. On the bright side, the company can use an existing $1 million manufacturing line, paid for with an SBA-backed loan, to produce the new candies. The high-tech line, Schmid points out, replaced low-skill, repetitious labor with highly skilled workers who can program the robots. In 2009, when it installed the line, which features robots named Lucy and Ethel, the company hired 40 new workers. Still, the development costs are substantial. Each new product requires new molds, which can cost $15,000 apiece, as well as new packaging and printing plates.

The company had a $3 million credit line but reduced it when it wasn't being used. Now the bank is reluctant to reinstate it. As for other options, he says, the company is too small to attract venture capital, and it is not plugged into angel investor networks.

"I don't think the solution is to stop sales growth and slow the business," says Schmid, who earned an MBA after serving in the Navy. "So local is the way to go. The local community knows and understands the brand."

Schmid would love to see Proffitt's LanX plans come to fruition. He says he would probably sell shares or bonds through a direct, in-state offering, and list on the exchange. "That would require us to disclose more, but if you're a company with integrity, that's not an issue. There's nothing I love more than talking about my company. Can an investor call up Cisco and talk to John Chambers? I think there's actually less risk involved by being able to invest in a brand that you know. And you always can call up Mike Schmid and talk."

The idea of a local exchange also appeals to Terry Brett, president of Kimberton Whole Foods. Started in 1986, the company has grown from one store in Kimberton to five in eastern Pennsylvania, with more than $10 million in annual sales. Today it is the largest-volume independent natural food retailer in the state. The stores, with their mix of local, organic, and biodynamic products and their community-centered events, are beloved by locals, as a quick glance online reveals.

"Way better than the now 'commercialized' other 'Whole Foods.' I'm able to buy more Local items and the service is friendlier!" writes one reviewer on Yelp.com.

"Hands down the best natural foods store in the area," raves another.

Kimberton Whole Foods' 84 employees receive full dental, disability, and health-care coverage, as well as profit sharing through a 401K plan. The company was named a "top workplace of 2010" by the *Philadelphia Inquirer, Philadelphia Daily News,* and Philly.com.

Still, that's not enough to keep Brett from worrying about competition from large-scale national chains that have already gobbled up many of the early independent retailers. In retailing, size counts. Suppliers and distributors favor big volume buyers. So in November, Brett gathered some of the remaining independent natural food retailers to discuss ways that they could work together to preserve their independence and fend off advances by national chains and deep-pocketed private equity firms, like one that recently approached him declaring that "locally owned" stores were the wave of the future. One idea is to form a sort of virtual chain akin to a buyers' cooperative, that would let the independents pool their purchasing for added clout with distributors.

Failing that, says Brett, the only option is to continue to grow and open new stores to stay competitive. But with margins already squeezed, it is hard to convince a bank to lend. He doesn't want to be forced to sell, like so many others before him, to a cash-rich investor that would likely discontinue many of the benefits and practices that make the Kimberton stores an attractive place to work and shop. That's got Brett thinking about other alternatives. "How can you create a partnership with investors that is not solely about money, where you get the participation and buy-in from the local population?" he wonders.

LanX, he thinks, may be a solution. "It's a wonderful idea. It's another way of supporting your regional economy. Investors and local stockholders would be less likely to vote their neighbors out of a job. I'd much rather see something like this than an equity group looking to buy up 300 stores and then selling them to an even bigger investor," all the while exploiting the fact that they are "local," he says.

A Working Model

Back in Lancaster, Trexler Proffitt is quixotically pursuing a complex feat of modern capitalism with a staff of student interns and no real budget to speak of. On the day I visited in September, a new group of interns had assembled for their first LanX staff meeting. Sitting around a classroom in flipflops and shorts, MacBooks propped open in front of them, the half-dozen or so students updated Proffitt on their first assignments—researching securities regulations, writing a business plan, contacting local government agencies, coming up with a fundraising list.

When I asked them why they applied for this particular internship, their answers were heartfelt and informed by current events. One student, Annie, explained that in her city and state government class, the context of all the discussions had been how so many cities—such as Harrisburg—and states are struggling financially. "You should to be able to invest in the place you live in and make a tangible difference."

For Erin, it was about creating a level of self-sufficiency and not having to depend on government bailouts. "People can put their money in something they can see has a real effect." Lorenzo, a soft spoken young man in a newsboy cap, believed that the local exchange was a new solution to many of society's problems. It was Jeannie, a returning intern, though, who expressed the excitement that was in all of their voices. "The greatest thing about this is that no one else is doing it," she chirped.

Indeed, the only real attempt at a local exchange to date has not been terribly promising. Called Investbx, it was created in 2008 to connect investors and small and midsized companies in England's West Midlands region. (England, too, once had thriving regional exchanges—as many as 22 a century ago). Companies can raise up to £2 million (or $3.2 million) on Investbx, which is regulated by England's FSA. The exchange has streamlined the process of issuing shares, and it commissions research on companies its lists.

It started out promisingly enough. Teamworks Karting, which runs a popular indoor go-cart center in the area, raised more than £735,000 from West Midlands investors to open another center. And Key Technologies, a high-tech firm with 232 employees and annual sales of £26 million, floated shares worth nearly £3 million on the exchange.

As of late 2010, however, Investbx listed just three companies— in addition to the Teamworks and Key Technologies, there is an investment firm. And trading has been light: The exchange holds a periodic auction to trade shares. Investbx will soon be put to the test. Launched with a £3 million government grant, the exchange will soon have to become self-supporting.

As Investbx illustrates, there are real challenges in creating a viable local exchange. The first is size. A community needs a certain mass to support a dedicated exchange. Proffitt figures that between the eight counties that LanX would serve, there are 2 million people and a GDP of $60 billion—about the size of Slovakia, which, incidentally, has its own exchange.

A local exchange would also have to attract a large enough pool of compelling companies to interest investors. Proffitt has drummed up enthusiasm for his idea among some area businesses. In addition to Wolfgang Candy and Kimberton Whole Foods, several other companies have expressed interest, including the manufacturer of an innovative, energy-efficient engine, a maker of recycled paper products, a regional water utility, and a restaurant and shared community kitchen. But getting them to take the plunge is another story.

On the flip side of the equation, an exchange must have sufficient investor participation to provide the necessary capital and liquidity. Once again, though, the idea seems to strike a chord. Janel Widdowson, a financial advisor based in Lancaster, says many of her clients, especially younger ones, feel disenfranchised from the financial system. "The complexity and instantaneous streaming of data has narrowed our time horizons. We don't invest anymore; we're traders," she says. A local stock exchange could "bring it back to its fundamentals." Her clients, she says, are hungry for alternatives. "LanX could satisfy that craving."

Then there is the question of support, such as research and sales, that Grant Thornton's Weild and Kim argue is vital to a well-functioning market. Who will vet the companies and tell their stories? Will there be a local equivalent of Moodys? These questions tie into the bigger issue of business model. Can local exchanges support themselves on listing and transaction fees? Or are they better structured as nonprofits or public-private partnerships? These are all questions that have yet to be answered.

The biggest challenge, however, may be navigating the legal hurdles. Exchanges are closely monitored by the SEC. The major exchanges, like the NYSE or NASDAQ, are what is known as self-regulatory organizations, meaning they are responsible for policing themselves. The SEC also has authorized Alternative Trading Systems (ATS), markets run by registered broker-dealers that electronically match buyers and sellers (typically accredited investors). The SEC would have to sanction any local exchange— a prospect many consider unlikely at the moment. Alternatively, a new exchange could partner with an existing exchange or ATS with regulatory approval.

A more immediate concern for Proffitt is funding to pull off his plan. Although all of these challenges loom large, he has lately found some promising support. He's been talking with groups in Maui, Detroit, Hartford, Connecticut, and Toronto that are looking to create their own local exchanges. In Hawaii, for example, where 85 percent of energy and food is imported, the hope is that a local exchange could help finance new ventures in these and other areas and help diversify the economy, says David Fisher, a consultant and former director of the Hawaii Small Business Development Center and one of the leaders of the initiative. There is plenty of capital in Hawaii, he says, but most of it is invested on the mainland. In March, the state senate approved a resolution convening a working group to investigate the creation of a Hawaii exchange.

In Toronto, the focus is on regional enterprises that make a positive social or environmental impact, but are often held back by a lack of capital. The Social Venture Exchange (SVX), as the market is called, has attracted a broad coalition of government, corporate, nonprofit, and local business supporters, and is expected to be up and running in June. Initially, the offerings will be available to accredited investors only, but the goal is to broaden the system to include retail investors within the next few years.

The groups have discussed collaborating, perhaps creating a nonprofit coalition of local exchanges that share a technology platform. "The movement needs one working model to show the way," says Proffitt. "We haven't started a new local stock exchange of this type in 80 years. We don't know how to do it anymore, and I'm talking about rediscovering that capability."[19]

DPO + Local Exchange = Game Changer

A lot of others are, too. In England, the local exchange concept has been talked up by politicians from local leaders all the way up to Deputy Prime Minister Nick Clegg. It is also being embraced in Wales, where just 20 Welsh companies are listed on the London Stock Exchange.[20] In the U.S., Slow Money is planning a series of regional exchanges to help food-related businesses raise capital. The idea behind all of the initiatives is to carve out a safe place where people can put their investment dollars to work in real companies engaged in productive businesses that benefit their communities. In doing so, they aim to reestablish a connection between investors and local companies, and to restore a sense of purpose and trust to our markets.

The reincarnation of local stock markets presents some interesting possibilities. For one, it offers a solution to the major drawback of so many locavesting models: liquidity. If investors can cash out of an investment when they need to, the proposition is much more appealing. In fact, many see the DPO-plus-local exchange model as the ultimate game changer for local investing.

At a time when many communities are promoting buy-local campaigns, the exchanges could serve as a focal point for local economic activity, as well as a branding tool for the region and its unique local enterprises. (If Virginia is for Lovers, why can't Lancaster be for Investors?) Like the early regional exchanges, they might reflect a specialization—maybe biotech in Boston, manufacturing in Detroit, or food and agriculture in Lancaster. Most would likely seek a diverse range of small and midsized companies based in the area that fall within the so-called funding gap. Activity on the exchanges may be slow, and there won't be the kind of volatility that allows traders to make a quick killing— but then, that's exactly the point.[21]

Despite a groundswell of interest in the topic, the local exchange concept has a giant "proceed with caution" sign hanging over it. The SEC is likely to take a keen interest, and any serious attempts that gain traction would likely come under fire from the financial industry. Even longtime advocates of local exchanges are wary. "The worst thing that could happen is for someone to rush out a local stock exchange without thinking it through, and have investors get burned," warns Don Shaffer, president & CEO of RSF Social Finance. That would create a black eye that might set back the local investing movement, he says.

And the technical and regulatory expertise required is daunting. "There's a lot of talk about creating community stock exchanges, but does anyone understand how to do that?" asks Michael Van Patten, a Wall Street veteran and founder of Mission Markets, an online marketplace for investments with a social or environmental impact that launched in 2010. (Workers Diners, for example, will be traded on the Mission Market's social capital market after its DPO.)

Van Patten, a triathlete who lives in the hedge fund haven of Greenwich, Connecticut, has become a respected voice in the local investing community. He shares a growing view that socially responsible investing, which often means simply screening out undesirable investments, is limited. The money invested in a large company, even if it is truly a good corporate citizen, does not necessarily trickle down to communities. "Investors need to have viable alternatives to invest in companies they know and have a relationship with," says Van Patten. Local investing is more like proactive impact investing, he says, where there are very clear benefits in addition to financial gain.

From Van Patten's vantage point, some of the local exchange ambitions are, well, naive. Rather than view Wall Street as the enemy, he says, the local exchanges must learn to embrace and work within the system. "It's a regulatory business. It's not like running a shoe shop," says Van Patten. "They've got to let the people who understand this business do what they do." It just so happens that Mission Markets, a registered broker-dealer, could serve as a platform and provide legal cover and expertise for emerging local exchanges. A local exchange could have its own distinct portal on the Mission Markets platform, for a fee. Among the small cast of aspiring local exchanges most are weighing that option against building their own systems. It's a question of economics. But also philosophy. The Lancaster-Toronto-Hawaii coalition favors a shared "open source" approach, with the goal of getting more people to understand the mechanics of a stock market, rather than it remaining a Wall Street black art. "I think this kind of openness and accountability will help businesses, investors, and the community," says Fisher.

Alternative Markets

If the idea of local exchanges seems farfetched or a little too retro for our globalized age, consider that it is just one concept being floated for an alternative to our casino-like markets. (And heck, if 1970s hair bands can make a comeback why not local stock exchanges?) In fact, ideas are bubbling up from some surprising corners of the industry, suggesting a growing sense that our public markets are failing us.

Former SEC commissioner Steve Wallman, now founder and CEO of online brokerage firm FOLIOfn, believes that investors could benefit from a safe-haven market. "The way the marketplace has evolved, not just with respect to capital raising but with respect to the ability for individual investors to invest fairly, has not been good. There is fast arising the question of whether there needs to be two separate markets," he says, one where professional traders can ply their high-frequency and algorithmic trading strategies, and one for those seeking to raise capital or invest for the long term. "A scenario that may need to be considered, therefore, is one in which dark pools and high-frequency trading exist as they wish, but are kept away from the investing, as opposed to trading, markets. That way, the public investing markets can be deployed once again to do what they do best: provide a means for investing where participants are engaged in reasonable price discovery and issuers can raise capital, all for the long term."

Meanwhile, David Weild and Edward Kim of Grant Thornton have proposed the creation of an alternative exchange that companies could choose to list on. This "alternative market segment," as they call it, would be open to all investors, and subject to all of the usual SEC regulations. Here's where they get really radical: While computers would display prices, all orders would be placed using that anachronistic communications device, the telephone. Weild and Kim envision recreating the ecosystem of old, with market makers, specialists, and brokers who would earn higher commissions and spreads in return for providing traditional services like market support, sales, and research. This, they believe, would attract small-cap companies that are typically ignored in today's markets.

It seems the way forward for our capital markets might be rooted in the past.

Game Plan for Locavestors

Local stock exchanges—like the kind that once dotted the land and served their regional economies—are staging a cautious comeback. They are seen by their proponents as an alternative to the frenzied speculation of modern markets and a way to reinvigorate capital investment in small, innovative firms and regional economies.

Pros:
- Liquidity. Liquidity. Liquidity. Investors would be able to sell shares if they needed to, rather than having to hold them indefinitely, making many types of local investments more attractive.
- Regional exchanges could lead to a greater volume and diversity of publicly traded companies and help offset the decline in listings at major exchanges.
- Investors would gain access to a diverse pool of qualified companies in their region to invest in.
- Local exchanges would be free of casino-like speculation and high-frequency trading—traders won't be attracted to markets where there is not a lot of action.
- Communities can take back control and promote their own economies.

Cons:
- Any new exchanges will likely take some time to get established.
- While the markets would provide liquidity, trading is likely to be light and even intermittent.
- Small companies of the type that may list on a local exchange may carry more risk than large, well-capitalized ones.
- The availability and quality of company research may not be the same as for large caps that trade on the major exchanges.

The Bottom Line: A very compelling idea that could, if well executed, provide a safe, alternative marketplace and important source of liquidity for small, locally based companies and investors.

For More Information:
- LanX - http://lancasterstockexchange.org/
- Hawaii Stock Exchange - http://hilocalexchange.org/
- Social Venture Exchange - http://socialventureexchange.org/
- Mission Markets - Missionmarkets.com

Conclusion

What would the world be like if we invested 50 percent of our assets within 50 miles of where we live?

That we may never know. But a shift of 10 percent or 5 percent or even 1 percent is within reach, and would have a significant and visible impact. As new models for local investing take shape and the infrastructure and ecosystem to support them evolves, exciting new possibilities are opening up for investors, entrepreneurs, and entire communities.

These developments are critical to our future competitiveness, and represent the kinds of financial innovations we should be encouraging—funding solutions, rather than more exotic ways to place bets. We have witnessed the failings of the unfettered free market system, tallied in lost jobs, rising inequality, and a creeping monoculture. Economic power and advantage increasingly accrues to a coterie of global corporations and financial institutions and the wealthy people who control them. Meanwhile, our government policies and financial markets are failing the most dynamic sector of the economy, small business, which is responsible for virtually all net job creation. It's not a winning formula.

Globalization is here to stay. But it's time for a backup plan. It's time to hedge our bets by investing in the kinds of enterprises that enrich us economically and socially, and help build healthy, productive local economies. Let's get back to investing in the native genius of America.

Local Funds

There are still many issues to be worked out. A fundamental challenge to all locavesting models is the economics associated with small investments. The process of due diligence—the research into the management, finances, and market positioning of a company—are a large but necessary cost of any investment. Yet it requires about the same amount of work to investigate a $50,000 investment as it does a $50 million investment, so the costs are disproportionately high for smaller deals. That cuts into the potential returns—one reason why Wall Street firms focus only on the largest, most profitable deals.

There is also a behavioral issue. As investors, we are used to investing our money the conventional way—in the stock market, mutual funds, bond funds, and CDs. The idea of taking a flier on a local business is alien to most of us.

One way to address these obstacles is through the creation of funds that can make investments on behalf of individuals. The funds could handle the legwork of identifying and vetting candidates, allowing investors to diversify their holdings over a range of companies in a particular geographic location. Initiatives such as the National Cooperative Business Alliance's co-op fund and the Opportunity Finance Network's CDFI fund—both being created in partnership with the Calvert Foundation—are promising. But we need more options like that.

In Brooklyn, for example, a creative army of young entrepreneurs is producing artisanal goods—like Nunu chocolates, Rick's Picks pickles, Liddabit candy, Salvatore Bklyn Ricotta, and Kombucha Brooklyn, to name just a few. There is also a new wave of craft distillers, microbrewers, and even wine makers in the borough. Many of these young entrepreneurs are growing quickly, expanding from flea markets to major retail stores and restaurants. (There's even a new restaurant in Manhattan devoted to Brooklyn-made products.) Why, I have wondered, couldn't we have a Brooklyn Artisanal Fund? That way the people who buy and appreciate these products could support their producers on another level and participate directly in their growth. Local funds wouldn't have to be limited to micro-enterprises; they could also serve established small and midsized businesses in a region.

For now, there are few, if any, funds like this, at least that are open to everyday, nonaccredited investors. Here again, economics come into play. Would the cost of vetting these tiny companies and maintaining a fund swamp its likely profits? Or, like the venture capital model, would one or two homerun companies carry the day? These questions have yet to be answered.

In the meantime, there are some interesting twists on the fund theme. Leslie Christian's Upstream 21 is one. It is an investment vehicle for accredited investors that acquires small, successful, sustainably run companies in the Pacific Northwest—so far, its portfolio of three companies reflects the region's forestry tradition. Upstream acts as a holding company, operating the companies as wholly owned subsidiaries and helping them improve their businesses. It's sort of a Berkshire Hathaway for local investing. Christian, a Wall Street veteran and Upstream's Warren Buffett, started the fund in 2004 after watching so many socially responsible pioneers get swallowed up by multinationals (hello, Ben & Jerry). Often, when a business owner needs to sell, that is the only option. But a multinational may move jobs out of the region and discontinue the values-based practices of the founders. Upstream provides an alternative, one that keeps jobs in the region and principles intact. In fact, Upstream 21's charter specifically mandates that it consider the best interests of employees, the environment, and suppliers along with those of shareholders—an idea that was expanded upon by B Labs with B Corporations, a new business structure being adopted by states that embeds triple bottom line accountability in its charter.

There are other conceptually similar funds, like Farmland LP, which acquires conventional farmland and converts it to more profitable and sustainable organic operations in Oregon's Willamette Valley. Like Upstream, it is open to accredited and institutional investors only.

As with all locavesting models, the real impact comes when all types of individuals can participate, not just high-net-worth investors. (If Upstream 21 were to go public, for example, ordinary investors could buy shares).

Christian believes there is strong momentum behind the local investing movement. Small businesses have always struggled to raise capital. The difference today, she says, is the demand from investors. "Normal everyday investors are saying we would like an option, we do not want to have all of our money in the global market, we want a local market. And that's what is new, I think." She pauses. "Well, not exactly new. A hundred years ago that's how it was done."

Eat Local, Buy Local, Invest Local

Locavesting is in its very early days. And the regulatory challenges cannot be overstated. The SEC is acutely aware of many of the issues holding back small business capitalization, but it must balance that with its duty to protect investors. "It's a tightrope we're trying to walk," one SEC official told me.

Several modest proposals could help, such as the crowdfunding exemption for small investments of up to $100, and a proposal to raise the threshold for when a company is considered public. (Right now, when a company reaches 500 shareholders and $10 million in assets, it automatically becomes a public reporting company even if their shares are privately held—a trigger that undermines the "pennies from many" crowdfunding and DPO models, and that has forced companies such as Google and Facebook onto an IPO path before they are ready).

The Kaufmann Foundation, which focuses on entrepreneurship, has a compelling proposal. It advocates exempting companies with a market capitalization of less than $100 million from securities regulations as a way to reinvigorate a languishing small cap marketplace. Others suggest simplifying the regulatory thicket of overlapping state and federal securities laws.

"These questions—how do we encourage small business, how do we encourage new ideas, how do we encourage entrepreneurs to do what they do best—are critically important for the future growth of the economy and for the innovation of new products and services that we want to bring to the marketplace of ideas," said Steve Wallman, founder of FOLIOfn and a former SEC commissioner. "It's a great challenge for people who care about public policy to figure out how to do that right."

Local, state, and federal governments also play a critical role. Like Illinois, they can stop looking to giant corporations for salvation and realize that, if each of their homegrown businesses could hire one person, they would have a stronger, more diverse, and less vulnerable economy—at a fraction of the cost. Many successful initiatives, such as Cleveland's Evergreen Cooperatives and Toronto's Social Venture Exchange, could not have happened without the support of enlightened local governments and institutions. I will leave the economic development and policy fixes for the experts. But as citizens and investors, we, too, have a vital role to play. As the Clare cops and the Brooklyn bookworms, and the Austin beer lovers showed, amazing things are possible when individuals get involved.

So check out your local merchants before reflexively heading off to that big-box store. Move your money to a community bank or credit union. Join a co-op. If you don't have local investment opportunities, join or start a local chapter of Slow Money or BALLE (Business Alliance for Local Living Economies). Think about where your dollars go. Support policies that actually help entrepreneurs, not just multinational business. And, whenever possible, eat local, buy local... and invest local.

Notes

Unless otherwise noted, all quotes come from interviews conducted by the author.

Introduction

1. From Christina Tosi interview on TheDairyShow.com, see http://vimeo .com/5569478.
2. Laura Conaway, "Wary of Wall Street? Invest in a Dairy Farm," NPR, March 12, 2009, www.npr.org/templates/story/story.php?storyId= 101794001.

Chapter 1

1. Matt Friedman, "President Obama meets small business owners at Edison Tastee Sub Shop," nj.com, July 28, 2010. David M. Herszenhorn and Jacki Calmes, "Obama Trumpets Democrats' Small-Business Bona Fides," *New York Times*, July 28, 2010. www.nj.com/news/index.ssf/2010/ 07/president_obama_greets_tastee.html.
2. Jake Sherman, "House Republicans unveil 'Pledge to America,'" Politico.com, Sept. 23, 2010. www.politico.com/news/stories/0910/ 42609.html; Dana Bash interview with John Boehner, CNN, Sept. 23, 2010, politicalticker.blogs.cnn.com/2010/09/23/exclusive-john-boehner-talks-with-dana-bash/.
3. "The Last Will and Testament of Benjamin Franklin," The Franklin Institute. www.fi.edu/franklin/family/lastwill.html.
4. Bruce H. Yenawine, *Benjamin Franklin and the Invention of Microfinance*, Pickering and Chatto Publishers, June 2010, London.
5. American Independent Business Alliance; see amiba.net/multiplier _effect.html.
6. Small Business Administration Office of Advocacy FAQ, Sept. 2010.
7. Kelly Edmiston, "The Role of Small Business and Large Business in Economic Development," Federal Reserve Bank of Kansas City, Economic Review, Second Quarter 2007.

8. Edward L. Glaeser, "Start-Up City," *City Journal*, Autumn 2010. www
.city-journal.org/2010/20_4_urban-entrepreneurship.html.

9. Kelly Edmiston, "The Role of Small Business and Large Business in
Economic Development."

10. Martin A. Sullivan, "U.S. Multinationals Cut U.S. Jobs While
Expanding Abroad," Sept. 13, 2010. http://taxprof.typepad.com/
files/128tn1102.pdf; Pallavi Gogoi, "Job Market Booming Overseas
for Many American Companies," Huffington Post, Dec. 28, 2010.
www.huffingtonpost.com/2010/12/28/job-market-booming-over-
seas_n_801839.html.

11. "Bailout May Cost $23.7 Trillion, Barofsky," Huffington Post, July 20,
2009. www.huffingtonpost.com/2009/07/20/bailout-may-cost-237-
tril_n_241512.html.

12. Damian Paletta, "Fight Over Consumer Agency Looms as Overhaul
Is Signed," *Wall Street Journal*, July 22, 2010. http://online.wsj.com/
article/SB10001424052748704746804575367502836650966.html

13. Steve Lohr, "Small Business: Job Role Highlighted," *New York Times*, Jan.
18, 1980. select.nytimes.com/gst/abstract.html?res=FA061FFF3B5A1
2728DDDA10994D9405B8084F1D3.

14. "The Cost of Winning an Election, 1986–2008," an analysis by the
Brookings Institution, can be found on The Campaign Finance
Institute Web site at www.cfinst.org/data/HistoricalStats.aspx.

15. Fred Wainwright, Center for Private Equity and Entrepreneurship,
Tuck School of Business at Dartmouth, Case # 5-0001, Jan. 10, 2005.

16. Q3 2010 Money Tree Report, PricewaterhouseCoopers and the
National Venture Capital Association.

17. "UNH Center for Venture Research: Angel Investors Flee Seed and
Start-Up Stage in First Half of 2010," Oct. 26, 2010, www.unh.edu/
news/cj_nr/2010/oct/lw26market.cfm.

18. John K. Paglia, Private Capital Markets Project, Pepperdine University,
Survey Report, Aug. 2009.

19. www.antiventurecapital.com/cboffer.html.

20. Catherine Clifford, "Bernanke: $40B in Small Biz Loans Disappears,"
CNNMoney.com, July 12, 2010 http://money.cnn.com/2010/07/12/
smallbusiness/small_business_credit_crunch/index.htm.

21. Nick Bunkley, "Fed Chief Urges Banks to Do More for Small
Business," *New York Times*, June 3, 2010. www.nytimes.com/2010/
06/04/business/economy/04fed.html.

22. Conor Dougherty and Luca Di Leo, "Banks Ease Loan Standards, but
Crunch Isn't Over," *Wall Street Journal*, Nov. 9, 2010.

23. Catherine Clifford, "Banks Pull Another $1 Billion from Small
Business Lending," CNN Money, Jan. 18, 2010. money.cnn.com/2010/
01/18/smallbusiness/small_business_lending_drop/.

24. National Small Business Association (NSBA), 2009 Year-End Report.
www.nsba.biz/surveys.shtml.

25. John K. Paglia, "2011 Economic Forecast," Private Capital Markets Project, Pepperdine University, Jan. 12, 2011.

26. Stacy Mitchell, "Taking Financial Reform into Our Own Hands," Huffington Post, July 14, 2010. www.huffintonpost.com/stacy-mitchell/talking-financial-reform-1_b_645587.html.

27. Institute for Local Self Reliance Community Banking Initiative www.newrules.org/news/charts-small-banks-small-business-lending.

28. Steven G. Craig and Pauline Hardee, University of Houston, "The Impact of Bank Consolidation on Small Business Credit Availability," *Journal of Banking and Finance,* April 2007, Volume 31, Issue 4.

29. IPOs counts vary, depending on who is doing the counting. This stat comes from David Weild and Edward Kim, "Market Structure Is Causing the IPO Crisis—and More," Grant Thornton Capital Market Series, June 2010. www.grantthornton.com/portal/site/gtcom/menuitem.91c078ed5c0ef4ca80cd8710033841ca/?vgnextoid=5bbe3429935bd110VgnVCM1000003a8314acRCRD. Other sources put the number of 2009 IPOs at 69.

30. Another cost is regulatory compliance, notably with Sarbanes-Oxley and its Section 404 requiring extensive internal company audits. The Dodd-Frank bill exempts companies with a market capitalization of less than $75 million from that requirement, but there are calls to raise the threshold further.

31. David Weild and Edward Kim, "Market Structure Is Causing the IPO Crisis—and More," Capital Market Series, Grant Thornton LLP, June 2010.

32. Ibid.

33. Calculated with data supplied by the NASDAQ OMX Group, Inc.

34. Report of the Advisory Committee on the Capital Formation and Regulatory Process, U.S. Securities and Exchange Commission, July 24, 1996. www.sec.gov/news/studies/capform.htm.

35. "B2B Finance: Credit Crunch Creates Opportunities for Large Corporations, Poses Policy Challenges," March 2010, Morgan Stanley.

36. Shuman arrives at $26 trillion by adding up the assets and liabilities held by households and nonprofits in 2009, including corporate equities, corporate bonds, mutual funds, pension fund reserves, and life insurance reserves, as detailed in the Fed's Flow of Funds data. By definition, these asset classes consist of publicly traded corporate equity and corporate bonds. See www.federalreserve.gov/RELEASES/z1/Current/z1.pdf.

Chapter 2

1. "Social networks of investors, mill managers, and mechanics raised the likelihood that new forms of textile production for the mass market would emerge in New England," explains David R. Meyer in his book *The Roots of American Industrialization,* John Hopkins University Press, 2003.

2   Will Payne, "How Kansas Drove Out a Set of Thieves," *Saturday Evening Post,* Dec. 2, 1911, courtesy of the Office of the Kansas Securities Commissioner, www.ksc.ks.gov/edu/bluesky.html.

3. Marilyn B. Cane and Peter Ferola, "Back to the Future: The States' Struggle to Re-Emerge as Defenders of Investors' Rights," *Business Law Journal,* May 1, 2005. Vol. 5, Issue 2. bizlawjournal.ucdavis.edu/archives/vol-5-no-2/Back-to-the-Future.html.

4. Dan Ernst, "Blue Sky Laws and the Progressive Regime," May 23, 2009 www.legalhistoryblog.blogspot.com/2009/05/blue-sky-laws-and-progressive-regime.html.

5. See Section 4(6) of the Securities Act.

6. In 1982 when Reg D was adopted, less than 2 percent of the population qualified as accredited investors. But given inflation and rising home values, the portion of the population that qualified climbed to more than 8 percent, according to the SEC. Home values have been battered, however, and the 2010 Dodd-Frank financial reform bill revised the accredited investor standard to exclude the value of an investor's primary residence, which for many people makes up the bulk of their net worth. So the number of accredited investors is probably closer to 2 percent of the population again.

7. In 2010, more than half of households with a net worth of $25 million or more invested in private equity and venture capital, according to *Wall Street Journal* columnist Robert Frank. http://blogs.wsj.com/wealth/2010/11/10/ultra-rich-pour-back-into-hedge-funds/.

8. SEC Office of Small Business Advocacy.

9. This is known as the *intrastate offering exemption* under section 3(a)(11) of the Securities Act.

10. For example, one Silicon Valley lawyer counsels, "When raising money, for a variety of reasons, it is generally recommended to only target accredited investors." "Clipping the Wings of Angels? New Accredited Investor Standards Contained in Dodd-Frank Wall Street Reform Act," *A View from the Valley,* July 20, 2010. www.mattbartus.com/clipping-the-wings-of-angels-new-accredited-investor-standards-contained-in-dodd-frank-wall-street-reform-act/.

11. Niall Ferguson, *The Ascent of Money,* Penguin, 2008, p. 91.

12. Adam Shell, "Will Stocks' 'Lost Decade' Usher in Another Bull Market?" *USA Today,* Jan. 4, 2010. www.usatoday.com/money/markets/2010-01-03-2010-outlook-stocks_N.htm.

13. Stephen Gandel, "The Case Against Goldman Sachs," *Time,* April 22, 2010. www.time.com/time/business/article/0,8599,1983747,00 .html.

14. Steve Fishman, "The Madoff Tapes," New York, Feb. 27, 2011 http://nymag.com/news/features/berniemadoff-2011-3/.

15. Louise Story, "A Secretive Banking Elite Rules Derivatives Trading," *New York Times,* Dec. 12, 2010. www.nytimes.com/2010/12/12/business/12advantage.html.

16. Binyamin Appelbaum, "Investors Bankroll Lawsuits to Profit From Payouts," *New York Times*, Nov. 14, 2010. www.nytimes.com/2010/11/15/business/15lawsuit.html.

17. Michael D. Hurd and Susann Rohwedder, "Effects of the Financial Crisis and Great Recession on American Households," National Bureau of Economic Research, Sept. 2010.

18. Michael Mandel, "A Lost Decade for Jobs," *Bloomberg Businessweek*, June 23, 2010. www.businessweek.com/the_thread/economicsunbound/archives/2009/06/a_lost_decade_f.html.

19. Kevin Phillips, *American Theocracy*, Viking, 2006, p. 267. The financial services sector includes banking, insurance, and real estate.

20. Arianna Huffington, *Third World America*, Crown Publishers, 2010, p. 21.

21. Simon Johnson and James Kwak, *13 Bankers*, Pantheon Books, 2010.

22. Robert E. Lighthizer, "Throwing Free Trade Overboard," *New York Times*, Nov. 13, 2010. www.nytimes.com/2010/11/13/opinion/13lighthizer.html.

23. Robert E. Scott, "The Burden of Outsouring," Economic Policy Institute, Oct. 2, 2008. www.epi.org/publications/entry/bp222/

24. Alan S. Blinder, "Our Dickensian Economy," *Wall Street Journal*, Dec. 17, 2010. online.wsj.com/article/SB10001424052748704828104576022002280730440.html.

Chapter 3

1. Evelyn M. Rusli, "Google's Bid for Groupon Portrayed as a Bargain," *New York Times*, Dec. 1, 2010. dealbook.nytimes.com/2010/12/01/googles-bid-for-groupon-is-seen-as-a-bargain/.

2. Stephanie Clifford, "Atlanta Hats? Seattle Socks? Macy's Goes Local," *New York Times*, Oct. 1, 2010. www.nytimes.com/2010/10/02/business/02local.html.

3. Jeff D. Opdyke, "Small Caps Loom Large," *Wall Street Journal*, May 1, 2010 online.wsj.com/article/SB100014240527487035725045752147229499936724.html.

4. Christine Hauser, "BP's Shareholders Take It on the Chin," *New York Times*, June 16, 2010. dealbook.nytimes.com/2010/06/17/bps-shareholders-take-it-on-the-chin/.

5. Azam Ahmed, "Investors Bet on Catastrophe Bonds," *New York Times*, Jan. 6, 2011. dealbook.nytimes.com/2011/01/06/looking-to-diversify-investors-bet-on-catastrophe-bonds/; Michael S. Schmidt, "New Exotic Investment: Latin Baseball Futures," *New York Times*, Nov. 17, 2010. www.nytimes.com/2010/11/18/sports/baseball/18investors.html; Mark Maremont and Leslie Scism, "Odds Skew Against Investors in Bets on Strangers' Lives," *Wall Street Journal*, Dec. 21, 2010. online.wsj.com/article/SB1000142405274870469400457601934429196
7866.html.

6. Don Grant, "Organizational Structures, Citizen Participation, and Corporate Environmental Performance," University of Arizona, 2001. cfpub.epa.gov/ncer_abstracts/index.cfm/fuseaction/display.abstractDetail/abstract/810

7. "Charitable Contributions Comparison," National Federation of Independent Business, Jan. 2003. www.nfib.com.

8. Okmyung Bin and Bob Edwards, "Social Capital and Business Giving to Charity Following a Natural Disaster: An Empirical Assessment," East Carolina University, March 2008. Ideas.repec.org/a/eee/soceco/v38y2009i4p601-607.html.

9. Stacy Mitchell, *Big-Box Swindle: The True Cost of Mega-Retailers and the Fight for America's Independent Businesses,* Beacon Press, 2006, pp. 73–77.

10. "Walking the Walk: How Walkability Raises Home Values in U.S. Cities," Joe Cortright for CEOs for Cities, Aug. 2009. www.ceosfocities.org/work/walkingthewalk.

11. www.soulofthecommunity.org.

12. Stacy Mitchell, "Holiday Sales Increase at Independent Businesses, National Survey Finds," New Rule Project press release, Jan. 14, 2010. www.newrules.org/retail/news/holiday-sales-increase-independent-businesses-national-survey-finds.

Chapter 4

1. http://web.sba.gov/faqs/faqindex.cfm?areaID=15.

2. Keith Olbermann, "Countdown Special Report: Small in Name Only," MSNBC, Sept. 22, 2010. www.msnbc.msn.com/id/39317328/ns/politics/.

3. Generally, S corporations do not pay federal taxes on their profits, like a regular C corporation does. Instead, the S corporation's income or losses are passed through to its owners, who report them on their own individual income tax returns. For businesses, S corps offer the limited liability protection of a corporation with the tax advantages of a sole proprietorship or partnership. For a full description, see "S Corporation Facts," www.nolo.com/legal-encyclopedia/article-30002.html.

4. corporate.tribune.com/pressroom/?p=253.

5. Allan Sloan, "Tribune Deal Makes Zell Ace of Tax Dodgers," *Washington Post,* May 1, 2007. www.washingtonpost.com/wp-dyn/content/article/2007/04/30/AR2007043001553.html.

6. Richard Rubin, "The Myth About Small Business," *CQ Weekly,* Oct. 2, 2010.

7. Lloyd Chapman, "Congressional Leaders Ignore Job Killing Contracting Abuse," Huffington Post, Jan. 11, 2011. www.huffingtonpost.com/lloyd-chapman/congressional-leaders-ign_b_805031.html.

8. "The Small Business Economy," U.S. Small Business Administration Office of Advocacy, 2008. http://archive.sba.gov/advo/research/sb_econ2008.pdf.

9. Sima J. Gandhi, "Eliminating Tax Subsidies for Oil Companies," Center for American Progress, May 13, 2010. www.americanprogress. org/issues/2010/05/oil_company_subsidies.html.

10. Greg Sargent, "Bipartisan Group of Senators Calls for Ethanol Subsidies to Expire," *Washington Post,* Nov. 30, 2010. voices.washington-post.com/plum-line/2010/11/bipartisan_group_of_senators_c.html.

11. Tom Philpott, "How Cash and Corporate Pressure Pushed Ethanol to the Fore," *Grist,* December 6, 2006. www.grist.org/article/ADM1/.

12. James Bovard, "Archer Daniels Midland: A Case Study in Corporate Welfare," Cato Institute, Sept. 26, 1995. www.cato.org/pub_display .php?pub_id=1100.

13. Philip Mattera and Anna Purinton, "Shopping for Subsidies: How Wal-Mart Uses Taxpayer Money to Finance Its Never-Ending Growth," Good Jobs First, May 2004. www.goodjobsfirst.org/sites/ default/files/docs/pdf/wmtstudy.pdf.

14. Arindrajit Dube, T. William Lester, and Barry Eidlin, "A Downward Push: The Impact of Wal-Mart Stores on Retail Wages and Benefits," University of California Berkeley Center for Labor Research and Education, Dec. 2007. http://laborcenter.berkeley.edu/retail/ walmart_downward_push07.pdf.

15. "Low Wages Fact Sheet," walmartwatch.com.

16. See: www.goodjobsfirst.org/corporate_subsidy/hidden_taxpayer_ costs.cfm.

17. "The Impact of an Urban Wal-Mart Store on Area Businesses: An Evaluation of One Chicago Neighborhood's Experience," Julie Davis, David Merriman, Lucia Samayoa, Brian Flanagan, Ron Baiman, and Joe Persky, Center for Urban Research and Learning, Loyola University Chicago, Dec. 2009. www.charlesvillage.net/walmart-loyola.pdf.

18. Stacy Mitchell, *Big-Box Swindle,* pp. 22–23.

19. Barry C. Lynn, "Breaking the Chain: The Antitrust Case Against Wal-Mart," *Harper's,* July 2006. harpers.org/archive/2006/07/0081115.

20. Stacy Mitchell, "Neighborhood Stores: An Overlooked Strategy for Fighting Global Warming," *Grist,* Aug. 19, 2009. www.grist.org/ article/2009-08-19-neighborhood-stores-strategy-for-fighting-global-warming.

21. Jacob S. Hacker and Paul Pierson, *Winner-Take-All Politics,* Simon & Schuster, 2010, pp. 274–275.

22. Catherine Rampell, "Corporate Profits Were the Highest on Record Last Quarter," *New York Times,* Nov. 23, 2010. www.nytimes. com/2010/11/24/business/economy/24econ.html.

23. Michael Powell, "Profits Are Booming, Why Aren't Jobs?" *New York Times,* Jan. 9, 2011. Jeffrey Sohl of the Center for Venture Research at the University of New Hampshire calls it "the capital gap"—the difficulty faced by entrepreneurs trying to raise between $250,000 and

$5 million, even if the companies are growing nicely. www.nytimes
.com/2011/01/09/weekinreview/09powell.html.

24. Don Lee, "U.S. Jobs Continue to Flow Overseas," *Los Angeles Times,* Oct. 6, 2010. articles.latimes.com/2010/oct/06/business/la-fi-jobs-offshoring-20101006.

25. Donna Smith, "Study Says Most Corporations Pay No U.S. Income Taxes," Reuters, Aug. 12, 2008. www.reuters.com/article/2008/08/12/us-usa-taxes-corporations-idUSN1249465620080812.

26. David Kocieniewski, "G.E.'s Strategies Let it Avoid Taxes Altogether," *New York Times,* March 24, 2011. www.nytimes.com/2011/03/25/business/economy/25tax.html?_r=1&src=me&ref=homepage.

27. Jesse Drucker, "Google 2.4% Tax Rate Shows How $60 Billion Lost to Tax Loopholes," Bloomberg, Oct. 21, 2010. www.bloomberg.com/news/2010-10-21/google-2-4-rate-shows-how-60-billion-u-s-revenue-lost-to-tax-loopholes.html.

28. Michael E. Porter and Mark R. Kramer, "The Big Idea: Creating Shared Value," *Harvard Business Review,* Jan. 2011. http://hbr.org/2011/01/the-big-idea-creating-shared-value/ar/1.

29. www.gallup.com/poll/141578/Americans-Three-Times-Confident-Small-Big-Business.aspx.

30. Alice Gomstyn, "Walmart CEO Pay: More in an Hour Than Workers Get All Year?" ABC News, July 2, 2010. abcnews.go.com/Business/walmart-ceo-pay-hour-workers-year/story?id=11067470.

31. Frank Rich, "Who Will Stand Up to the Superrich?" *New York Times,* Nov. 14, 2010. Citing data from *Winner-Take-All-Politics* by Jacob S. Hacker and Paul Pierson. www.nytimes.com/2010/11/14/opinion/14rich.html.

32. Nicholas D. Kristof, "A Hedge Fund Republic," *New York Times,* Nov. 18, 2010. www.nytimes.com/2010/11/18/opinion/18kristof.html.

33. James P. Miller, "Rural Towns Feel Chill of Shutdowns—Maytag's Exit in Galesburg Shows Globalization's Ills," *Chicago Tribune,* Sept. 1, 2003.

34. "Maytag in Illinois, Iowa, and Michigan," Good Jobs First, May 25, 2006 www.goodjobsfirst.org/news/article.cfm?id=120.

35. Charles Piller, Edmund Sanders, and Robyn Dixon, "Dark Cloud over Good Works of Gates Foundation," *Los Angeles Times,* Jan. 7, 2007. www.latimes.com/news/la-na-gatesx07jan07,0,2533850.story.

Chapter 5

1. "Dudley Davis," *Vermont Business,* Dec. 2004, www.vermontbiz.com/article/december/editorials-bellows-falls-and-dudley-davis.

2. Gary S. Corner, "The Changing Landscape of Community Banking," *Central Banker,* Fall 2010. www.stlouisfed.org/publications/cb/articles/?id=1997.

3. Gary S. Corner and Rajeev R. Bhaskar, "The Demographics of Decline in Small-Business Lending," *Central Banker,* Spring 2010. www.stlouisfed.org/publications/cb/articles/?id=1933.

4. Oral statement of Thomas M. Hoenig, president, Federal Reserve Bank of Kansas City, before the House Subcommittee on Oversight and Investigations, Overland Park, Kan., Aug. 32, 2010. www.kansascityfed.org/speechbio/hoenigpdf/hearing-testimony-8-23-10.pdf.

5. Credit Union National Association.

6. Hoening, oral statement.

7. www.newrules.org/banking/news/too-big-are-now-even-bigger.

8. Stacy Mitchell, Bank and Small Business Lending, Huffington Post, Feb. 10, 2010.

9. "Quick Facts on Overdraft Loans," Center for Responsible Lending, April 9, 2009, www.responsiblelending.org/overdraft-loans/research-analysis/quick-facts-on-overdraft-loans.html.

10. Julianne Pepitone, "Bank Overdraft Fees to Total $38.5 Billion," CNNMoney.com, Aug. 10, 2009. money.cnn.com/2009/08/10/news/companies/bank_overdraft_fees_Moebs/index.htm.

11. Jeremy Hobson, "Are Savings Accounts Worth It Anymore?" American Public Media, Aug. 26, 2010. marketplace.publicradio .org/display/web/2010/08/26/pm-are-savings-accounts-worth-it-anymore/.

12. "November Oversight Report, Examining the Consequence of Mortgage Irregularities for Financial Stability and Foreclosure Mitigation," Congressional Oversight Panel, Nov. 16, 2010. cop.senate.gov/reports/library/report-111610-cop.cfm; Also see Gretchen Morgenson, "Opening the Bag of Mortgage Tricks," *New York Times,* Dec. 18, 2010. www.nytimes.com/2010/12/19/business/19gret.html.

13. sonomacounty.golocal.coop/stories/why_bank_local/95/.

14. Rob Cox and Fiona Maharg Bravo, "Large Banks Still Have Financing Advantage," *New York Times,* Nov. 23, 2010. www.nytimes.com/2010/11/24/business/24views.html.

15. "Two Steps Forward: After the Credit Card Act, Credit Cards Are Safer—But Challenges Remain," Pew Health Group, July 2010. www .pewtrusts.org/our_work_report_detail.aspx?id=60075.

16. Stacy Mitchell, "Big Banks Want you Back," Huffington Post, March 11, 2010. www.huffingtonpost.com/stacy-mitchell/big-banks-want-you-back_b_494908.html.

17. David Hilzenrath, "2010 Worst Year for Bank Failures Since 1992," *Washington Post,* Dec. 28, 2010. www.washingtonpost.com/wp-dyn/content/article/2010/12/28/AR2010122803649.html.

18. Eric Dash, "F.D.I.C. Says Many Small Lenders Are Still at Risk," *New York Times,* Nov. 23, 2010. www.nytimes.com/2010/11/24/business/24fdic.html.

19. Josh Harkinson, "How the Nation's Only State-Owned Bank Became the Envy of Wall Street," *Mother Jones*, Mar. 27, 2009. http://mother jones.com/mojo/2009/03/how-nation%E2%80%99s-only-state-owned-bank-became-envy-wall-street.

20. Josh Harkinson, "How the Nation's Only State-Owned Bank Became the Envy of Wall Street."

21. Amy Merrick, "In North Dakota, the Good Times Are Still Rolling," *Wall Street Journal*, June 5, 2009. online.wsj.com/article/SB124415780405186905.html; Dale Wetzel, "ND Budget Outlook: $1B budget surplus in July," Associated Press, Sept. 22, 2010. www.businessweek.com/ap/financialnews/D9ID269O0.htm.

22. Karen Bouffard, "Bernero Lobbies for State Bank," *Detroit News*, Sept. 30, 2010. detnews.com/article/20100930/POLITICS02/9300381/Bernero-lobbies-for-state-bank.

23. Katherine Yung, "Bernero Wants a State-Owned Bank to Boost Small Businesses," *Detroit Free Press*, Oct. 6, 2010. www.istockanalyst.com/article/viewiStockNews/articleid/4560452

24. Center for State Innovation, "Washington State Bank Analysis," Dec. 2010. www.stateinnovation.org/Home/CSI-Washington-State-Bank-Analysis-020411.aspx

Chapter 6

1. Opportunity Finance Network, CDFI 2008 Stats. www.opportunity finance.net/industry/industry_main.aspx?id=234.

2. In August 2010, ShoreBank was closed by the FDIC and taken over by Urban Partnership Bank, a newly chartered bank owned by financial institutions including American Express, Bank of America, and Citigroup.

3. Micheal Hassett, "Citigroup Reinvents Banking Wheel with Communities at Work Fund," Justmeans.com, May 12, 2010. www.just-means.com/Citigroup-Reinvents-Banking-Wheel-With-Communities-At-Work-Fund/14410.html.

4. Opportunity Finance Network CDFI Market Conditions Report, Fourth Quarter 2009; Federal Deposit Insurance Corporation, Quarterly Banking Profile. www.opportunityfinance.net/store/downloads/cdfi%20market%20conditions%20report%204thq09.pdf.

Chapter 8

1. Peter Applebome, "A Store Kept Afloat by the Generosity of Customers," *New York Times*, Aug. 4, 2010. www.nytimes.com/2010/04/05/nyregion/05towns.html.

2. online.wsj.com/article/SB120062371134999641.html.

3. Nathaniel Popper, "Who's Buying the Bookstore?" *Wall Street Journal*, Jan. 18, 2008. http://online.wsj.com/article/SB120062371134999641 .html.

4. Nathaniel Popper, "The Book Angels" *New York Times*, Oct. 28, 2007, www.nytimes.com/2007/10/28/nyregion/thecity/28book.html.

5. www.brownstoner.com/brownstoner/archives/2008/02/streetlevel _par.php.

6. abookstoreinbrooklyn.blogspot.com/2008/07/magic-and-money -thing.html.

7. Mike Kilen, "Bookstore Turns to Final Page," *Des Moines Register*, Aug. 24, 2006.

8. www.sheepless.org/magazine/video/greenlight-bookstore-tells- different-story.

9. Allison Batdorff, "Powell Mercantile Serves as Model for Others," *Billings Gazette*, Nov. 16, 2004. trib.com/news/state-and-regional/article _6d486760-b33d-5dd0-b065-0add0f7c0d45.html.

10. "Big Society at Risk of Ignoring Potential of Enterprising Rural Communities," Plunkett Foundation press release, Nov. 25, 2010. www.plunkett.co.uk/newsandmedia/news-item.cfm/newsid/458; Caroline Davies, "The Archers Helps to Save Village Shops," *Guardian*, Dec. 2009. www.guardian.co.uk/uk/2009/dec/30/archers- village-shops-community-owned.

Chapter 9

1. The threshold for poverty in the United States in 2009 was $21,756 for a family of four.

2. Jacob S. Hacker and Paul Pierson, *Winner-Take-All Politics*, Simon & Schuster, 2010, p. 3.

3. GrameenAmerica.com.

4. Vikas Bajaj, "Microlender, First in India to Go Public, Trades Higher," *New York Times*, Aug. 16, 2010. www.nytimes.com/2010/08/17/busi- ness/global/17micro.html.

5. http://techcrunch.com/2010/06/02/diaspora-project/.

6. A security, as defined by the Securities Act of 1933 and later ampli- fied by the Supreme Court, is essentially any stock, bond, or note, as well as "the countless and variable schemes devised by those who seek the use of the money of others on the promise of profits." *Marine Bank* v. *Weaver*, 455 U.S. 551, (1982). http://supreme.justia. com/us/455/551/.

7. Mark Gimein, "You Are Unlikely to Prosper," The Big Money, Jan. 18, 2010, www.thebigmoney.com/articles/money-trail/2010/01/18/ you-are-unlikely-prosper.

8. Cahal Milmo, "Trade Soars for New Lending Website," *Independent,* March 8, 2010. www.independent.co.uk/news/media/online/trade-soars-for-new-lending-website-1917784.html.

9. www.fundingcircle.com.

10. Thirty-five is the somewhat arbitrary cutoff point for nonaccredited investors in many private offerings; if that threshold is exceeded, higher SEC requirements kick in.

11. www.panix.com/~pspinrad/prospectus/.

12. www.profounder.com/about/.

Chapter 10

1. Woody Tasch, *Inquiries into the Nature of Slow Money,* Chelsea Green Publishing, 2008, p. 18–19.

2. The Greenhorns FAQ, www.thegreenhorns.net.

3. Fred Pearce, "The Nitrogen Fix: Breaking a Costly Addiction," Yale Environment 360, Nov. 5, 2009. e360.yale.edu/content/feature.msp?id=2207; Robert J. Diaz and Rutger Rosenberg, "Spreading Dead Zones and Consequences for Marine Ecosystems," *Science,* Aug. 15, 2008. http://www.sciencemag.org/content/321/5891/926.abstract.

4. www.restaurant.org/pressroom/social-media-releases/release/?page=social_media_whats_hot_2011.cfm.

5. Lindsey Lusher Shute, "How the Next Farm Bill Could Plant a New Crop of Farmers," *Grist,* Feb. 2, 2011.

6. Melissa Weinman, "Locally Grown Food Could Boost State's Economy," *Gainesville Times,* July 27, 2010. www.gainesvilletimes.com/archives/35847/

7. Brad Masi, Leslie Schaller, and Michael H. Shuman, "The 25% Shift, The Benefits of Food Localization for Northeast Ohio & How to Realize Them," Dec. 2010. www.neofoodweb.org/resources/92.

Chapter 11

1. Lee Nichols, "From Beer to Infinity," *Austin Chronicle,* Jan. 22, 2010. www.austinchronicle.com/food/2010-01-22/940758/.

2. Always the innovator, Benjamin Franklin founded a mutual fire insurance company called the Philadelphia Contributorship in 1752 (almost a century before Rochdale) that still exists. But the Rochdale association pioneered the unique governance structure and ethos of co-ops that continues today. www.co-op.ac.uk/our-heritage/rochdale-pioneers-museum/about-the-museum/about-the-pioneers/.

3. International Co-operative Alliance, Statistical Information on the Co-operative Movement. See www.ica.coop/coop/statistics.html.

4. Steven Deller, Ann Hoyt, Brent Hueth, and Reka Sundaram-Stukel, "Research on Economic Impact of Cooperatives," University of Wisconsin Center for Cooperatives, June 19, 2009, http://reic.uwcc .wisc.edu/summary/.

5. Melanie Warner, "Wal-Mart Eyes Organic Foods," *New York Times,* May 12, 2006. www.nytimes.com/2006/05/12/business/12organic. html.

6. The 2010 NCB Co-op Top 100 Report can be found at www.coop100. coop.

7. Joop De Boer, "The Reinvention of the Co-Op," part of "The Top 10 Trends for 2011," The Pop-Up City, Jan. 3, 2011. http://popupcity. net/2011/01/top-10-trends-for-2011/.

8. Aaron Smith, "When Workers Take Charge," CNNMoney.com, Sept. 23, 2009. money.cnn.com/galleries/2009/smallbusiness/0909/gal-lery.worker_owner_coop.smb/index.html.

9. "Steelworkers Form Collaboration with Mondragon, the World's Largest Worker-Owned Cooperative," United Steelworkers Media Center, Oct. 27, 2009. www.usw.org/media_center/releases_advisories? id=0234.

10. Jane Burns, "Willy St. Co-op Members Raise $1 Million for 'Willy West' Project," Wisconsin State Journal, May 13, 2010.

11. www.ontario.coop/cms/documents/212/2008_Quebec_Co -op_Survival_Report_Summary.pdf.

Chapter 12

1. For an initial listing on NASDAQ's Capital Market (formerly called the NASDAQ SmallCap Market), companies must have a minimum market value of $15 million or have net income of at least $750,000 in the latest fiscal year or in two of the last three fiscal years, as well as a minimum of one million publicly held shares. Requirements for its Global Market listings are much higher. Listing fees are a minimum of $50,000. Source: Listing Standards & Fees, July 2010. NASDAQ. The "Big Board" NYSE has even higher hurdles. See www.nyse.com/ regulation/nyse/1147474807344.html.

2. In its more familiar form, Reg D, rule 504 offers an exemption for private placements (to accredited investors) of up to $1 million. But when used with certain state securities laws and the SCOR form, the rule provides a flexible basis for a DPO with no limits on advertising or the types of investors. For a good discussion of Reg D, rule 504, see http://katovichlaw.com/2010/09/29/the-dual-nature-of-rule-504/. For a fuller explanation of federal securities exemptions for small businesses, see: www.sec.gov/info/smallbus/qasbsec.htm#eod6.

3. Lorrie Grant, "Small Firms Take Direct Route to Stock Offerings," *USA Today,* April 29, 1997.
4. Andrew Klein, "WallStreet.com," *Wired,* Feb. 1998. www.wired.com/wired/archive/6.02/wallstreet.html.
5. CityMade, Inc. prospectus can be found at www.citymade.com/dpo.php.
6. For an initial listing on NASDAQ's Capital Market (formerly called the NASDAQ SmallCap Market), companies must have a minimum market value of $15 million or have net income of at least $750,000 in the latest fiscal year or in two of the last three fiscal years, as well as a minimum of one million publicly held shares. Requirements for its Global Market listings are higher. Listing fees are a minimum of $50,000. Source: Listing Standards & Fees, July 2010. NASDAQ. The NYSE has even higher hurdles.

Chapter 13

1. Kristina Fietkiewicz and W. Trexler Proffitt Jr., "U.S. Capital Markets and Their Effects on Regional Economic Development, 1790 to 1930," Franklin & Marshall College, 2010.
2. "Little Markets," *Time,* June 1, 1936, www.time.com/time/magazine/article/0,9171,756196,00.html#ixzz174K7IVRS.
3. Fietkiewicz and Proffitt Jr., "U.S. Capital Markets and Their Effects on Regional Economic Development, 1790 to 1930."
4. "Little Markets," *Time.*
5. "NYSE Euronext Announces Fourth Quarter and Full-Year 2009 Financial Results," www.nyse.com/press/1265627527144.html.
6. "Study Reveals Surprising Insights on Private Equity-Backed IPOs," Renaissance Capital, LLC, Sept. 2, 2010. www.renaissancecapital.com/ipohome/Review/PEIPOs.aspx.
7. "US IPO Market Presents Challenges During Q3 2010 Financial Sponsors & Non-US Issuers Lead Growth of a Robust Pipeline," PriceWaterhouseCoopers, Oct. 6, 2010. www.pwc.com/us/en/press-releases/2010/US-IPO-Market-Presents-Challenges.jhtml.
8. David Weild and Edward Kim, "A Wake-up Call for America," Capital Market Series, Grant Thornton LLP, Nov. 2009. www.grantthornton.com/staticfiles/GTCom/Public%20companies%20and%20capital%20markets/gt_wakeup_call_.pdf.
9. Graham Bowley, "Wall Street, the Home of the Vanishing I.P.O.," *New York Times,* Nov. 18, 2010. www.nytimes.com/2010/11/18/business/18place.html.
10. Brian G. Cartwright, General Counsel, U.S. Securities and Exchange Commission, "The Future of Securities Regulation," Oct. 24, 2007, speech. www.sec.gov/news/speech/2007/spch102407bgc.htm.

11. Ibid.

12. NYSE Euronext, see www.nyse.com/about/history/1022221392987 .html.

13. "Duration of Stock Holding Periods Continue to Fall Globally," http://topforeignstocks.com/2010/09/06/duration-of-stock-holding-period-continues-to-fall-globally/; Julie Creswell, "Speedy New Traders Make Waves Far From Wall St.," *New York Times,* May 16, 2010. www.nytimes.com/2010/05/17/business/17trade.html.

14. Graham Bowley, "Lone $4.1 Billion Sale Led to 'Flash Crash' in May," *New York Times,* Oct. 1, 2010. www.nytimes.com/2010/10/02/ business/02flash.html.

15. Jesse Westbrook, "High-Frequency Traders Lobby, Donate to Head Off U.S. Rules," Bloomberg, Nov. 9, 2010. www.bloomberg. com/news/2010-11-09/high-frequency-firms-accelerate-lobbying-donations-to-head-off-u-s-rules.html.

16. Graham Bowley, "The Flash Crash, in Miniature," *New York Times,* Nov. 9, 2010. www.nytimes.com/2010/11/09/business/09flash.html.

17. Graham Bowley, "In Striking Shift, Investors Flee Stock Market," *New York Times,* Aug. 22, 2010. www.nytimes.com/2010/08/22/ business/22invest.html.

18. Jonathan Spicer, "Globally, the Flash Crash Is No Flash in the Pan," Thomson Reuters, Oct. 2010. www.reuters.com/article/2010/10/ 15/us-flashcrash-europe-idUSTRE69E1Q520101015.

19. As quoted in "Local Stock Exchange Plan Gains Momentum," *The Diplomat,* Franklin & Marshall College, Aug. 27, 2009.

20. Andy McFarlane, "Local Stock Exchanges to Return?" BBC News, Oct. 26, 2009. http://news.bbc.co.uk/2/hi/uk_news/8314840.stm.

21. It is worth noting that only 2,000 of the 9,000 or so publicly listed companies in the United States have actively traded shares.

Acknowledgments

Little did I realize what I was getting myself into when I embarked upon this project. It was like diving into an endless canyon. That is why I am so grateful to all of the people who helped me along the way and gave so generously of their time. They are too numerous to mention individually by name. But I especially want to thank Dante Hesse and John Friedman (John, I hope you get your pig); Michael Shuman, John Katovich, and Jenny Kassan, who patiently answered my questions about securities law; Trexler Proffit, David Fisher, and Adam Spence; the folks at The Reinvestment Fund, Accion, the Opportunity Finance Network, and the New Hampshire Community Loan Fund; James Frazier; the many bright crowdfunding and co-op entrepreneurs I spoke with and the inspirational individuals, including Jessica Stockton-Bagnulo, Tom Stearns, Chris Michael, and Melinda Little, who are showing how modern-day barns are raised. I also want to acknowledge the great debt I owe to the Business Alliance for Local Living Economies (BALLE), Slow Money, Michael Shuman, and Stacy Mitchell at the New Rules Foundation for the incredible groundwork they have laid in this important area.

This book would never have come into being had it not been for my agent, Mel Parker, who saw the seed of a book in a small article I wrote for the *New York Times Magazine* amid the market turmoil of 2008. I could not have asked for a more trusted guide throughout this process. I also want to thank Debra Englander and her team at John Wiley & Sons, including Emilie Herman, Claire Wesley, Sharon Polese, and Adrianna Johnson. You have been a pleasure to work with and extremely accommodating.

Friends and family were a lifeline. I am grateful for the friendship and astute editorial advice of Sheri Prasso, Geoff Lewis,

Dan Keeler, and Cliff Reeves, and the fact-checking prowess of Jason Mose. Owen D. Murnane, family historian and pub-crawler-in-chief, helped illuminate my own entrepreneurial links to the past. Uncle O, you are deeply missed. Finally, I could not have done this without the support of my partner in love and life, Robert McCanless. In addition to his patience and many helpful suggestions, he nurtured me throughout this journey in every sense of the word.

Index